CONQUERING the DRAGON WITHIN

**God's Provision for Assurance and Victory
in the End Time**

MARVIN MOORE

To go forward without stumbling, we must have the assurance
that a hand all-powerful will hold us up, and an infinite pity be
exercised toward us if we fall. God alone can at all times hear our
cry for help (*Sons and Daughters of God*, 154).

Pacific Press Publishing Association
Boise, Idaho
Oshawa, Ontario, Canada

Edited by Kenneth R. Wade
Designed by Tim Larson
Cover illustration by Ron Lightburn
Typeset in 11/13 New Century Schoolbook

Unless otherwise indicated, Scripture quotations are from the New International Version. Emphasis in these quotations has been added by the author.

Library of Congress Cataloging-in-Publication Data

Moore, Marvin, 1937-
    Conquering the dragon within : God's provision for assur-
ance and victory in the end time / Marvin Moore.
        p.   cm.
    ISBN 0-8163-1252-4
    1. Christian life—Seventh-day Adventist authors.
2. Seventh-day Adventists—Doctrines. 3. Justification.
4. Sanctification. 5. Sin. 6. Temptation. I. Title.
    BV4501.2.M5817 1995
    248'.8—dc20   94-39860
                                                        CIP

95 96 97 98 99 • 5 4 3 2 1

TABLE OF CONTENTS

DEDICATION

To
Elder M. D. Lewis
and
Carol Cannon

Key to Abbreviations of the Works of Ellen G. White

AG	*God's Amazing Grace*
CCh	*Counsels for the Church*
CDF	*Counsels on Diet and Foods*
COL	*Christ's Object Lessons*
CTBH	*Christian Temperance and Bible Hygiene*
DA	*The Desire of Ages*
GC	*The Great Controversy*
Mar	*Maranatha*
MB	*Thoughts From the Mount of Blessing*
MCP	*Mind, Character, and Personality*, 2 volumes
MH	*The Ministry of Healing*
MR	*Manuscript Releases*, 12 volumes
PC	Paulson Collection
RH	*Review and Herald*
SC	*Steps to Christ*
SD	*Sons and Daughters of God*
SM	*Selected Messages*, 3 volumes
#T	*Testimonies for the Church,* 9 volumes (# = volume number)
TSB	*Testimonies on Sexual Behavior*

INTRODUCTION

I began writing this book in January 1991, but I soon discovered that I had a full-blown case of writer's block. That's rather unusual for me, since I've written a great deal in the last twenty years. Finally I decided that it still was not time for me to write this book, so I started on another one that I had been thinking about for a long time. The result was *The Crisis of the End Time*, which you may have read. Now, three years later (early 1994), I'm trying again to write the first one. The fact that you are reading these words is evidence that this time I made it.

My purpose in this book is to share what I've learned about becoming the kind of person that I want to be. I do not mean that I have actually become all that I want to be. Far from it. But I've learned that I am not doomed to live with my weaknesses and my defects forever. Change is possible. In *Conquering the Dragon Within* I will share with you what I've learned about the change process.

You will read a great deal about both justification and sanctification in this book. My basic foundation in these issues came from the late M. D. Lewis, my Bible teacher at Southwestern Junior College in Keene, Texas. What I learned from him back in the mid-1950s has helped me to thread my way through the Adventist theological controversies over righteousness by faith. Even more significantly, Elder Lewis's foundation in righteousness by faith helped me to establish a meaningful and theologically-sound relationship with Jesus. For this reason I have chosen to dedicate this book to Elder M. D. Lewis.

I also want to acknowledge the contribution made by Carol Cannon, the program director and head therapist at The Bridge Fellowship in Bowling Green, Kentucky. I thought I was getting along quite well in life when I attended Carol's codependency treatment program in March 1992. Was I ever in for a surprise! I learned more about spiritual life and character change in those two weeks than I had learned in any previous five-year period. Since then I have continued to learn by reading literature on addiction and codependence and by attending Twelve-Step meetings. Again, Carol pointed me in that direction. She also read the manuscript, and her suggestions have made the final product more useful to you, the reader. So I have also chosen to dedicate this book to Carol Cannon.

One other person deserves a special word of thanks for his contribution to this book—my editor, Ken Wade. Almost without exception, the books I have written have been improved by the editors who worked on them after I did. Ken's editing of *Conquering the Dragon Within* achieved this while maintaining throughout my own style of writing. Thanks, Ken, for a good job.

Since 1990, I have conducted seminars on the subject of this book all over the United States and Canada. Many of you who attended these seminars have challenged my thinking with your questions, and for this I am deeply grateful. Many of the ideas in this book were refined by your questions. Thank you for your willingness—and your courage—to ask.

Many of the points that I make in this book I have illustrated with experiences from my own life and the lives of others. The stories about myself that do not involve other people happened, for the most part, about the way I have told them. Where the stories involve other people, I have altered names, places, and details to conceal the actual identity of these other individuals.

You will probably notice some repetition of ideas in this book. To a certain extent this is inevitable, since I will be discussing the same idea from varying points of view. Also, because the repetition will help to fix important points in your mind, I have not eliminated every instance when the same idea shows up twice.

My prayer is that God will bless you as you read *Conquering the Dragon Within* so that what I share from my experience can help you to be better prepared for the critical days I believe, and I know many of you, my readers, believe, lie just ahead.

Marvin Moore

PROLOGUE

"The dragon was enraged at the woman and went off to make war against the rest of her offspring—those who obey God's commandments and hold to the testimony of Jesus" (Revelation 12:17).

This text is very familiar to Seventh-day Adventists. The dragon, of course, is Satan, and the woman is the church. We believe this verse predicts the trials that God's people will go through during the final days of earth's history. We also believe that we are among those people and that God has commissioned us to warn the world about the dragon's roar.

As we anticipate earth's final crisis, it's easy to focus the majority of our attention on the events that will transpire during those weeks, months, and years. It's also easy to suppose that the majority of the dragon's wrath during those days will be focused on external persecution. The truth is, though, that from the day he was cast into the earth, the dragon has been working primarily on human hearts. The real battle that each of us has to fight is not against the dragon *without* but against the dragon *within*. That's why, as we anticipate the final crisis, our most earnest efforts need to be focused on conquering the dragon *within*.

We dare not wait to conquer him until the final crisis begins, though. We need to be using every strategy that heaven has to offer for conquering him every day, right now.

Because we believe that God ordained the advent movement 150 years ago to warn the world of this coming crisis, we have focused a great deal of attention on that crisis. Regrettably, many of us have spent more time on the externals than on the internal. But fortunately, during all these years, we have had the benefit of the gift of prophecy; Ellen White continually focused on the internal conflict, even on those pages of her writings where she described so vividly the external conflict.

Unfortunately, sometimes we have misunderstood her counsel about the conflict within, which in some cases has led to an unhealthy perfectionism. I would like to share with you two of her statements that frequently are misunderstood:

> Those who are living upon the earth when the intercession of Christ shall cease in the sanctuary above are to stand in the sight of a holy God without a mediator. Their robes must be spotless, their characters must be purified from sin by the blood of sprinkling. Through the grace of God and their own diligent effort they must be conquerors in the battle with evil. While the investigative judgment is going forward in heaven, while the sins of penitent believers are being removed from the sanctuary, there is to be a special work of purification, of putting away of sin, among God's people upon earth (GC, 425).

> Now, while our great High Priest is making the atonement for us, we should seek to become perfect in Christ. Not even by a thought could our Saviour be brought to yield to the power of temptation. Satan finds in human hearts some point where he can gain a foothold; some sinful desire is cherished, by means of which his temptations assert their power. But Christ declared of Himself: "The prince of this world cometh, and hath nothing in Me" John 14:30. Satan could find nothing in the Son of God that would enable him to gain the victory. He had kept His Father's commandments, and there was no sin in Him that Satan could use to his advantage. This is the condition in which those must be found who shall stand in the time of trouble (GC, 623).

Our misunderstanding of these statements especially concerns the perfection Ellen White described. Some Adventists insist that we must be "absolutely perfect" in order to be spiritually prepared for the final crisis. I will not attempt to respond to that idea here. This book is my response, though I will address the issue specifically in the Epilogue.

For now, I would like to call your attention to one sentence in the first statement above. Speaking of God's people who live after the close of probation, Ellen White said, "Their robes must be spotless, their *characters* must be purified from sin by the blood of sprinkling." Notice the word *characters*, which I italicized.

In another significant statement about the end time in *Christ's Object Lessons,* Ellen White said, "It is in a crisis that *character* is revealed" (COL, 412, emphasis added). Statements such as these suggest that a righteous *character* is the preparation we all need in order to conquer the dragon in earth's final crisis. Ellen White went on to point out that it will be too late to shape the character after the final crisis has begun (see GC, 623). If we are to have the necessary preparation then, we must be conquering the dragon within right now.

That is why I wrote this book. In *The Crisis of the End Time* I focused partially on this theme. However, that book was a combination of end-time events and character development. With the exception of the Prologue and the Epilogue, this book focuses exclusively on the spiritual preparation we must make for the end time. I plan to focus again on end-time events in a later book, but I believe that this one is the more urgent.

I would like to say a few words about the content and organization of this book. As you can see from the table of contents, it is divided into two sections. The first section deals with justification and the second with sanctification. I have discussed them separately because doing so helps us to understand them. However, in actual experience they form a single whole. I have emphasized this by referring to each of them repeatedly in both sections.

With respect to justification, there are several trends of thought in Adventism today. If you are at all familiar with these issues, you will see as you read through Section I that I have adopted and attempted to clarify one of these. I would ask one favor of those who question the validity of the position I have taken in Section I. Before you pass judgment on what I say there, please complete your reading of Section II. In other words, please interpret Section I in the context of the book as a whole. Otherwise, you are very likely to misinterpret my meaning in Section I.

You will notice as you get into Section II that I make significant use of the concepts that arise out of the modern "recovery movement," including the Twelve Steps of Alcoholics Anonymous. I have been in recovery (not from alcoholism, but from *work*aholism) for nearly three years now. I have found the concepts expressed in the Twelve Steps to be extremely useful in helping me understand and apply the biblical principles of sanctification and character development. Some people question the validity of the recovery movement and the Twelve Steps as a useful tool for Christians in their struggle against sin. Again, please read everything I say before passing judgment on any part of what I say.

Nothing is more important for character development and victory over sin—conquering the dragon within—than a relationship with Jesus. And nothing is more conducive to a relationship with Jesus than a consistent devotional life. While I refer to the devotional life from time to time, I have chosen not to belabor the point in the main body of the book. The major emphasis comes, rather, in a set of devotional exercises at the end of each chapter.

Each exercise is divided into two parts. The first part is a biblical reflection on the principles discussed in that chapter. The second part is a devotional study of 1 Samuel. In the early part of the book, the devotional exercises from 1 Samuel may seem to be only incidentally related to the subject matter of the book. However, as you come to the later chapters, you will discover a great deal of relationship between the devotional exercises and the subject matter of the book.

I hope that *Conquering the Dragon Within* will help you to begin gaining the victory in those areas of temptation where you may so often have felt discouraged by failure in the past. And I hope that it will help prepare you to conquer the dragon without during the terrible time of trouble that in many ways appears to lie just ahead. Most important, I hope the character you develop today, tomorrow, and the next day will prepare you to welcome Jesus when He comes.

SECTION I

*How Jesus Treats Sinners
Who Want Victory
(Justification)*

Chapter
One

DESPAIR

One morning back in 1974, I browsed through the March 19 issue of *Insight*, the Adventist youth magazine. The following paragraphs in the letters-to-the-editor section caught my attention:

> Just what *is* the solution when one has asked for forgiveness and made his confession, is willing to forsake his sins, has prayed earnestly, and consecrated himself to God only to find himself falling right back into sin? . . .
>
> Somewhere a vital link in the chain of becoming like Christ is missing for me—has anyone who has trod the road ahead found the answer—the really workable solution that results, at the close of the day, in triumphant, heartfelt praise to such a Friend who could do so much for you? What a change that would be! I'm all for "victory to victory," but HOW?

The author of that letter was listed as "name withheld," so you and I will never know who wrote it. But one thing is certain: Whoever it was felt desperate.

Have you ever felt that way?

I have.

Preachers used to tell me that victory over sin would surely come if I'd just turn my will over to Jesus. "Make His will your will," they'd say. "Come to the foot of the cross. Fall on the Rock and be broken."

Nice words. Cheerful words. Even encouraging words—or so it seemed at first glance. But the reality was usually far different. When I went home, I discovered that I was living the same old life—trying to overcome my temptations but failing about as often as I succeeded.

God knows how hard I tried turning my will over to Jesus! But it seemed that the harder I tried, the farther away the "foot of the cross" got. And as for "falling on the Rock," Jesus said it, but for the life of me, I couldn't figure out how to do it.

Maybe the Bible will help, I'd say to myself. Didn't Paul promise that "I can do all things through Christ, who gives me strength" (Philippians 4:13)?

Great idea!

I hope it worked for someone out there, because back then it sure wasn't working for me. I felt a whole lot more like Paul's man in Romans 7: "What I want to do I do not do, but what I hate I do" (verse 15). I was losing far more encounters with the dragon than I was winning!

I have bad news for you. The person who wrote that letter to *Insight* was not alone. Millions of Christians, including thousands of Adventist Christians, understand the feeling all too well. They don't need the Bible to tell them their special sin is destroying their happiness and maybe their sanity. Quite apart from any biblical pronouncement, they know they ought to quit for their own good. The Bible just adds a moral perspective that makes each failure a reason for whipping themselves a little harder.

Most of us find that it works part of the time. "God, help me not to do it!" we say under our breath. Then we clench our fists and grit our teeth, and sure enough, we don't do it. We're clean! Accepted! Back in a right relationship with God. Saved at last. After all, didn't God just prove it by giving us the victory? Unsaved people don't gain those kinds of victories, do they?

Here's more bad news: People who start out like that will almost invariably fall to the old temptation again. Maybe not for a week. Maybe not for a month or a year. But sooner or later . . . Sometime . . . . Almost certainly . . . . The dragon will win.

I wonder, is that what *Insight*'s correspondent was talking about? Is that how he felt—on the mountain one day, in hell the next? A hell he got sucked into in spite of his best intentions and hardest efforts? A hell from which it seemed there was no escape, from which apparently God Himself was powerless to extract him?

Yes, for some Christians it's been perpetual hell for years. They put up a good front. They keep the masks on their faces. Every week they're in church, smiling and telling everyone how wonderful it is to be a Christian. They may even bury the past down in the basement of their psyches for a while. But one day the temptation becomes too overwhelming, and they're down in hell again.

The world mustn't know, though, least of all, the church! There's an image to maintain, a reputation to protect. They go back to church the next Sabbath with the familiar smile pasted on their faces.

Other Christians are more honest. When it doesn't work, they take off the mask. They quit the church. Some even quit God. I suspect that many of those so-called "backsliders" would still be with us, had they been able to make the Christian life work for them. It's not that they wouldn't *like* to be in the church. Quitting is just easier, and far less frustrating, than trying and failing time after time.

That's the bad news.

Fortunately, I have good news for you as well. God *has* provided a way out. It's called "the plan of salvation." I will not go into any detail about it here, though, since that's what the rest of this book is about. It describes how you can experience victory over temptation. It explains how you can conquer that besetting sin you thought would be with you the rest of your life.

I wrote this book to share with you two kinds of hope that God has given me: hope that victory over sin *is* possible for you and hope that God will stick by you during the process. I hope that by the time you come to the Epilogue, you will realize that you, too, can conquer the dragon of sin that lurks inside of you.

DEVOTIONAL EXERCISES

Biblical reflection on chapter 1

1. Read Romans 7:14-25. Write a paragraph or two expressing ways in which you feel or have felt like Paul.
2. If you have experienced victory, write a paragraph or two about that. Especially explain what you did that gave you the victory, and comment on how successful your efforts were over a long period of time—six months or more.

Devotional study of 1 Samuel 1

1. How did Hannah's inability to have children affect her feelings toward her husband, toward Peninnah, and toward God?

2. How did Elkanah and Peninnah each relate to Hannah's sorrow? How do you think their responses made her feel? Were their responses appropriate? If not, why not? How might they have responded better?

3. Two people tried to help Hannah deal with her depression. Who were they? Which one was more helpful? Analyze the efforts of both people, and explain why one was helpful and the other was not.

4. Which of Hannah's relationships mentioned in question 1 most needed healing in order to lift her out of her depression?

5. In what ways do the lessons of 1 Samuel 1 apply to your problems and the way you feel today? How can you apply the lessons of this chapter to your present relationships with others?

Chapter
Two

HOW GOD TREATS CHRISTIANS WHO MAKE MISTAKES

A number of years ago, when I was pastoring a church in Texas, I had to ask a Sabbath School teacher to resign. This was particularly difficult, because he was a retired minister who, for a number of years, had held quite a responsible position in the Adventist Church. The problem was a particular point of view he held on salvation that I felt was incorrect and very discouraging. I would not have objected had he brought his view up once or twice and left it at that, but he turned his theology into quite a campaign. His class soon divided over the issue, and I could sense a threat to the unity of the congregation if he continued.

At issue was the question of how God deals with Christians who sin after they have been converted. The Sabbath School teacher insisted that any time a Christian sins, he immediately breaks his relationship with Jesus, and he doesn't get that relationship back until he confesses his sin. Presumably, he would be lost if he were to die between the time of commission and confession.

At first glance, this bit of theology almost makes sense. We humans like concise definitions, and this one is so concise it's actually a formula: Act A leads to Result A. Act B reverses the process, and we get Result B. As a formula, it looks like this:

Act A ———>	**Result A**
Sin ————>	**Broken relationship**
Act B ———>	**Result B**
Confession –>	**Restored relationship**

Unfortunately, for all its precision, which makes it seem so right, this idea is very wrong. I've talked to a number of people who used to believe this, and they told me that it nearly drove them crazy. They never could find peace of mind in their Christian experience. They felt as if they were bouncing in and out of salvation like a basketball dribbling down the court. One woman told me this teaching actually drove her into spiritualism!

Some people who believe this theory insist that bouncing in and out of salvation is not a problem, because once a converted person learns that something is wrong, she or he stops doing it. I've even heard people say that once a person has been saved, he or she stops sinning. That makes the theological alarms *really* start going off in my head!

Justification

The real issue in this discussion is the doctrine of justification. In order to know how God treats Christians who sin after they have been converted, we must have a clear understanding of justification, so let's talk about it. Justification means two things:

Forgiveness
Declared Righteous

Let's look at each of them.

Forgiveness. Paul makes it very clear in Romans 4:4-8 that justification means forgiveness. Let's begin with verses 4, 5:

> When a man works, his wages are not credited to him as a gift, but as an obligation. However, to the man who does not work but trusts God who *justifies* the wicked, his faith is credited as righteousness.

Did you see the word *justifies* in that last sentence? There's no doubt about it—Paul is talking about justification in this paragraph. However, he doesn't want us to take his word for God's attitude toward sinners, so he reinforces his point with a quote from the Psalms that talks about forgiveness:

> Blessed are they whose transgressions are *forgiven,*

whose sins are covered.
Blessed is the man whose sin the Lord will never count
against him (verses 7, 8).

Clearly, *justification* means "forgiveness." Justification is one
of those long theological terms that puzzle some people. So next
time someone says to you, "What on earth does justification
mean?" use this shorthand definition. Tell them it means "forgiveness."

Declared righteous. The other definition of *justification* is "declared righteous." While this definition is equally simple, it is a
bit more complicated to explain. It's a key point, though, so pay
careful attention. We will begin by looking at Romans 3:20, where
Paul is again talking about justification. In order for the point to
be as clear as possible, we need to read the quote from both the
King James Version and New International Version:

KJV	NIV
Therefore by the deeds of the law there shall no flesh be *justified* in his sight.	Therefore no one will be *declared righteous* in his sight by observing the law.

Notice that where the King James Version says "justified," the
New International Version says "declared righteous." That's not
a contradiction, though. The Greek word *dikaios*, from which we
get our English word *justified*, means "to declare righteous." Thus
a person who has been justified has been declared righteous.

Ellen White says exactly the same thing on page 62 of her book
Steps to Christ, though her wording is slightly different:

He lived a sinless life. He died for us, and now He offers to
take our sins and give us His righteousness. If you give yourself to Him, and accept Him as your Saviour, then, sinful as
your life may have been, for His sake you are *accounted righteous*. Christ's character stands in place of your character,
and you are accepted before God just as if you had not sinned.

Declared righteous and *accounted righteous* are practically syn-
onymous terms. If there is a difference between them, it doesn't

matter here. The question is, What do those terms mean? What does it mean to be declared, or accounted, righteous?

Let's examine Paul's term *declared righteous* more closely. To declare means to say something with vigor, to proclaim it as true and very important. Righteousness means goodness, perfection. Putting these two ideas together, to declare righteous means to proclaim that something or someone is essentially good and perfect. Justification, then, is righteousness by proclamation. God proclaims that the sinner is righteous.

In Paul's day, *dikaioō* (declared righteous) was a legal term. In one of its shades of meaning, *dikaioō* was a judicial proclamation of innocence. The issue was not whether a person was actually innocent, because the judge issuing the proclamation might not have enough information to determine the innocence of the accused with absolute certainty.

The New Testament writers picked up this Greek term and applied it in a way that goes beyond what it meant in the legal terminology of the time. God *knows* you and I are guilty, but by grace He proclaims us innocent. A judicial pardon is much the same today. The governor or judge issuing the pardon knows that the accused is guilty but chooses to treat him as though he were not. That's why the English word *justify* can mean both "to declare righteous" and "to forgive" or "to pardon."

It's important to understand that justification means to declare righteous *in spite of the evidence of wrongdoing by the sinner.* In Romans 3—one of the most significant discussions of justification anywhere in the New Testament—Paul states unequivocally that "there is no one righteous, not even one"; "all have sinned" (Romans 3:10, 23). The issue is not whether sufficient evidence exists to condemn us. Our sins are recorded in the books of heaven for the whole universe to see. *Every human being stands guilty before God!* Our only hope is a judicial proclamation, a declaration that we are righteous in spite of our obvious wrongdoing.

That's justification.

Justification is almost a fiction. We *have* sinned. We *are* guilty. But in spite of this plain fact, God treats us as though we were perfect.

Christ's character/our character

I'd like to go back now and pick up on another thought in Ellen White's statement that we read a moment ago. To give you the context, I will quote the sentence in which she uses the expression *accounted righteous.* However, I especially want you to notice the sentence that follows, which I have italicized:

> If you give yourself to Him, and accept Him as your Saviour, then, sinful as your life may have been, for His sake you are accounted righteous. *Christ's character stands in place of your character, and you are accepted before God just as if you had not sinned.*

In that last sentence, Ellen White explains in greater detail how justification works. She says that Christ's righteous character stands in place of your sinful character and mine, and that is why God can accept us as if we had not sinned.

This statement by Ellen White actually adds an important dimension to justification that we have not yet discussed.[1] Up to this point we have talked about justification in the sense of pardon for sinful deeds committed in the past. However, Ellen White's statement carries this a step farther and applies justification to our sinful character in the present as well.

Character is what a person is on the inside—his or her thoughts, feelings, attitudes, and motives. The Bible makes it clear that human beings are sinful, not just in their outward deeds, but in the innermost part of their being. "Surely I was sinful at birth," the psalmist said, "sinful from the time my mother conceived me" (Psalm 51:5). At conception, and even at birth, a person has not had a chance to do anything bad—certainly not by any conscious choice. Thus to be sinful at conception means to be sinful in one's innermost being.

In Mark 7:20-23, after mentioning a long list of sins such as murder and adultery, Jesus said, "All these evils come from *inside*, and make a man [unclean]." Again, the sin problem goes beyond the sinful deeds we humans commit. We are sinful on the inside, that is, in our characters.

And, according to Ellen White, God declares, or accounts, our characters to be righteous in spite of our record of past sins.

"Christ's character stands in place of your character, and you are accepted before God just as if you had not sinned." In other words, God attributes what Jesus is like on the inside to you and me as though we also were like that on the inside![2]

Again, justification is almost a fiction. We *are* sinners on the inside. Our characters *are* evil. But in spite of this plain fact, God treats us as though we were perfect on the inside. He can do this because "Christ's character stands in place of" our character. What Jesus is like on the inside becomes what God considers us to be like on the inside.

Let me explain it with an analogy. Imagine that you are standing at the edge of a lake that is surrounded with pine-covered mountains. Several rocky crags jut into the sky above the tree line, and white clouds billow over the mountains. "I *must* get a picture of this beautiful scene," you say as you dash to your car. You grab your camera, rush back to the lake, and point and shoot. When you get home, you mail the film off to be developed. Two weeks later you open your mailbox, and there it is—the package from your friendly film processor.

You tear open the envelope and start flipping through the prints. Soon you come to *the* picture. The lake is there, the mountains, the trees, and the rocky crags. But what happened to the clouds? They're all washed out—almost invisible. You can hardly tell where the clouds end and the sky begins.

Why did your picture turn out like that?

Because you failed to use a filter. A filter is a piece of glass that photographers put in front of the lens to alter the light as it enters the camera. The right filter would have removed the part of the light spectrum that washes out clouds, and the clouds in your picture would have snapped out just as beautifully on the print as they were in real life.

Jesus is a sin filter.

Let's say that you are standing before God's throne in heaven. Of course, any sinner who should presume to do that (none ever has) would be instantly consumed. But in your imagination you are not consumed. Why? Because Jesus stands between you and the Father, and Jesus is a sin filter. Your character is very flawed, but God looks at you through Jesus, and Jesus filters out all those flaws. When God looks at you through Jesus, He sees you as though you had Jesus' character.

That's what Ellen White means when she says, "Christ's character stands in place of your character, and you are accepted before God just as if you had not sinned."

That's quite a transaction, wouldn't you say? Now let's talk about why it's so important.

Why it's so important

At the same time that God justifies you, He saves you. He gives you eternal life. To be justified is to be saved. If you were to die the moment after God justified you, you would spend eternity in His kingdom.

And this leads to an amazing conclusion: God saves you and me while we are still sinners. He does not demand that we overcome all our sins first, or even a certain number of sins or a certain kind of sin. He does not demand that we have a perfect character to be saved. He accepts us with the horrible record of our past sins, and He accepts us with the present sinful condition of our character. No wonder Paul could exclaim:

> Oh, the depth of the riches of the
>   wisdom and knowledge of God!
> How unsearchable his judgments,
>   and his paths beyond tracing out! (Romans 11:33).

In later chapters you will see that God's acceptance of us and Christ's acceptance of us while we are yet sinners has powerful implications, not only for our peace of mind, but for our ability to conquer in the struggle with sin.

For now, let's just rejoice in the fact that it's true!

---

[1] See Additional Note 1 at the end of chapter 2.

[2] See Additional Note 2 at the end of chapter 2.

DEVOTIONAL EXERCISES

Biblical reflection on chapter 2

  1. Read Romans 3:19–5:21. Make a list of all the reasons Paul gives that explain why the doctrine of justification is impor-

tant to our attitude toward God.
2. What difference can these thoughts make in your attitude toward God today? How does it change your understanding of God's attitude toward you? How does it affect your peace of mind? Write a paragraph or two in response to these questions.

Devotional study of 1 Samuel 2:1-26
1. Read through Hannah's prayer, and choose the statement that means the most to you. Write a paragraph or two about how it applies to your life today. If you have time, repeat this exercise with one or two additional statements.
2. What differing attitudes in Eli's sons and in Samuel made the difference in the way they related to life? How does this apply to your life today?

Additional Note 1

Justification is a biblical term, and it is best to let the Bible define its own terms. That is why I began my definition of justification from the Bible. However, Ellen White at times used biblical terms in ways the Bible writers did not. This does not mean her usages and definitions are wrong, as long as they do not contradict what the Bible writers said. Adventists believe that she also spoke for God, and therefore it is appropriate for us, among ourselves, to discuss her insights and to accept them as true.

Additional Note 2

I'm not sure the Bible ever addresses the question of justification as it applies to character quite as clearly as Ellen White does. However, the idea is implicit in what Paul says about justification. While he never uses the word *character,* he does use a word that is closely related. He speaks of the sinful *mind.* Thus in Romans 1:28 he says that God "gave them [the wicked] over to a depraved *mind.*" He goes on to define sin, not merely in terms of behavior, but in terms we would call character: "They have become *filled with* every kind of wickedness, evil, greed, and depravity. They are *full of* envy, murder, strife, deceit and malice" (verse 29). To be "filled with" evil and "full of" evil suggests an inner evil condition, not just outward evil deeds. Also, words such as *greed, depravity, envy,* and *malice* that Paul used to describe sinners refer to more than deeds. They describe the condition of the mind and heart. Thus he clearly has in mind the sinful character and not just sinful deeds.

Since comments such as these set the stage for Paul's later explanation of justification as God's answer to sin, it seems obvious that justification must declare righteous the entire human condition—the sinful mind (character) as well as sinful deeds.

Thus I believe Ellen White is correct in applying justification to our sinful character in the present as well as to our sinful deeds of the past, even though the Bible does not state this concept as explicitly as she does.

Chapter
Three

THE OIL-WELL PLATFORM

I've never been on an oil-well platform in the ocean. I don't recall so much as having seen one from the air. But I've seen lots of pictures of oil-well platforms, and I'm sure you have too, so we both know what they look like.

Four massive pillars jut up from the sea, their lower extremities anchored deep in the ocean floor. A huge steel platform is built on top of these pillars, and an oil rig is raised on top of the platform. Service areas for equipment, along with living quarters for the workers, are built on top of and within the platform. When the platform is completed, workers swarm across it, and work begins.

Now please notice this, because it is crucial: *The platform has just one purpose—to provide a safe place where work can be done.*

Even when the sea below is raging, work continues. The platform sits high above the waves. It really doesn't matter how high the waves toss, or, up to a point at least, how strong the wind blows. Those massive pillars anchored deep in the ocean floor keep the platform secure. The work on top goes on. Because, you see, *the platform is built to provide a safe place where work can be done*. If no work is done, the platform is a multimillion-dollar boondoggle.

This is an analogy of sin and salvation. I'd like to compare the ocean to sin and the platform on those pillars above the ocean to justification. The work that is done on the platform we will call character development. The diagram on the next page will help you understand what I'm saying:

Character
Development

Justification

Ocean		Ocean
SIN		SIN
Ocean floor		Ocean floor

The platform represents justification. God built it to provide a safe place for work to be done, and the work He wants done on it is character development.

The good things and the bad things you and I *do* arise out of what we *are* on the inside. Good deeds spring from a good character, and bad deeds spring from a bad character. Since every human being is a sinner who does bad things, we can safely say that every human being has a flawed character. Our goal as Christians is to change what we are like on the inside from bad to good. That way we can produce good deeds instead of bad deeds.

The point of the diagram above is that justification is the platform on which the work of character development can take place. *Character development must be supported by justification.* Until you and I are justified, character transformation in the Christian sense is impossible.

You will notice that the ocean beneath the platform is called "sin." When you and I started out in life, we were swimming around in the ocean of sin, and we loved it. But when Jesus came into our lives, He lifted us out of that ocean and put us on the platform of justification. It's crucial to understand that justification happens the moment you and I accept Jesus as our Saviour. We are justified the instant our feet touch the floor of the platform, and at that very instant we are saved. At that point God begins looking at us through Jesus, the sin filter, and He treats us as though we had Christ's perfect character, even though we

29

don't. If we were to die right then, we would be guaranteed a place in God's eternal kingdom.

Our good deeds have absolutely nothing to do with getting us onto the platform. *We can't even make a start at doing good deeds until our feet are on the platform.* The work of character development that we do after God has placed us on the platform is what makes good deeds possible.

What I say next is crucial to your peace of mind as a Christian, and my analogy of the oil-well platform helps to explain what I mean. So please keep reading even if it seems like theological hair splitting at first.

Occasionally I hear of Christians who believe that character transformation happens instantly. They claim that people who have been truly converted stop sinning. "If you find yourself still falling into sin," they say, "that's proof you haven't been converted."

This is simply not true.

Character transformation does not happen in an instant. This should be obvious to any Christian who has struggled against even one sin. However, let's nail down the point with some inspired evidence.

Paul said, "Not that I have already obtained all this, *or have already been made perfect*" (Philippians 3:12). After many years as a Christian, Paul admitted that he was still far from perfect. And Peter said that we are to *add* to our faith goodness, "and to goodness, knowledge; and to knowledge, self-control," etc. (2 Peter 1:5). We do not achieve all of these character traits at once. We add them one at a time.

Ellen White understood that character transformation takes time. She even used Peter's words to make the point:

> *Christian character is not achieved in an instant,* but day after day we are to add to our faith virtue, and to virtue knowledge, and to knowledge temperance, and to temperance patience, and to patience brotherly kindness, and to brotherly kindness charity. It is in this way that we are to be made ready for the coming of Christ (RH, 4 April 1891 emphasis added).

Some of you reading this book may be saying, "It's true that *character development* takes time. But any time a Christian discovers a sin he hadn't been aware of before, he should stop doing that sin immediately." Again, that's a nice-sounding theory, but it does not square up either with the inspired evidence or with the facts of Christian experience.

Let's go back to Paul. Paul struggled mightily with sin, and he did not achieve victory on the first try. "What I want to do I do not do," he said, "but what I hate I do" (Romans 7:15). Paul wasn't talking about unknown sin here, or a sin of ignorance, for he said that he *wanted* to do good and he *hated* doing evil. Later he said that he delighted in God's law, "but I see another law at work in the members of my body, waging war against the law of my mind and making me a prisoner of the law of sin at work within my members. What a wretched man I am! Who will rescue me from this body of death?" (verses 23, 24).

Paul was desperate! He sounds like *Insight*'s correspondent whom I quoted in chapter 1. Is he talking your language? I suspect so. If you're like me—and Paul—you can think back on many times in your life when you did something you knew full well was wrong, but something drew you to it like a magnet draws iron.

John acknowledged that victory is God's desire for us, but he agreed with Paul that Christians don't overcome sin instantly, the moment they become aware of it. He said, "My dear children, I write this to you so that you will not sin." But notice what he added: "If anybody does sin, we have one who speaks to the Father in our defense—Jesus Christ, the Righteous One" (1 John 2:1). Complete victory is God's goal for us, but He is very realistic about the probability of our achieving that victory on the first try.

Ellen White said it plainly: "Wrong habits are not overcome by a single effort. Only through long and severe struggles is self mastered" (4T, 612).

Here's the bottom line: Don't expect to overcome all your temptations on the first try. In fact, don't expect to overcome them without a *long* and *severe* struggle.

In another place, Ellen White said, "We shall often fail in our efforts to copy the divine pattern" (SM, 1:337). Does that sound like victory on the first try to you?

Some time ago, I ran across a real gem of a quotation in a book that was written by a group of Christians involved in a Twelve-Step recovery program: "It is foolish not to anticipate relapses" (*The Twelve Steps: A Spiritual Journey*, 26).

Some Christians I've met get very upset (dare I say angry?) at that statement. "There's never any excuse for sinning!" they cry.

I agree. I never said there was an excuse for sinning. I am only being realistic about the probability that you and I will achieve instantaneous, total victory every time we become aware of a new sin in our lives. God doesn't demand it, and *we are foolish to expect it.*

Let's get back to the oil-well platform out in the ocean.

You do not fall off the platform every time you make a mistake. The oil-well platform was built so work could be done on it, and that work is character development. You will make mistakes in the process of developing character. Some of those mistakes will be sins. God knew that mistakes and sins would happen on the platform. Let me assure you that He built it plenty strong enough to hold you up through every mistake.

My Sabbath School teacher in Texas believed that we break our relationship with Jesus—we fall off the platform—every time we sin. This is actually a form of righteousness by works. It makes our acceptance with God dependent on our good works. According to this theory, the only time God accepts us apart from our good works is when we first come to Jesus and He forgives us of our sins of the *past*. Our acceptance *from then on* depends on our maintaining good works.

That's heresy!

Let me say it plainly: *God provided the oil-well platform—justification—to be a secure place where you and I can live while we make mistakes as we learn not to make mistakes.*

But if our acceptance with God does not depend on our good behavior, what does it depend on? Aren't we excusing sin if we say we can continue in known sin and still be accepted by God? Isn't that opening the door to presumption?

Keep reading.

DEVOTIONAL EXERCISES

Biblical reflections on chapter 3
1. Read Jude 24, 25. What does *falling* mean in this text? Is God giving us a guarantee that He can keep us from ever sinning? If not, what does He mean?
2. Read Philippians 3:12-15 from the New International Version and from the King James Version. What differences do you notice between them with respect to perfection? Write a paragraph or two about the insights each text provides for better understanding the other.

Devotional study of 1 Samuel 2:27–3:21
1. Did God treat the sin of Eli's sons the way chapters 2 and 3 of this book say that God treats sinners? Explain why or why not.
2. How does God speak to Christians today? How can you know when God is speaking to you?
3. How do you think Samuel felt about revealing to Eli what God had told him? Compare this story about Samuel with the story of Jonah. How would you feel if God were to give you an assignment such as He gave to Samuel or Jonah? What would be the best way to deal with those feelings?

Chapter
Four

THE CONDITIONS FOR RECEIVING JUSTIFICATION

Imagine a town with exactly one thousand citizens. We'll call it Centerville. Unfortunately, the people in Centerville are in a desperate situation. Everyone has been unemployed for a whole year. Nobody has the money to buy anything. The town is threatened with starvation if something doesn't happen soon.

Fortunately, something does happen. A wealthy businessman happens to drive through Centerville one day, and when he stops to buy gas, he learns of the people's terrible plight. Being a kind man, he feels sorry for them, and he decides to give away a million dollars. He obtains the name and address of every citizen, and he asks his accountant to write each of them a one thousand–dollar check. When all the checks are written, he drops them in the mail. A day or so later, each person receives his or her one thousand dollars.

Some of the people hurry to the bank, cash their checks, and buy food. Others, however, are skeptical. "Nobody would be so foolish as to send everyone a thousand dollars for nothing," they say, and they refuse to cash their checks.

Think of this for a moment. Every one of those citizens *owns* a full one thousand dollars. However, only those who go to the bank and cash their checks actually *possess* their one thousand dollars. The others own it but do not actually possess it. And as long as they don't possess it, it does them no good whatsoever.

This parable illustrates an important point about justification: Everyone in the whole world has been justified, just as everyone in Centerville received a one thousand–dollar check.

"I thought only Christians got justified," you say.

I realize that it's common in Christian circles to think that

God justifies people only when they become Christians, which leaves out people who never accept Christ. And in a sense that is true. We will be talking about that a bit later in this chapter. For now, though, please read the following verse from Romans 5:18:

> Consequently, just as the result of one trespass [Adam's] was condemnation for *all* men, so also the result of one act of righteousness [Christ's] was justification that brings life for *all* men.

When Adam sinned, the entire human race became sinners with him. We hardly need the Bible to tell us that, do we? One good look at the morning news is enough to dispel any doubt about humanity's sinfulness. However, Christ came to reverse what Adam did. Where through Adam the entire human race became sinners, through Christ the entire human race has been justified. Many theologians agree that in this verse Paul means that when Jesus died on the cross, *He justified every person who has ever lived.*

Wait a minute! you say. Does that mean that every human being who ever lived on the face of the earth will spend eternity in heaven?

That's not what Paul said, and it's not what he meant. When Paul said that every human being has been justified, he meant that when Christ died on the cross, He paid the debt for every human being's sins. However, it's not enough to have the debt paid. Each sinner must also accept it. That's where our parable about the thousand-dollar check for every citizen in Centerville comes in.

Every citizen *owned* a thousand dollars, but not every citizen *possessed* their thousand dollars. Only those who cashed their checks at the bank benefited from what they owned.

It's the same with justification. Jesus paid the price for every human being. Every sinner who ever lived *owns* justification. Jesus deposited it to their account when He paid for their sins on the cross. However, only those who "cash their checks" actually *possess* the justification that Jesus has already given them.

The question is, What does it mean to "cash the check"? Or, to put it another way, What is the condition for receiving the justification that is already ours?

Let me begin answering that question by telling you what is *not* the condition for receiving justification: Good behavior. Good works. "No one will be declared righteous [justified] in his sight by observing the law," Paul said in Romans 3:20. And in Ephesians 2:8, 9 he said, "It is by grace you have been saved, through faith, ... *not by works.*" One of the greatest temptations we Christians face is to think that we must in some way clean up our behavior, even if it's just a tiny bit, in order to make ourselves acceptable to God. That is precisely what's wrong with the theology of my Sabbath School teacher in Texas—that God breaks His relationship with Christians (rejects them, if you please) every time they make a mistake.

But saying that we are not saved by works merely tells us how *not* to get our one thousand dollars. It doesn't say a word about how to get it. If every human being has already been justified but only certain ones will benefit from it, what is the condition for *possessing* the justification that we already *own*?

I will mention two qualifications for receiving justification. Both are biblical, and both are crucial to our peace of mind as Christians.

Faith. The first condition for receiving justification is faith. "It is by grace you have been saved, *through faith*," Paul said (Ephesians 2:8). And in another place he said that "righteousness from God comes *through faith*" (Romans 3:22). We'll come back to faith a bit later in this chapter. But first we need to spend a little time looking at the other condition for possessing justification.

Repentance. The second condition for possessing justification is repentance. This is a thoroughly biblical concept. John the Baptist and Jesus both said, "Repent for the kingdom of heaven is near" (Matthew 3:2; 4:17). When the people who heard Peter's sermon on the day of Pentecost realized that they had crucified the Son of God, they asked what they should do, and Peter said, "Repent!" (Acts 2:38).

Why is repentance so crucial to salvation and to receiving justification? Because repentance is our attitude toward *sin*. God saves us from *sin*. When He justifies us, He declares that we are not guilty of *sin*. That's why He asks us to repent of our *sins*. I like Ellen White's simple definition of repentance:

Repentance includes sorrow for sin and a turning away from it (SC, 23).

Let's break that sentence down for closer analysis. It has two parts. Repentance includes:

Sorrow for sin
Turning away from sin

Now please notice:

Sorrow for sin is an	**Attitude**
Turning away from sin is an	**Action**

By action, I don't mean good works that merit us salvation. The story of the prodigal son helps to make this point clear.

You will recall that the prodigal son left home with one-third of his father's wealth in his pocket.[1] After wasting it all by living it up in the city, he found himself taking care of pigs. Out there in the mud and the filth, he finally realized how good home really was, and a great longing arose in his heart.

"My father's servants are better off than I am," he said to himself. "I'm going to go home and say, 'Dad, I've sinned against heaven and against you, and I no longer deserve to be called your son. Just pay me to be a servant around the place. Anything, just so I can live here' " (see Luke 15:18, 19).

Having said these words, he put his feet on the path and went home. And when he got there, he said, "Father, I've sinned against heaven and against you, and I no longer deserve to be called your son."

This young man had both of the elements of genuine repentance that Ellen White mentioned in the statement above: sorrow for sin (attitude) and turning away from sin (action).

The *attitude* (his sorrow for sin) is obvious in what he said: "I have sinned against heaven and against you, and I no longer deserve to be called your son."

The *action* (his turning away from sin) is obvious in what he did: He put his feet on the path and went home, and when he got there, he confessed to his father.

And what did the father say to the servants? "Quick! Bring the best robe and put it on him" (Luke 15:22).

Please notice this, because it's crucial: There's no indication in the story that the father said, "Before we put this robe on you, son, I'd like you to run through the shower. Also, let's have Mother wash those dirty clothes. We don't want to soil the family's best robe with the filth from the pig sty, do we?"

No! The robe went right over the dirty clothes, symbolizing that the robe of Christ's righteousness covers us, sins and all. God does not require us to clean up our act—to overcome all of our sins or even some of them—before He covers us with Christ's robe of righteousness. Christ's righteousness covers all our sins. His perfect character stands in place of our flawed character, and we are accepted before God just as if we had not sinned.

Now let me ask you a very practical question: Does Jesus *remove* the robe every time we make a mistake?

The answer again is No! A thousand times No!

Why can I say this so positively? Because of a statement Ellen White made that has come to mean a great deal to me:

> When it is in the heart to obey God, when efforts are put forth to this end, Jesus accepts this disposition and effort as man's best service, and He makes up for the deficiency with His own divine merit (SM, 1:382).[2]

Please notice that we have in this statement both of the elements of genuine repentance:

> "When it is in the heart to obey God"
>   That's sorrow for sin: **Attitude**
> "When efforts are put forth to this end"
>   That's turning away from sin: **Action**

When these two are present, Jesus "makes up for the deficiency with His own divine merit."

Let's get practical: What is the deficiency? You know the answer to that as well as I do. The deficiency is the mistakes we make in the process of trying to overcome. To put it bluntly, *the deficiency is our sins.*

Does Ellen White say that "Jesus makes up for the deficiency" by *breaking His relationship with us*"? That He jerks off the robe of His righteousness every time we sin?

No! Again, a thousand times No!

I trust all Adventists agree that when we first come to Christ He pardons us and declares us righteous in relation to those sins we committed in the past. But I'm telling you that justification is also a robe that God puts over you, which you continue to wear as you live your Christian life. As long as you keep that robe on, He justifies you instantly when you make a mistake, and your relationship with Him—your assurance of salvation—remains unbroken.

I'm telling you that justification is a platform on which you live. As long as you stay on the platform, you have a relationship with Jesus, and you are assured of salvation. In the process of character development, you will make mistakes. God knows that. He built the platform for the purpose of giving you a foundation on which to develop character, including the mistakes you will make in the process. *The platform was built to give Christians a secure place on which to live while making mistakes as they learn not to make mistakes.*

When you make those mistakes, "Christ's character stands in place of your character, and you are accepted before God just as if you had not sinned."

Back to faith

Earlier I told you that we'd discuss faith again before concluding this chapter. An experience I had at the Oklahoma camp meeting during the summer of 1993 is a good illustration of the point. After I had presented this concept, a woman came up to me with downcast eyes, and she said, "Is it true? Is it *really* true?"

I assured her that it was.

She kept looking at the floor, and she shook her head and said, "I just can't believe it. I just can't believe it."

Poor soul. She couldn't believe the best news in the world.

Two things are especially likely to cause Adventists to disbelieve what I've been sharing with you here. The first is shame and false guilt. I don't mean the guilt we feel when we've done something that is truly wrong and we need to confess it. That's very healthy guilt. False guilt is the shame we continue feeling after we've confessed our sin. Some people feel unworthy just because they're alive!

The other cause of disbelief among Adventists is false theology. I made this same presentation at another camp meeting during the summer of 1993, and afterward a minister friend told me that he'd heard a number of people complain that I was teaching "new theology." Conservative Adventists tend to emphasize standards and correct behavior as a mark of genuine Christian experience, and some of these people have a hard time understanding that God accepts them, defects and all.[3]

But this is precisely where faith comes in. Paul says that justification—the oil-well platform, the robe of Christ's righteousness—is for those who *believe.*

The Pharisees accused Jesus of teaching new theology too. And the Bible tells us that "he came unto his own, but his own did not receive him." But then it says that "to all who received him, to those who *believed* in his name, he gave the right to become children of God" (verse 12).

My point is this. If you are anxious to overcome and you're doing all you know to overcome, Jesus accepts that as the best you have to offer at that moment. He does not reject you. He accepts you, imperfections and all. And *anything that causes you to disbelieve this gift of righteousness that Jesus offers you is jeopardizing your eternal life.* Satan doesn't care whether the cause of your disbelief is false guilt or false theology, or the cares of this world or rationalism or . . . or . . . or . . . . All he cares about is getting you to disbelieve. The method doesn't matter.

But let's turn that around:

- To all . . . who *believed* in his name, he gave the right to become children of God (John 1:12).
- This righteousness of God comes through *faith* (Romans 3:22).
- For it is by grace you have been saved, through *faith* (Ephesians 2:8).

The next time you're tempted to feel that the sins you commit every day make you far too great a sinner for Christ to accept, claim the promise by *faith.* As long as you believe, it's yours. Even if you don't feel like it.

The next time you're tempted to let your theology get in the way of the peace that comes from knowing that Jesus accepts you, claim the promise anyway, and ask Jesus to help you understand.

---

[1] According to Jewish custom, the oldest son in the family inherited twice as much as the other sons.

[2] See the Additional Note at the end of this chapter for a further comment on this statement.

[3] I am not saying that all conservative Adventists disbelieve. Many of the conservative Adventists I've met have welcomed this message warmly! I am only saying that there is this *tendency* among conservative Adventists, or among conservative Christians of any denomination, for that matter.

DEVOTIONAL EXERCISES

Biblical reflection on chapter 4

Was David saved or lost between the time he committed adultery and the time he confessed his sin to the prophet Nathan? Study the evidence carefully in 2 Samuel 11:1–12:11. Then reflect on the following questions:

1. Make a list of the sins David committed during this series of events.
2. For which one(s) did Nathan rebuke him?
3. When did David confess each one? (Where the Bible does not say, make a guess based on what you know about David's character.)
4. Make a list of the possible reasons why David waited so long to confess the sin(s) Nathan rebuked him for.
5. Was David saved or lost between the time he sinned and the time he confessed to Nathan? Answer this question for each of the items on your list under 1.

Devotional study of 1 Samuel 4

1. Why did the presence of the ark of the covenant not give Israel a winning advantage in their battle with the Philistines?
2. In what way did the glory depart from Israel when the ark

of the covenant was captured? Why?

3. What privileges has God given to Christians today, and how can we misuse them?

Additional Note

Some people have questioned my interpretation of this statement by Ellen White because of what she says in the remainder of the paragraph. Here is the full statement:

> When it is in the heart to obey God, when efforts are put forth to this end, Jesus accepts this disposition and effort as man's best service, and He makes up for the deficiency with His own divine merit. But He will not accept those who claim to have faith in Him, and yet are disloyal to His Father's commandment. We hear a great deal about faith, but we need to hear a great deal more about works. Many are deceiving their own souls by an easygoing, accommodating, crossless religion. But Jesus says, "If any man will come after me, let him deny himself, and take up his cross, and follow me" (SM, 1:382).

It is true that Ellen White emphasizes the importance of works in the second part of this paragraph. However, taken as a whole, the second half supports the first half. Two points in the second half make this clear. First, Ellen White says that Jesus "will not accept those who claim to have faith in Him, and yet are *disloyal* to His Father's commandment." Loyalty and disloyalty have to do with attitudes, the set of the mind, not behavior. Disloyalty is quite a different matter from the disobedience of a person who is struggling for victory. The struggling Christian who knows God's will and wants nothing more than to obey is completely loyal to God's commandments in his mind even in those instances when, in his human frailty, he disobeys. The disloyal person, on the other hand, is antagonistic toward God's will in his heart, which is exactly the condition I have described thus far as one that Christ's merits will not cover.

Second, Ellen White said, "Many are deceiving their own souls by an easygoing, accommodating, crossless religion. But Jesus says, 'If any man will come after me, let him deny himself, and take up his cross, and follow me.' " The person who is living an easygoing, accommodating, crossless religion does not want victory enough to struggle for it with all his heart. He wants the broad way that leads to destruction. He is unwilling to put forth the effort required to walk the narrow way.

The issue in what I am saying is not whether obedience is important. I do not hesitate to affirm that obedience is *very important*. The issue is how God treats us when we want to obey but fail. The person who does not care about disobedience disqualifies himself as much from the first half of Ellen White's statement as he does from the second half, for he does not have it in his heart to obey, nor is he putting forth efforts to obey. That's whom Ellen White is talking about in the second half of her statement and not the loyal person she describes in the first half. We must not use the second half of her statement to deny what she so positively affirms in the first half.

Chapter
Five

SALVATION:
THE PARTS AND THE WHOLE

Recently I bought a Toyota 4-Runner, a four-wheel drive sports-utility vehicle. My wife and I have already made two trips into the mountains of Idaho on back roads where only a four-wheel drive can go, and we're looking forward to many more.

When I get into that 4-Runner and start up the engine, I'm not usually aware of the engine, nor do I stop to think about the transmission, the wheels, or the brakes. I *know* about these various parts on a car, of course, but when I drive a car, I think about the vehicle as a whole. I *experience* the car as a whole. With the 4-Runner, I can say that I *enjoy* the car as a whole, and I don't have to understand anything about its various parts to do that. In fact, the more I stop to think about the various parts, the less I'll enjoy the car as a whole.

However, if something goes wrong with the car I'm driving, then I become keenly aware of its parts, and I start looking for the one that's defective. If I can't figure out the problem and fix it myself (and usually I can't), then I take it to a person who is trained to figure out car problems and fix them. We call such an individual a "mechanic." Mechanics are trained to know every detail about every part of a car and to fix whatever has gone wrong.

It's not quite enough, however, to say that a mechanic needs to understand the various parts of a car. He also has to understand the car as a whole, but in a different way than you do when you drive it. The mechanic needs to understand how the various parts of a car relate to each other. Often, he can't fix one part properly unless he knows how it relates to other parts.

God's plan of salvation is something like that. Theologians break the plan of salvation down into its various parts, but God wants us to *enjoy* His plan of salvation, and we can't do this and at the same time concentrate on every fine point of theology. However, if something goes wrong—if we sin—then it's very important that we understand something about the various parts of God's plan of salvation so we can fix the problem.

I hope you are enjoying your Christian experience so much that you don't need this book. Why? Because this book is what we might call a "manual" for dealing with sin problems, and I hope you don't have any of those. However, since every human being but Christ has been a sinner, I am going to assume that you need more than to merely *enjoy* God's salvation. You also need to understand its various parts so you can apply the right one to your sin problems.

As you know, this book is divided into two major parts: justification and sanctification. We might liken them to the engine and transmission of a car. We don't need to understand the difference between justification and sanctification when our Christian experience is running along smoothly, but it's crucial that we understand the difference between them when things start to go wrong. And, like the mechanic, we also need to understand God's plan of salvation as a whole in the sense that we need to know how its various parts relate to each other. In other words, we need to understand clearly how justification and sanctification relate to each other.

Actually, it's impossible to talk about justification very long without getting into sanctification, at least a little bit. You may not have noticed it, but that's already happened in this book. Remember the oil-well platform analogy in chapter 3? The platform itself is justification, but it was built so that character development—sanctification—could be done on it. Justification supports sanctification. Sanctification can only happen when it has a firm platform of justification on which it can rest.

Please read the following sentence carefully, because it states one of the most important reasons why you need to understand justification:

You cannot grow in sanctification
if you don't understand justification.

Why can I be so positive about that statement? Because of something Ellen White wrote that I read a few years ago. Here is her statement:

> To go forward without stumbling, we must have the assurance that a hand all-powerful will hold us up, and an infinite pity will be exercised toward us if we fall. God alone can at all times hear our cry for help (SD, 154).

Let's analyze that statement a phrase at a time.

To go forward without stumbling.

I'm sure you can agree that in this phrase Ellen White is not talking about the condition for walking down the sidewalk without hitting our toes on a piece of broken cement and falling down. In her statement, *stumbling* is a metaphor, a symbol, for "sinning." So let's say it that way: "To go forward without sinning . . ."
Ellen White goes on to say:

To go forward without stumbling [sinning], we must have . . .

Wonderful! We are about to learn the requirement—what we must have—in order not to sin. Why didn't someone give us the formula a long time ago?

To go forward without stumbling [sinning], we must have the assurance . . .

Did you read that? Ellen White didn't say that to go forward without sinning we must have some super power or access to some secret knowledge. All we need is assurance.
What kind of assurance do we need?
Two kinds:

To go forward without stumbling [sinning], we must have the assurance that:
1. A hand all-powerful will hold us up, and

2. An infinite pity will be exercised toward us if we fall.

Most of us can understand the "all-powerful hand" part well enough. Every time we sin, we recognize our weakness and our need of power from outside of ourselves to stop. Paul said, "I can do all things through Christ, which *strengtheneth* me" (Philippians 4:13, KJV). Ellen White stated a true principle when she said that we cannot overcome our sins unless we have access to a power outside of ourselves to help us. We will be talking a great deal more about that power in Section II.

But let's look at the second point of assurance we need in order to go forward without sinning: To go forward *without* sinning, we must have the assurance that when we *do* sin God won't abandon us. He will pity us—and not with mere human pity, but with infinite pity!

That's why it is so crucial that you and I understand justification. Justification is the assurance of infinite pity that we need *when* we sin in order to *stop* sinning.

I am now teaching you how to be a "mechanic" of the plan of salvation. I am helping you to understand the various parts of the plan and the relationship between them, not so much for you to enjoy them (that will come in due time), but so you can cooperate with God to fix the sin problems in your life.

Can I say it plainly?

Unless you understand that a sinner who has accepted Christ remains under justification when he sins, you will not succeed in overcoming your sins.

If you find that hard to believe, then please go back and read Ellen White's statement over again. That's exactly what she says, and that's exactly what she means.

Section I, which we are in right now, is about justification. And as you read, it's crucial that you understand *why* I am talking about justification. You and I are each mechanics of salvation, working on the defects in our own lives. Justification is intimately related to sanctification, and, as mechanics of the plan of salvation, we must understand that relationship correctly in order to make the salvation process as a whole work in our lives.

Now that you understand this relationship, let's go back to talking about justification.

DEVOTIONAL EXERCISES

Biblical reflection on chapter 5
1. Read Romans 5:6-11 and 6:1-7. What does chapter 5:6 mean when it says we "were still powerless"? What were we powerless over?
2. Compare your conclusion in question 1 with chapter 6:1, 2. Do Romans 5:6 and 6:1, 2 contradict each other over whether Christians can overcome sin? Explain your answer in a paragraph or two.
3. How does your answer to question 2 help you understand the relationship between justification and sanctification?

Devotional study of 1 Samuel 5
1. Who benefited most from the way God treated the Philistines during the time the ark of the covenant was in their midst?
2. Have you ever felt afraid of God? If so, what was the reason for your fear as you understood it then? Would you explain the cause of your fear any differently today?
3. Has God ever cast down any false gods in your life? How did He do it? How did you feel about it at the time? In what ways did you benefit?

Chapter
Six

IS IT IN THE BIBLE?

I've spent a good bit of time reflecting on the doctrine of justification during my life. Several years ago, I began asking the question we've been dealing with thus far in this book: How does God relate to Christians who sin after they have been converted? I found several statements by Ellen White that responded to that question, but for quite some time I wasn't sure the Bible even addressed it. However, as I continued studying, I found a clear teaching emerging in the Bible regarding God's relationship to the imperfections of born-again Christians.

I would like to share my conclusions with you in the rest of this chapter. I will divide my comments into three parts.

The general tenor of the New Testament

First, the whole tenor of the New Testament suggests that God accepts His people with all their imperfections. This is clearly evident in the epistles of Paul. Let's examine an example in Colossians 3:1-10:

Paul begins this chapter with language that makes it very clear these Christians were converted: "You have been raised with Christ," he says. "You died, and your life is now hidden with Christ in God" (verses 1, 3). But notice the sins that these people have yet to completely overcome:

> Put to death, therefore, whatever belongs to your earthly nature: sexual immorality, impurity, lust, evil desires and greed, which is idolatry. . . . Rid yourselves of all these things: anger, rage, malice, slander, and filthy language. . . Do not lie to each other (verses 5-9).

These people have been born again, yet they are still struggling with a long list of sins. The conclusion seems inescapable that God has not broken His relationship with them just because of their imperfect behavior.

Peter in the upper room

Was Peter converted or unconverted at the time of the last supper the disciples celebrated with Jesus just before His crucifixion? The answer to that question depends partly on which Gospel writer you happen to be reading. Luke says that after Jesus and the disciples had finished eating, "a dispute arose among them as to which of them was considered to be greatest" (Luke 22:24). Jesus gently reproved them, and then turning to Peter He said, "Simon, Simon, behold, Satan hath desired to have you, that he may sift you as wheat: But I have prayed for thee, that thy faith fail not: and when thou art converted, strengthen thy brethren" (verses 31, 32, KJV).

According to Luke, Peter was not converted at the time he was in the upper room. And, given Peter's denial of Christ a few hours later, we don't have a hard time believing Luke's account.

But we get a completely different impression from John's Gospel. In chapter 13 John tells us how Jesus handled the disciples' argument over who would be the greatest: He assumed the role of a servant and washed their feet. Peter felt very embarrassed and said to Jesus, "You shall never wash my feet."

Jesus said, "Unless I wash you, you have no part with me."

Whereupon Peter replied, "Not just my feet, but my hands and my head as well!" (verses 8, 9).

Notice how Jesus answered Peter's declaration:

"A person who has had a bath needs only to wash his feet; his whole body is clean. And you are clean, though not every one of you." For he knew who was going to betray him, and that is why he said not everyone was clean (verses 10, 11).

Jesus made it very clear that with the exception of Judas, all the disciples were clean. At the very least, we can conclude that Jesus meant all except Judas were converted. Yet according to Luke it was on this very occasion—the Last Supper—that Jesus said to Peter, "*When* you are converted."

So was Peter converted or unconverted in the upper room?

I believe the answer is both. John leaves no doubt that Peter had received the new birth. This is the conversion that every Christian experiences at the beginning of his or her walk with Christ. This is the conversion that saves us and assures us of a place in God's eternal kingdom.

On the other hand, in the part of the upper-room conversation that Luke quoted, Jesus seems to have had in mind the more immediate problem of Peter's upcoming denial (see Luke 22:33, 34). He was talking about a specific character defect that Peter had yet to overcome.

My point is this: It is possible for a Christian to be converted in the sense of the general direction of his or her life, while at the same time being unconverted on specific sins that she or he has not fully surrendered. Our eternal life, of course, is based on our overall commitment to Jesus—our general conversion—not on the unconverted details of our lives.

Adventists have always understood baptism to symbolize the Christian's overall commitment to Christ, while the periodic footwashing service symbolizes a cleansing of the sins committed by the converted Christian since the last time his or her feet were washed.

The man of Romans 7

For two thousand years theologians have debated whether the man of Romans 7:14-25 was converted or unconverted. I have thought a lot about this question, and I would like to share with you my answer. So that you can be aware of exactly what this passage says, I will quote it below. Unless you are very familiar with it, I suggest that you read it through before continuing with this chapter:

We know that the law is spiritual; but I am unspiritual, sold as a slave to sin. I do not understand what I do. For what I want to do I do not do, but what I hate I do. And if I do what I do not want to do, I agree that the law is good. As it is, it is no longer I myself who do it, but it is sin living in me. I know that nothing good lives in me, that is, in my sinful nature. For I have the desire to do what is good, but I cannot carry it out. For what I do is not the good I want to do; no, the evil I do not want to do—this I keep on doing. Now if I do what I do not want to do, it is no longer I who do it, but it is sin living in me that does it.

So I find this law at work: When I want to do good, evil is right there with me. For in my inner being I delight in God's law; but I see another law at work in the members of my body, waging war against the law of my mind and making me a prisoner of the law of sin at work within my members. What a wretched man I am! Who will deliver me from this body of death? Thanks be to God—through Jesus Christ our Lord.

The question we're trying to answer is whether the man in this passage is converted or unconverted. Here's an exercise I suggest you try. Draw a line down the middle of a sheet of paper. Then read through the passage, and in one column list the clues that suggest the man of Romans 7 is converted and in the other column write the clues that suggest he's not converted.

After you've completed your two lists and reflected on them, ask yourself, Do converted people experience the struggle that Paul describes here or only unconverted people? What does your answer suggest about your own conversion? What does it suggest about your relationship to Jesus?

I hope it's clear to you now that the question of whether the man of Romans 7 is converted or unconverted is not just so much theological hair splitting. It has profound implications for your Christian experience and mine—for whether we feel accepted or rejected by God.

I'm sure by now you've guessed that I believe the man of Romans 7 is very much a converted Christian. I'd like to show you why I believe that. However, let's be fair to those who say he's not converted. Let's examine the evidence on both sides. We'll begin with the evidence that those who believe he's not converted point to.

The man of Romans 7 is not converted. Paul makes a number of statements that suggest the man of Romans 7 is unconverted. For example, in verse 14 he says, "We know that the law is spiritual, but I am unspiritual, sold as a slave to sin." Those who believe that the man of Romans 7 is unconverted call attention to the fact that by his own admission, he is unspiritual. "Converted people are spiritual," they say. "The fact that this man is unspiritual means he's unconverted."

Another point in favor of the view that the man of Romans 7 is unconverted is his total lack of victory. He says over and over again that while he would like to overcome temptation, he is unable to do so.

Finally, Paul says that the man he is describing is "sold as a slave to sin" (verse 14); he is "a prisoner of the law of sin at work within [his] members" (verse 23). When we compare these words with chapter 6:16-18, we come away with the distinct impression that the man of Romans 7, who is enslaved to sin, is unconverted. Here is what Romans 6:16-18 says:

> Don't you know that when you offer yourselves to some-one to obey him as slaves, you are slaves to the one whom you obey—whether you are slaves to sin, which leads to death, or to obedience, which leads to righteousness? But thanks be to God that, though you used to be slaves to sin, you wholeheartedly obeyed the form of teaching to which you were entrusted. You have been set free from sin and have become slaves to righteousness.

Notice Paul's contrast: Disobedient people who are slaves to sin (unconverted people) versus Christians who are slaves to righteousness (converted people). Paul said to the Roman Christians, "You used to be slaves to sin." This is clearly a reference to their life as pagans, before they accepted Christ. That being the case, his statement in Romans 7:14 that he is "sold as a slave to sin" seems like a powerful argument in favor of the idea that the man of Romans 7 is unconverted. However, let's look at the evidence on the other side.

The man of Romans 7 is converted. Notice that Paul writes in the first person. He says, "*I* am unspiritual." "*I* do not understand what *I* do." "What *I* want to do *I* do not do, but what *I* hate *I* do" (verses 14, 15). Paul is not talking about some hypothetical Christian. He is sharing with us his own experience. He's telling us what it's like when he struggles against temptation.

Those who believe that the man of Romans 7 is unconverted acknowledge that Paul is describing his own experience, but they claim that he is describing his experience prior to the time Christ approached him on the Damascus Road. However, that is ruled out by the fact that Romans 7 is written in the present tense. Paul says, "I *am* unspiritual," not, "I *was* unspiritual." He says, "I *do not* understand what I *do*," not, "I *did not* understand what I *did*."

If we take Paul to mean exactly what he said, then he is describing his own experience in the present, which would be at the time he wrote his letter to the Christians in Rome. Since he wrote that letter many years after he had accepted Christ as his Saviour, we can conclude that in Romans 7:14-25 he is describing his own experience as a converted Christian. This is a strong argument in favor of the idea that the man of Romans 7 is converted.

Those who claim that the man of Romans 7 is converted also point out that he talks very much like a converted person. He says, "I have the desire to do what is good, but I cannot carry it out"; "in my inner being I delight in God's law" (verses 18, 22). This language is almost identical to David's words in Psalm 119:47, where he said, "I delight in your commands because I love them." I think we would all agree that in Psalm 119 David was describing his own experience and that his words sprang from a converted heart. Unconverted people don't love God's law. Unconverted people don't delight in God's law. They hate it. They think it's stupid.

The solution. So is the man of Romans 7 converted or unconverted? What is the solution to this problem? It lies, I believe, in noticing a significant difference between Romans 6 and 7.

As I pointed out, in Romans 6 Paul is clearly contrasting the preconversion experience of the Roman Christians with their postconversion experience. Thus he says in verse 17, "Thanks be to God that, though you used to be slaves to sin [preconversion], . . . you have . . . become slaves of righteousness [postconversion]." In Romans 6 the two sides that Paul describes appear to be mutually exclusive:

- Unconverted people who are slaves of sin.
- Converted people who are slaves of righteousness.

Romans 6 suggests that the entire person is either on one side or the other. He is either converted or unconverted. It would appear he or she cannot be both at the same time. However, as we have seen, the person that Paul describes in Romans 7:14-25 has both converted and unconverted characteristics:

Unconverted characteristics
- He is unspiritual (verse 14).
- He is sold as a slave to sin (verse 14).
- Nothing good lives in him (verse 18).
- He is a prisoner of the law of sin in his members (verse 23).

Converted characteristics
- He has a desire to do what is good (verse 18).
- He delights in God's law in his inner being (verse 22).
- He wants to do good (verse 21).

The key to solving the puzzle of the man of Romans 7 is to notice that in Romans 7 Paul differentiates between his true self that wants to do what is good and the sinful nature within him that keeps pulling him into sin. There are actually two Pauls in Romans 7:1-14. One is the committed Paul who loves God's law and wants to obey it. The other is the sinful Paul who has not yet learned how to obey. Please notice also that Paul considers only one of these to be the *real* Paul—his converted self. The sinful nature that causes him to do bad things dwells within his body and thus influences his behavior, but it is not the real Paul. Notice what he says:

> If I do what I do not want to do, I agree that the law is good. As it is, *it is no longer I myself who do it, but it is sin living in me* (verses 16, 17).

The word *I* in the italicized phrase is emphatic in the Greek, which is why the NIV translates it "I myself." Paul is making a distinction between his true self and the sin that lives within him that is not a part of his true self. The same thought is expressed in verses 22 and 23:

For *in my inner being* I delight in God's law; but I see another law at work in the members of my body, waging war against the law of my mind and making me a prisoner of the law of sin at work within my members.

Again, Paul distinguishes between his true self that delights in God's law and the sin that lives within him, which is not a part of his true self, but that makes him sin.

Paul's clearest statement of this idea is in the second half of verse 25:

So then, I myself in my mind am a slave to God's law, but in the sinful nature [Greek: the flesh] a slave to the law of sin.

Notice that Paul distinguishes between his mind and his body. The real Paul—the Paul who delights in God's law and wants to obey it—dwells in his mind. The sinful Paul dwells in his body. I think we can all agree that while our bodies are of crucial importance, the most real part of our existence as humans is in our minds. This distinction is unquestionably Paul's intention when he says, "So then I myself in my mind am a slave to God's law, but in the sinful nature a slave to the law of sin."

Clearly, the converted Paul and the unconverted Paul live together in the same person in this passage, but they do not have equal standing. Paul leaves us in no doubt that his true self is his converted self, not his unconverted self. It is his converted self that counts, not the sinful nature that dwells within him.

Paul also says that this true self is what counts with God, not his sinful self. This is clear from the very next verse—Romans 8:1. This verse begins with the word *therefore*, which links it to what Paul said in the previous verse about the two Pauls: "*Therefore*, there is now no condemnation for those who are in Christ Jesus." If God does not condemn the sinner who has two natures within him, then we can conclude that He accepts the sinner who in his innermost being longs to be like Jesus but still has not conquered the sinful nature that dwells within his body.

This interpretation of Romans 7 agrees exactly with the thought that I have expressed thus far and will continue to express throughout the rest of this book—that God accepts us for the perfect people we long to be, not for the imperfect, sinful people our sinful nature causes us to be. Paul is stating the same thought expressed by Ellen White: "When it is in the heart to obey God, when efforts are put forth to this end, Jesus accepts this . . . as man's best service."

DEVOTIONAL EXERCISES

Biblical reflection on chapter 6

Read in Genesis 27 and 28 the story of how Jacob defrauded Esau of the birthright and of his flight to Haran to escape his brother's anger. Also, read Ellen White's account of these events in *Patriarchs and Prophets*, 180-187.

1. How did Jacob feel about his deception (see *Patriarchs and Prophets*, 180, 183)? What is the most recent time in your life when you felt this way?
2. How would you describe Jacob's greatest need after his sin? Compare that with your feelings at the time you mentioned in your answer to question 1.
3. How did God meet Jacob's need?
4. Write a few paragraphs comparing Jacob's needs and God's response with your needs and God's response to you.

Devotional study of 1 Samuel 6:1–7:1

1. Chapter 6:1 says that the Philistines consulted their priests and diviners about how to return the ark of God to Israel. Why do you think God cooperated with the advice of these pagan religious leaders and caused the ark to go back to Israel in just the way they said it would? What can we learn from this about how God may relate to people today who do not understand His truth the way we do?
2. In verses 19 and 20, God seems to have dealt very harshly with His own people. What "statement" was God making? What did He want the people to understand?
3. What lesson can we learn from this for our relationship with God today?

Chapter

Seven

WILLFUL SIN

I still remember the first time I gave a public presentation of the ideas we've discussed so far. I'd known for some time that I needed to speak on this subject but had never found the time to organize my thoughts. Then in the spring of 1991 the Georgia-Cumberland Conference invited me to give a series of camp-meeting talks at Southern College in Tennessee, and I discovered after arriving that I'd been allotted one more hour than I had planned on.

The time had come for my talk on justification.

One thing I've learned about making a new presentation is to expect questions I have never thought about. I was not disappointed on this occasion. I had not even finished my talk when a hand shot up in the audience. "God saves us *from* our sins, not *in* our sins." Another hand went up. "There's never an excuse for breaking the law!"

I responded to these questions, and then I saw a third hand waving for my attention.

"You're not talking about willful sin, are you?" my questioner asked.

I don't remember how I answered this question on that occasion, but I do know that for the next several months, nearly every time I made this presentation, someone would come up to me afterward and say, "Of course, you're not talking about *willful sin*, are you, Pastor Moore?" Often, their tone of voice and the look in their eye betrayed that they were more than a little worried I *was* talking about willful sin.

I pondered that question quite a while before I found the answer—or perhaps I should say, before I found an answer that made sense to me. Now I present my answer as part of the seminar, and nobody has asked that question for a long time. When you see my answer, I hope you'll agree that it's right. If it is, it's also more good news.

Sins that God will not cover

Before we can say whether or not justification covers willful sin, we have to define what we mean by willful sin. Let's look at three kinds of willful sin that God will not forgive and will not cover with Christ's righteousness.

Rebellion. If by willful sin we mean a sin that a person chooses to do with the full knowledge that it's wrong and with no desire to do what's right, then I agree. Justification does not cover that kind of willful sin.

This is what I call "sin with a high hand." It's actually a form of rebellion against God. The world is full of people who think God's standards of morality are foolish, that Christians who obey His laws are prudes, and they'll thank you for not pointing out their sins. Such people have no repentance in their hearts. As long as they maintain that attitude toward their sins, they cannot expect to receive God's justification. The robe of Christ's righteousness will never cover a sin that we refuse to repent of.

Presumption. Another kind of willful sin that God will not forgive or cover with Christ's righteousness is the sin we make excuses for. I heard an example of this at a seminar that I conducted in southern California during the winter of 1993. When I had finished the part of my presentation about willful sin, a woman raised her hand.

"I have a friend who smokes cigarettes," she said. "He tells me that it's impossible for him to overcome his smoking habit, and he's sure God understands that and will forgive him anyway."

That's presumption. I want to share with you a principle that I will be talking about in later chapters in a different context, but I must say it here too: *Victory over every sin is possible for every Christian. There is no such thing as a sin that is impossible to overcome.* Repentance means you believe that statement and commit yourself to it. You may struggle a long time before you experience complete victory, but you never give up your commitment to victory. You never give up trying to gain the victory.

The man who said he couldn't overcome his smoking habit but felt certain that God would understand and forgive him anyway was unwilling to believe that victory was possible for him. Or, if he was willing to believe, he was unwilling to pay the price in pain that victory demands. He was saying, in essence, "I like my sin too much to give it up, so I'll rationalize a way to enjoy it and believe I can be saved anyway." I do not hesitate to say to any Christian who thinks that way: *You are in grave danger of breaking your relationship with Jesus—if you haven't already done so!*[1]

Presumption—excusing our sins because we refuse to believe (or do not want to believe) that we can overcome them—is a form of willful sin that God cannot forgive and will not cover with Christ's righteousness.

Deadly doctrine. A third form of willful sin that is fatal to eternal life is sin that is based on what I call "deadly doctrine." I found an excellent illustration of this in an article on homosexuality that appeared some time ago in *Christianity Today*. Before quoting the paragraph, I want to assure you that the editors of *Christianity Today* do not approve of the attitude it expresses. They are merely passing along information. Here's the paragraph:

> Gail, a lesbian in a monogamous relationship, speaks with passion of her Christian faith. . . . She argues that true Christian faith does not get bogged down in repentance and forgiveness but is empowered by love of any kind (*Christianity Today*, 19 July 1993).

For the purpose of our discussion, the primary issue in Gail's statement is her denial that repentance has any place in the Christian life. This is what I call "deadly doctrine."

No human being has a perfect theology, regardless of how sincere he may be or how well he knows the Bible. Every person who is saved will be saved in spite of his or her flawed theology. The requirement for salvation is not perfect theology. It's faith in Jesus. However, some forms of theology—some doctrines—are not merely flawed; they are deadly. For example, John said that anyone who denies that Jesus came in the flesh is antichrist (see 1 John 1:1-3). I'm sure you would agree with me that the antichrist will not have a part in God's eternal kingdom!

Another deadly doctrine is the teaching that Jesus is not the Saviour of the world, that He did not die to save people from their sins. I'm sure many people will be in heaven who never knew about Jesus, or, if they knew about Him, they did not fully understand who He was and what He had done for them. But nobody can be saved who knows the truth about Jesus and refuses to believe it. That's another deadly doctrine.

Gail believes a deadly doctrine. She believes that "true Christian faith does not get bogged down in repentance and forgiveness." John the Baptist said, "Repent!" Jesus said, "Repent!" Peter said "Repent!" (Matthew 3:2; 4:17; Acts 2:38). How can Gail say that repentance is not important to Christian faith!

God can accept people who believe something is right when in His eyes it is wrong, as long as they are not excusing their behavior or rebelling against His laws. Wrong as I believe homosexuality to be, Gail's "deadly doctrine" that we're talking about here is not her belief that homosexuality is an acceptable form of behavior for Christians. My concern is that she does not believe in repentance.

I can't help but wonder, has Gail chosen to believe this because she doesn't *want* to give up her homosexuality? Only God knows, but if this is her reason, then her deadly doctrine is as much a form of excusing sin as saying that victory is impossible. This is another form of willful sin that God cannot forgive and will not cover with Christ's righteousness.

Sins that God will cover
Now that we have examined three kinds of sin that God cannot accept, I would like to mention one that I believe He can. I am referring to what some people call "known sin." The issue is this: Does the awareness of doing something wrong constitute a willful sin that God cannot forgive or cover with Christ's righteousness? And my answer is, Not necessarily.

Allow me to explain.

I will begin my explanation by quoting a short piece that I found in a newsletter published by The Bridge—a chemical dependency and codependency treatment center in Bowling Green, Kentucky. The Bridge is operated by Paul and Carol Cannon, who are dedicated Seventh-day Adventists. I had the privilege of going through their codependency treatment program in March of 1993, and my wife Lois went through the program two months later. We were greatly blessed.

The item I want to share with you is actually a letter that an addict wrote to The Bridge:

> I have been an addict since the age of 13. I have two younger sisters and had two younger brothers who died due to the hell that comes from alcohol and drugs. My father also died of the same hell. My mother, who I believe was bordering on insanity [due to alcohol], has been living virtually homeless.
>
> My own drinking and drug abuse is getting worse. I've been experimenting with cocaine, smoking, and shooting. This past weekend I spent $75.00, our trailer lot rent money, on cocaine. I make $5.75 an hour, and that's a big chunk out of my paycheck.
>
> Each time after I use and drink, I tell myself, my wife, my older son, and the Lord, that I am sorry and that I want to stop. I want each time to be the last, but it never is; only a month or so and I fall again.
>
> My wife, along with other people who care, keeps telling me the only way to overcome this is through total dependence on Jesus. My wife is typing this letter for me and is asking me what else I want to say, but my mind is so confused I can't think right now what else to say, except, can you help me?

Let's reflect on that letter a bit. Specifically, I'd like to ask you three questions.

- When this young man drinks and shoots cocaine, does he know what he is doing?
- Is he sorry for his sin?
- Is he turning away from sin—is he trying to quit?

When I make this presentation on a Sabbath morning, I usually ask the people in the congregation to answer those questions by raising their hands to Yes and No. The vast majority always raise their hands with a Yes to all three.

Now here is another tough question:

> If genuine repentance includes sorrow for sin (attitude) and a turning away from it (action), was this young man genuinely repentant?

My audiences have never hesitated to say Yes in answer to that question. This young man hated his sins of drinking alcohol and shooting drugs. He was desperate for victory (attitude). Furthermore, like the prodigal son, he was making an effort to quit (action). By his own admission, he had on numerous occasions promised God, his wife, and his family that he would quit, and each time he did—for a while. Finally, out of utter desperation, he dictated a letter to The Bridge asking for help.

Clearly, this young man *wanted* to quit and was *trying* to quit. He had all the marks of genuine repentance.

Now let me ask you a couple more questions:

> If Jesus is willing to apply His divine merit to the deficiencies of anyone who has it in his or her heart to obey God and is putting forth efforts to obey God, does this young man qualify?

My audience has always said Yes to that question too. Now here's the toughest question of all:

> If this young man knows what he's doing when he drinks and shoots cocaine but is sorry for what he's doing and wants to stop, does Jesus make up for his deficiency with His own divine merit even while he's doing it? Does Jesus cover him with His righteousness in the very act?

I am glad to tell you that the vast majority of Adventists raise their hands Yes in response to that last question too.

But how can this be true? Here's a young man who knows full well how terribly wrong it is to drink alcohol and shoot drugs, yet he does it anyway. Is God supposed to cover *that* sin with His own divine merit?

Suppose I had told you about a woman whose besetting sin is gossip. One Sabbath morning as she listens to the preacher's sermon, God convicts her that gossiping is wrong. Immediately she repents. She feels very sorry for her sin, and she vows to quit. Sure enough, for two weeks she doesn't gossip. But then one day she hears that the head elder and the choir director are involved in an affair, and she can't resist the temptation. She picks up the phone and shares the bad news with her best friend.

Do you think Jesus would make up for that woman's gossip—an obvious deficiency—with His divine merit?

Most of the Adventists I've met have no trouble saying Yes. "After all, that's only a little sin," they say.

How interesting! God's plan for saving people who are guilty of little sins is different from His plan for saving people who are guilty of big sins!

The truth is that God saves everyone the same way. It may be more palatable to you and me to suppose that God will cover only little sins with His righteousness and not the big ones, but I can assure you that the degree of sinfulness does not change God's method for dealing with sin. He's willing to reach as far down into the pit as necessary to rescue a sinner, and He saves those at the very bottom in exactly the same way He does those near the top.

Let me explain what's really going on here. It's called *addiction*. I'd like to share with you something Ellen White said about addiction. She doesn't use the word, but there's no question that she's talking about addiction. The quote comes from *Steps to Christ*, page 47. I'll share it with you in bits and pieces so that I can comment on it as we read it. Ellen White's words are in bold-faced type:

You desire to give yourself to Him, but you are weak in moral power, in slavery to doubt, and controlled by the habits of your life of sin.

That's an addict. An addict has absolutely no control over his sinful habits.

Your promises and resolutions are like ropes of sand.

That's an addict. An addict will say, "I'll never do it again," and five minutes later he'll be back at it.

You cannot control your thoughts, your impulses, your affections.

That's an addict. If an addict feels like doing it, he has to do it. He cannot say No to his passions.

The knowledge of your broken promises and forfeited pledges weakens your confidence in your own sincerity, and causes you to feel that God cannot accept you.

Does Ellen White say that God cannot forgive the addict, or does she say that the addict *feels* God cannot forgive him? The answer is obvious. God is willing to forgive, but the addict finds it difficult or impossible to believe God can forgive. The first time or two, of course He will forgive. He will probably forgive the tenth time, and by a stretch of divine grace He may forgive the hundredth time. But the thousandth time?

Do you remember the letter to *Insight's* editor that I quoted in chapter 1? Allow me to refresh your memory:

Just what *is* the solution when one has asked for forgiveness and made his confession, is willing to forsake his sins, has prayed earnestly, and consecrated himself to God only to find himself falling right back into sin? . . .

Somewhere a vital link in the chain of becoming like Christ is missing for me—has anyone who has trod the road ahead found the answer—the really workable solution that results, at the close of the day, in triumphant, heartfelt praise to such a Friend who could do so much for you? What a change that would be! I'm all for "victory to victory," but HOW? (*Insight*, 19 March 1974).

Believe me, millions of Christians feel exactly like that. My guess is that *Insight's* desperate correspondent was an addict. Was she or he addicted to alcohol, tobacco, or drugs? Perhaps, but it could as well have been to food, sex, anger, coffee, television, or racy novels. I don't know what *Insight*'s correspondent was addicted to, but I know that addiction was the problem, because he or she couldn't say No. The inability to say No is one of the primary characteristics of addiction.

And addicts are the kind of people Jesus lifts onto the oil-well platform so they can work at overcoming their addictions.

I submit to you that Ellen White's statement about Jesus covering our deficiencies with His divine merit applies to all addicts who are desperate to overcome, but because of their failures they feel that God cannot accept them. Do they know what they're doing when they yield to their addiction? Absolutely! How can an alcoholic *not* be aware that he's lifting the cup to his lips? How can the drug addict *not* be aware that he's thrusting the needle into his arm?

"Why don't they just say No?" you ask.

Because an addict can't "just say No."

Review with me the opening statement in that paragraph by Ellen White that I quoted a page or two back: "You desire to give yourself to Him, but you are weak in moral power, in slavery to doubt, and controlled by the habits of your life of sin." Notice what she said: "You *desire* to give yourself to Him." This person isn't rebelling against God. He's not excusing his sin. He wants victory. He's desperate for victory. But Ellen White says he is "weak in moral power, in *slavery* to doubt, and *controlled* by the habits of [his] life of sin."

A slave has no choice. A slave can't *"just say No."* It's for this very kind of person that Jesus makes up the deficiency—the person who has it in his heart to obey God and is putting forth efforts to obey God, but is not yet *able* to obey God.

At this point I can hear someone say, "So you mean that a person can be saved in the very act of adultery."

Some Pharisees posed that question to Jesus once upon a time, and He seemed quite willing to save the addict (see John 8:1-11).

I knew a woman once whose marriage was a wreck. Her husband was physically and emotionally abusive to her, and she felt starved for affection. She succumbed when an understanding man at work began paying attention to her. Within a matter of weeks, she was deep into an affair. She was a Christian, though, and she knew that what she was doing was wrong. "We slept together eight or ten times," she said, "then I broke it off. It was the hardest thing I ever did, but I knew I couldn't live with myself if I kept up the relationship."

When she had finished telling me her story, I said to this woman, "You were a Christian while this affair was going on. Did you feel that God ever abandoned you during that time?"

"Oh no!" she said. "No, no. I never thought that."

Am I condoning sin? Absolutely not—or as Paul would say, "God forbid!"

But how easy it is to stand on the outside and judge another human being when all we can see is her behavior. We have no idea of the pain, the hell, that's driving her to find relief. We have no idea of her weakness, the master passion she is desperate to control but hasn't learned how. I'm so thankful for a statement by Ellen White that we've already seen once or twice in this book. It helps me to leave the judging to God:

> To go forward without stumbling we must have the assurance that a hand all-powerful will hold us up, and an infinite pity will be exercised toward us if we fall. God alone can at all times hear our cry for help (SD, 154).

Please notice two things about this statement. First, "An infinite pity will be exercised toward us if we fall." That applies to all but sexual sin, doesn't it? Dare we say that God sticks by people during their struggle with addiction, *except* for sexual addiction? Does God break His relationship with people who commit sexual sin?

Do I really need to answer that question for you? I hope you've figured out the answer for yourself.

The second thing I want you to notice about that statement is the last sentence: "God alone can at all times hear our cry for help." Frankly, all I can do is listen when my friend says that she knows she was a Christian in a saving relationship with Jesus the entire time she was involved in an affair. Was she *really* sorry for her sin and anxious to do right, even while engaged in the sinful act, but just unable yet to handle the combination of pain and passion? God alone knows for sure, because He alone could at all times hear her cry for help.

Does this mean the church should withhold its discipline in cases like this? Not at all. If it is done properly, discipline can be a step toward restoration. Misguided kindness that refuses proper discipline may actually strengthen the sinner in his or her sin. But those who are responsible for disciplining serious sin need to understand the power of addictions and offer help, not condemnation, especially when there is evidence of genuine repentance.

I'd like to summarize what we've said so far in this book. Justification is like an oil-well platform. When we accept Jesus as our Saviour, He immediately sets us on the platform, and from that moment on we are saved. From that moment on we also engage in the work of character development—a task that is impossible while we are floundering in the ocean of sin. Jesus knows that we will make mistakes in the process of developing a character that reflects His. That's why He built a strong, solid platform—one that won't collapse every time we make a mistake. God built the oil-well platform to be a secure place where you and I can develop character, mistakes and all, without fear of falling off. Jesus does not push us off the platform every time we make a mistake while learning not to make mistakes. When we sin in the process of learning not to sin, *He keeps us from falling off!* And that applies to gossip and sexual sin and every kind in between.

That's the most marvelous news in the world to people who are struggling with temptation!

---

[1]At the same time, we must remember that when we do break our relationship with Jesus, He is always willing to take us back.

DEVOTIONAL EXERCISES

Biblical reflection on chapter 7
1. What Bible stories or Bible passages can you think of that illuminate the various kinds of willful sin God *cannot* forgive or cover with His righteousness?

    a. Rebellion (see, for example, John 13:18-30).

    b. Presumption (see, for example, Romans 2:1-4).

    c. Deadly doctrine (see, for example, 1 Timothy 1:1-7, 18-20).

2. Can you think of an example in the Bible of someone who was addicted and wanted out? (See, for example, Romans 7:14-25.)
3. Review the examples you have given, and see what each one suggests about God's relationship to this person or persons.

Devotional study of 1 Samuel 7:2-17

1. In order to return to the Lord, the Israelites had to put away their false gods and commit themselves to the true God. What false gods do some Christians serve today? What attitudes and actions show that they are serving these gods? Do you serve any false gods? How can you put them away? How can you "commit" yourself to God?
2. If you continue sinning, is that an indication that you have not committed yourself to God? Explain your answer.
3. In what ways can you expect God to work on your behalf when you put away the false gods in your life and commit yourself to Him?

Chapter

Eight

EXPERIMENTAL RELIGION

Someone told me once that Thomas Edison performed 3,000 experiments in the process of making the first incandescent light bulb. It was not merely a case of making a glass ball and stringing a filament through it, though. One of the first things Mr. Edison learned was that if the filament was thin enough to glow, it would burn up, but if it was thick enough not to burn up, it wouldn't glow bright enough to make a light. He had to conduct many experiments in the process of finding just the right materials to make a filament that was thin enough to glow without burning up.

This story illustrates a concept of character change that Ellen White held, which I have found very helpful. She called it "experimental religion." She spoke of experimental religion on numerous occasions. Here are a couple of representative statements:

> Experience is knowledge derived from experiment. Experimental religion is what is needed now (Mar, 74).

> Experimental religion must be urged upon those who embrace the theory of the truth (MR, 12:284).

The word *experiment* is the key to understanding what Ellen White meant by her expression *experimental religion.*

Scientists conduct experiments to discover how nature works and also to make nature work for them. For you and me, flipping a switch to turn on a light bulb is an instantaneous event. However, Mr. Edison had to endure a long, tedious process to make that possible. He surely must have felt frustrated at times, but he didn't give up. When one experiment failed to turn out the way he wanted it to, he changed the process slightly and tried again.

It would have been impossible for Edison to make a light bulb on the first try. He didn't understand enough about the scientific concepts underlying light bulbs to do that. He had a lot to learn, and the only way to learn was by repeated experiments. Each experiment taught him something that contributed to the overall understanding he needed in order to perfect his invention.

Mr. Edison did not succeed on the first try, but he did on the last try. It's easy to suppose that his last try was the one that counted most. But the truth is that the last try could never have happened without the first try and every other try in between, because with each try Mr. Edison learned a little bit more, either about how to make a light bulb or how *not* to make a light bulb. Viewed in this way, failure is as important as success.

Character development a learning process

Character development is like that. It's a learning process. And we learn to develop character in the same way that Thomas Edison learned to make a light bulb—by experimenting, "failing," and experimenting again. That's what Ellen White meant by her expression *experimental religion*.

When Mr. Edison's first effort at making a light bulb didn't work, he didn't give up. He tried something else, and something else. Each time an experiment "failed," he changed the parameters just a bit and tried again. And each time he learned something; he gained some new insight into what it takes to make a light bulb.

It's the same with character development. Most of us find that our first effort at overcoming a particular temptation doesn't work, but that doesn't mean we should give up. Rather, like Thomas Edison, we should try to understand what went wrong and try again. If that doesn't work, we should fine-tune our strategy and try again. That's the learning part of character development and victory over sin. Those who keep refining the strategy and learning from each so-called failure discover that eventually character does change; eventually they do gain the victory.

Victory over sin is not an event. It's a process. While our goal is the event at the end that we call victory, it's impossible for the event to happen apart from the process. And during the process, failure is as important as success as long as we are learning from each failure. That's true in nearly everything else we humans do. Why should we be so horrified that it's true in spiritual matters too?

Experimental science is the way scientists learn about nature and how to harness nature for the benefit of humanity. In the same way, experimental religion is how Christians learn to develop character and overcome sin.

Unfortunately, too often Christians think victory should be an event that happens every day on every try. And, failing to realize that victory is a process that takes time, they become discouraged. They think they've failed just because victory doesn't happen *now*. That's exactly the problem *Insight's* correspondent whom I quoted in the first chapter faced:

> Just what *is* the solution when one has asked for forgiveness and made his confession, is willing to forsake his sins, has prayed earnestly, and consecrated himself to God only to find himself falling right back into sin? . . .
>
> Somewhere a vital link in the chain of becoming like Christ is missing for me—has anyone who has trod the road ahead found the answer—the really workable solution that results, at the close of the day, in triumphant, heartfelt praise to such a Friend who could do so much for you? What a change that would be! I'm all for "victory to victory," but HOW?

The sense of urgency in that letter—that something's wrong if victory doesn't happen *right now*—is overwhelming. The writer failed to understand that victory is a process that looks forward to success at the end, but in between are many other events that *look* like failure but really are not *if we are learning from them.*

Success is a process, not just an event. The event comes to those who are patient enough to endure the process, and that includes Christians engaged in the process of developing character and overcoming sin. It's easy to focus our attention so exclusively on the victory at the end that we fail to appreciate the importance of the process that's required to get there.

Mr. Edison did not think of those 2,999 experiments as failures. Each one was a success, because each one contributed to the overall understanding he needed to eventually make a light bulb. You and I need not think we've failed just because victory didn't come with this particular effort or that. As long as we are learning from each effort, then each one is a success.

Sin is sin

Having said this, I must hasten to point out that the fact we learn through falling into a particular sin does not make it less of a sin. God never excuses sin. He doesn't say, "We'll just overlook it this time, since you were learning from it."

This may seem like a total contradiction of everything else I've said so far in this chapter, but *it's not*. People who have a shallow view of sin don't understand that they've failed when they sin. They think they had a good time. Only those who recognize that sin is sin are in a position to realize that they've failed and need to try again.

I affirm absolutely that our so-called failures are sins that need to be repented of and overcome. We need to feel guilty for committing those sins. We *must* feel guilty about them. Something would be terribly wrong if we didn't recognize them as sins and feel guilty about them. People who excuse their sins and refuse to feel guilty about them and confess them have bowed out of the victory process. The only ones who will ever achieve the victory *event* are those who are willing to call every sin they commit by its right name—*sin*—and hang in with the victory *process*.

The problem is that some Christians carry their recognition of sin as sin too far. They wallow in the guilt they feel for the sins they've committed. They allow the guilt to go on and on until they become very discouraged. *Insight*'s correspondent was doing that.

Here is where a bit more of the story about Thomas Edison and the light bulb can help. I'm told that when he was about half through with those 3,000 experiments, a reporter interviewed him. "Mr. Edison," the reporter said, "you've conducted 1,500 experiments in your effort to make a light bulb, but so far you've failed every time. Don't you think it's time you just gave up and acknowledged that it's impossible to make a light bulb?"

Whereupon Mr. Edison replied, "Young man, I have not failed 1,500 times. To the contrary, I have successfully identified 1,500 ways that will not work to make a light bulb."

I like that. Thomas Edison understood how to make each failure a steppingstone to success. You and I need to do the same with the sins we commit.

Most Christians don't think that way about sin, and in one sense that's good. We should never brush sin off as casually as Mr. Edison brushed off the reporter.

There is an error at the other extreme, though. People who torment themselves endlessly with guilt need to keep in mind Mr. Edison's reply to the newspaper reporter. When one of his experiments failed to produce the light bulb that Edison hoped for, he observed carefully what had happened, then varied the experiment and tried again. People who wallow in guilt can't do that. Their overwhelming feelings of shame block out any rational thinking that might help them to objectively evaluate what happened and try something different.

Paul had some good advice for Christians who wallow in guilt. "Forgetting what is behind," he said, "I press on toward the goal" (Philippians 3:12, 14). I believe Paul means Christians are to forget the shame and guilt. Once we've confessed, we should immediately turn our attention to examining carefully what happened and see if we can't find a way to vary the experiment next time. Much of the rest of this book will give you ideas for varying the experiment, so I won't go into detail about that here. However, a couple of suggestions may help you get started.

Ask yourself, What was I doing five minutes (or perhaps even five hours) before I sinned? What was I thinking? What were my feelings? One variation on the experiment might be to recognize those feelings earlier and intervene earlier. Try different types of intervention. Bible reading and prayer are two possibilities, and combining them is a third.

This kind of experimentation is quite rational. It's almost like detaching yourself from yourself and looking at what you did as though someone else had done it and you were going to advise them. *But you and I can't do that while we're wallowing in guilt.* That's why it's imperative to get rid of the guilt as soon as possible by confessing it. Only then is it possible to deal objectively with the cause of the failure.

You may be wishing desperately that you *could* confess a sin and be done with the guilt. If guilt has you in its control like a vice grip and confession won't relieve it, much of what I say later in this book will help you. However, here's a suggestion for now.

When guilt continues after confession, it's not guilt you're feeling. It's not the Holy Spirit talking to you. It's shame. Shame has a place in our lives, but it is one of the most easily distorted of our natural emotions. Ever since Adam and Eve fled from God after eating of the tree of the knowledge of good and evil, the human race has been plagued by shame, often quite apart from any wrong we may have done (though what Adam and Eve did was obviously wrong). If you are experiencing this unhealthy shame, I suggest that you ask God to remove it. A word of caution, though: Don't expect Him to do it in a minute, an hour, or a day. Getting rid of shame and other unhealthy emotions is a lifelong process. But you can get started today.

The importance of faith

Before he conducted the first experiment, Thomas Edison believed that a light bulb could be made. He'd never seen one, but he believed that he would see one some day, *and he believed that he would be the one to make it.* Mr. Edison made it his goal to create the first functioning incandescent light bulb. Had he ever allowed himself to believe that any of those first 2,999 experiments were failures, he would have given up his goal, and someone else would eventually have gotten credit for inventing the light bulb.

This helps me to understand Paul's words in Hebrews 1:1: "Faith is being sure of what we hope for and certain of what we do not see." Mr. Edison felt absolutely certain about the reality of light bulbs, even though he'd never seen one. That's why he succeeded in making one.

Our "failure" to achieve victory over our most cherished sins may cause us to feel that victory is impossible. But that's not God's plan for us. God's plan is that we have faith—absolute certainty—that complete victory is possible for us, even though we've never experienced it. If we hold to that certainty, never giving up on the process, even when it seems long and discouraging, *we will experience complete victory in due time.*

There are two reasons why Christians become discouraged in their effort to overcome sin. One is a lack of faith, which we've just talked about. The other is that they are not practicing the process correctly. Each of those 3,000 experiments that Mr. Edison conducted was slightly different from the one before. After each experiment, he analyzed the results and decided how to conduct the next experiment.

One of the major causes of the continual failure that so many Christians experience is that they never refine their strategy for victory. They may put more determination into each succeeding effort, but greater determination is not necessarily the key to victory. One of the worst forms of insanity is trying the same thing over again and expecting different results. Experimental religion means varying the strategy with each new effort (not just trying the same thing a little harder) and then reflecting on the results, paying careful attention to what works and what doesn't work. This is essentially what Ellen White says in one of her most insightful statements on experimental religion:

> Real experience is a variety of careful experiments made with the mind freed from prejudice and uncontrolled by previously established opinions and habits. The results are marked with a careful solicitude and an anxious desire to learn, to improve, and to reform on every habit that is not in harmony with physical and moral laws (3T, 69).

Ellen White is not talking about people who are in search of an excuse for doing whatever they want. To the contrary, those who are genuinely in search of spiritual growth as they carry out their experiments in religion will be anxious "to learn, to improve, to reform on every habit that is not in harmony with physical and moral laws."

If you experiment with your religion in that way, I guarantee you, Jesus will never leave you.

Never!

DEVOTIONAL EXERCISES

Biblical reflection on chapter 8
1. Read Romans 5:6-11 and Philippians 2:12, 13.
2. According to Romans 5:6-11, who is responsible for our salvation? According to Philippians 2:12, 13, who is responsible for our salvation?
3. Write a paragraph explaining the relationship between your answers to the two questions in item 2. Also explain where the experimental religion we discussed in this chapter fits into these concepts.

Devotional study of 1 Samuel 8
1. Write a paragraph describing what you think were Samuel's feelings in this chapter. Mention specific biblical evidence that supports your conclusion.
2. Were Samuel's feelings justified? Explain why or why not.
3. How did God respond to Samuel's feelings?
4. Can you think of a situation in your life in which you felt the way Samuel did? Explain ways in which God's response to Samuel helps you understand what may have been God's attitude toward you in your situation.

Chapter
Nine

THE FOOTBALL COACH

In his book *The Claim*, Dwight Nelson tells the story of a little boy who was drawing a picture on a piece of paper. "What are you drawing?" his mother asked.

"A picture of God," the little boy replied.

"But, son, how can you draw a picture of God when nobody knows what He looks like?" his mother asked.

"They will when I get finished," the little boy said.

We smile at this story, but it conveys an important truth: To a great extent, we understand God through pictures. Indeed, God has revealed Himself to us largely through pictures of things we can see. The stories of a lost sheep, a lost coin, and a lost boy come to mind. So do the story of the Flood and the story of the cross—both powerful revelations of God's attitude toward sinners.

Justification is nothing more than a picture of a God who loves us and does not hold our sins against us. Yet some of us have the most difficult time grasping this concept. We think we *must* have a God who demands obedience and punishes us for our sins.

To each one of us, God is real in our minds. Our "picture" of Him is the way we understand Him in our minds. It's our attitude toward Him. Each of us has an attitude, a picture about God, that is a bit different from that of anyone else. There are as many pictures of God as there are people in the world. One of the major challenges of the Christian life is to straighten out our warped pictures of God. God revealed Himself in the Bible in order to give us a more accurate picture of Himself than we could get from observing nature.

Actually, God is much more than any one picture of Him can

encompass. There is some truth to the Flood picture of a God who demands obedience and who judges and punishes sinners. But it must be held in balance—in tension, if you please—with the picture of God on a cross who forgives us our sins and *stays with us during the victory process.* Because some of us have such great difficulty with this latter concept, in this chapter and the one that follows, I would like to share with you two pictures of God that may help you to grasp it more easily. I call the first one "the football coach" picture of God.

Imagine that you are a football player, and Jesus is your Coach. You probably know that during a football game, each team's coach sits on the sidelines. However, Jesus doesn't sit on the sidelines during the game. He's out on the ball field, running beside you, whispering in your ear, telling you when to run, where to run, when to throw the ball, whom to throw it to, etc. You are the most successful player on the team, because Jesus coaches every move you make.

You probably know that occasionally it's necessary for a football player to run toward the opposing team's goal post for a few yards in order to find an opening where he can head back toward his own goal post. The question is this: Does Jesus run beside you when you're running the wrong direction?

Every Christian runs the wrong direction from time to time. Some of us manage to do it every day. It's so easy to think that Jesus stops running with us—that God abandons us—when we sin. I hope that by now you've learned that He doesn't.

Unfortunately, some Christians have a hard time with the idea that God really doesn't demand performance in any sense before He will save us.

In an earlier chapter, I explained that the two conditions for receiving justification are faith and repentance. But for some people this isn't enough. They point to statements in the Bible that seem to suggest that our salvation in some way depends on obedience. For example, James said that "faith by itself, if it is not accompanied by action, is dead" (James 2:17). He went on to point out that Abraham's "faith and his actions were working together, and his faith was made complete by what he did" (verse 22). In his most cryptic statement, he said that "faith without deeds is useless" (verse 20).

First, it's important to understand that good works are very important to God. Jesus Himself said, "Let your light shine before men, that they may see your good deeds, and praise your Father in heaven" (Matthew 5:16). And Paul followed up one of his most famous "salvation by faith alone" statements with these words: "For we are God's workmanship, created in Christ Jesus to do good works, which God prepared in advance for us to do" (Ephesians 2:10).

Several years ago, I was talking with a preacher who puts a great emphasis on salvation by faith apart from works, so I decided to have a little fun. I said, "You know, God loves good works. Our good works are very important to Him."

There was a long pause as my words sank in. My preacher friend didn't say anything. Finally, I broke the silence. "Of course," I said, "our good works have nothing to do with our salvation."

Sometimes I think we are so afraid of works that we'd like to believe they have no place whatsoever in the Christian life. But that simply is not true! Good works were very important to both Jesus and Paul, as well as to James. Paul went so far as to say that God *created us* to do good works. If the plan of salvation doesn't prepare us to do good works, then Jesus' death on the cross was in vain. God never intended that His people should be satisfied with living in sin. That's why Paul said so emphatically, "Shall we go on sinning so that grace may increase? By no means!"—or as the King James Version says, "God forbid!" (Romans 6:1, 2).

How can we reconcile these two ideas—we are not saved by works, but the plan of salvation has failed if we don't do good works? The parable of Jesus the football Coach provides us with some insight that helps to solve this problem.

I asked a question at the end of the story about Jesus the football Coach, but I didn't answer it. The question was, Does Jesus run beside the player when he runs the wrong direction? And the answer is, Yes, as long as he is still on Jesus' team. As long as he still has Jesus' goal post in mind. If he switches to the other team and has their goal post in mind, then Jesus will no longer run beside him.

It's the same with you and me in the game of life. Jesus is perfectly willing to run beside us when we run the wrong direction, so long as we are still on His team. But if we join the devil's team, He can no longer run beside us. He will run beside us so long as we have His goal post in mind, but He cannot run beside us when we switch to the devil's goal post.[1]

That's essentially what Paul means in a statement that I referred to earlier:

> Brothers, I do not consider myself yet to have taken hold of it [perfection, victory over sin]. But one thing I do: Forgetting what is behind and straining toward what is ahead, *I press on toward the goal* to win the prize for which God has called me heavenward in Christ Jesus (Philippians 3:13, 14).

Notice that Paul kept pressing toward the goal. In order to keep our relationship with Jesus, we must maintain our goal of victory over sin. Even when we run the wrong direction—when we sin after we've been saved—we do not endanger our relationship with Jesus as long as victory is still our *goal*. We endanger our relationship with Him by giving up the goal, by refusing to repent of our sins, by saying to Jesus, "I don't care about Your commandments. I just want what I want." But as long as good works is our goal, then Jesus accepts us for what we *want* to become, not for what we *are*.

"But James said that faith without deeds is useless!" you protest.

That's true. But God is realistic enough to know that we aren't going to produce those good deeds to perfection on every single try. That's why He accepts our sincere *intention* to do good as though we had *already done it*. That's what Ellen White means in the statement I've already quoted several times:

> When it is in the heart to obey God, when efforts are put forth to this end, Jesus accepts this disposition and effort as man's best service, and He makes up for the deficiency with His own divine merit (SM, 1:382).

When it is in your heart to obey God and you are trying to obey God, there can be no doubt that obeying God is your goal, and Jesus accepts you even when you run the wrong direction; even when you sin after you've been saved.

Thus the question you have to ask yourself is not whether you've obeyed perfectly, because none of us has. The question you must ask is whether obeying God is your goal.

As long as it's your goal to obey God, He treats you as though you had. Christ's character stands in place of your character, and you are accepted before God just as if you had not sinned.

---

[1]Even when we "join the devil's team," Jesus continues running beside us in the sense that He keeps inviting us to rejoin His team. A broken relationship with Jesus does not have to be permanent. He certainly does not want it to be permanent! His grace is always available to us on a moment's notice. However, the fact that His grace is always available does not mean that it is impossible for us to break our relationship with Him.

DEVOTIONAL EXERCISES

Biblical reflection on chapter 9

1. How many verses in the New Testament can you think of in which God challenges us with a goal? (See, for example, Matthew 5:43, 44; 22:34-40; Philippians 2:5; 3:12-14; 1 Peter 1:5-7.)
2. Which of these passages sounds more like a command that God expects us to obey immediately, and which ones sound like we grow into obedience?
3. Write a paragraph or two explaining the relationship between these ideas.

Devotional study of 1 Samuel 9

1. Write a paragraph describing Saul's personality and character as it is portrayed in this chapter.
2. What evidences do you see in this chapter that God was leading Saul toward being king of Israel? What evidence is there that he was aware of God's leading in his life?
3. Has God ever led you toward a certain destiny that you were unaware of at the time? Looking back, could you have been more aware of God's leading? *Should* you have been? Write a paragraph reflecting on these questions.

Chapter
Ten

BABY MIKE

Imagine that you are a father with an eleven-month-old baby who has been walking by holding onto the furniture for several weeks. We'll call him Baby Mike. One day you're seated in an easy chair in the living room, and across the room, Baby Mike is walking along by holding onto the couch. You are naturally anxious to see Baby Mike walk without holding onto things, so you call to him. He turns and looks at you, and you can tell he's thinking really hard. It must be very frightening to a baby to take those first few steps on such wobbly legs.

"Come here," you say. "Come to Daddy." You keep encouraging Baby Mike to come till finally, after a couple of minutes, he lets go of the couch and starts across the floor. Naturally, he's very unstable on his legs, and about halfway across the living room his right toe catches on the carpet, and down he goes.

You jump up from your chair, leap over to where Baby Mike is lying on the floor, jerk him up by one arm, and swat him a good one on the bottom. "You bad boy," you yell. "You can do better than that!"

Baby Mike is crying by now, but you ignore that and set him down on the floor. "Now let me see you stand on those feet of yours and walk like a man!" you say.

I don't know about you, but I'm horrified just thinking about a father who would spank a baby that was engaged in experimental walking. Yet it's amazing how many Christians think that's how Jesus treats sinners who are engaged in experimental religion. They think that when they sin, Jesus jumps to their side, jerks them up by the arm, swats them on the bottom, and says, "You bad sinner! You can do better than that!" Then He shoves them down on the floor and says, "Now, let me see you walk like a real Christian should!"

I have just shared with you a picture of God—a picture that I believe is horribly false, but a picture nonetheless. Almost no one would paint God in those graphic terms, but it's amazing how many of us have that picture of God in our heads. Even when our rational minds tell us otherwise, we *feel* that that's God's attitude toward us when we make a mistake.

Let's see if we can't find a different picture of God. We're back in the living room, watching Baby Mike let go of the couch and walk across the living-room floor. Again, Baby Mike stumbles and falls, but this time, Daddy goes over and picks Baby Mike up, holds him tight in his arms, and says, "I'm so glad to see that you want to walk and you're trying to walk!" Then he puts Baby Mike down on the floor, holds his two little hands, and says, "Now, let me help you learn how to walk."

In this picture, you participate with Baby Mike in his experimental walking. You help Baby Mike learn. You help him through the mistakes.[1]

This picture, I believe, illustrates God's true attitude and Jesus' true attitude toward us when we sin in the process of learning not to sin. Jesus picks us up in His arms, hugs us tight, and says, "I'm so glad you want to overcome and that you're trying to overcome." Then He puts us down, places a hand around our shoulder, grasps one of our hands with His other hand, and says, "Now let Me help you learn to do it the right way."

How can anyone say that Jesus' putting His arm around us and holding our hands when we sin as we learn not to sin is a broken relationship? He died for the very sins we are trying to overcome. At the very least, He's going to stick by us as we learn to overcome. Jesus does not hold back His kindness until we get our performance in order. He's looking for all the reasons He can possibly find for sharing His kindness with us in spite of our performance, to help us improve our performance. "He who did not spare his own Son, but gave him up for us all—how will he not also, along with him, graciously give us all things?" (Romans 8:32).

As I have said so many times already in this book, if you want nothing more than to serve Jesus and simply are not yet able to do so completely, you can rest assured that Jesus is on your side.

You do not break your relationship with Him just because you yielded to that master passion that still exercises some control over your life. To the contrary, He is beside you to encourage you and help you do better next time.

But for that to happen, you must have the right picture of God in your mind. You must have the right picture of Jesus in your mind.

In Exodus 20:3 God said, "You shall have no other gods before me." None of us has ever seen God, of course. Whatever the God we believe in is like, He is a perception in our minds—a picture, if you please. Our relationship with God and our relationship with Jesus are determined by the picture we have of Them in our minds. A false picture of God is a false god. One of the main reasons why God gave us the Bible is to provide us with an accurate picture of Himself.

It goes without saying, of course, that no one has a perfect picture of God. We are all growing in our understanding of God. Even the nice picture of God that I painted for you in the illustration of the father who hugs his baby and helps him learn to walk is only partial. It only shows God's mercy. It says nothing about His justice, which is equally as important as His mercy. No single illustration or metaphor is adequate to encompass all that God is. Indeed, no collection of human metaphors is adequate to encompass all that God is. Yet God teaches us about Himself through metaphors and illustrations. Many of Jesus' parables are pictures that help us to understand God.

I pointed out earlier that even the theological term *justification,* which we've been discussing in this first section of the book, is a picture of God. It shows us a God who declares us righteous, even though we are still very imperfect on the inside. My purpose thus far in this book has been to expand on the snapshot of God that we get in the word *justification.* I've tried to paint in the details a little more clearly. And to a great extent, I've used more pictures to fill in the picture. I've used metaphors such as the oil-well platform, the town of Centerville with one thousand starving citizens, Jesus the football Coach, and the father whose baby is learning to walk.

I must hasten to add, however, that justification is much more than a picture in our minds. Justification is an actual transaction in heaven—God's crediting Christ's righteousness to our account in heaven's record books. And that is an event that happens outside of our minds, trillions of miles away from us, yet our understanding of that transaction is another picture of God.

And the picture in our minds is crucial. We receive justification by faith, and faith *is* in our minds. In one sense, we can say that faith itself is a picture in our minds. Justification implies a picture of a God who forgives our sins and refuses to hold them against us. Faith means to accept that picture as real. It means making that the picture of God by which we order our lives.

If justification is required for salvation, and if faith can be defined as the picture we have of God in our minds, then we can say that our salvation depends on having the right picture of God in our minds. No wonder God said, "You shall have no other gods before me." A false God—a false picture of God, if you please— can cost us our eternal life!

I would like to suggest that conquering the dragon within— victory over sin—also depends on having the right picture of God in our minds. If we hold a false picture of God, such as the picture of the father who spanks his baby when he stumbles and falls, victory will be impossible for us. May I remind you of Ellen White's statement that "to go forward without stumbling [sinning], we must have the assurance that . . . an infinite pity will be exercised toward us if we fall"? Without that assurance—without that picture of God—sooner or later, we will stumble; we will sin.

To *keep* from falling, we must have a picture in our minds of a God who accepts us *when* we fall.

---

[1]In reality, the best fathers probably let their babies learn to walk by themselves. I'm sure there's a sense in which God does that for us too, but that's not the point of this analogy.

DEVOTIONAL EXERCISES

Biblical reflection on chapter 10

1. Can you think of a story in the Bible that illustrates God's acceptance of our *desire* to obey Him, even though we have sinned? (Possible examples: Genesis 28:10-22; John 8:1-11; Luke 22:31-34.)

2. What made the difference between God's acceptance of these people and His harsh response to the sin of Ananias and Saphira in Acts 5:1-11?
3. When you sin, how can you tell whether God thinks of you the way He thought of the woman caught in adultery or the way He thought of Ananias and Saphira?
4. What evidence can you see in your life that God accepts you and is encouraging you even when you make mistakes?

Devotional study of 1 Samuel 10
1. What additional insights into Saul's character and personality do you find in this chapter? Add to the material about his character that you wrote for chapter 9.
2. Samuel told Saul that "the Spirit of the Lord will come upon you in power, . . . and you will be changed into a different person" (verse 6). Then, "as Saul turned to leave Samuel, God changed Saul's heart" (verse 9). Did this experience change Saul's character or personality? Did it have the potential for changing him? Write a paragraph explaining your answer.
3. What could Saul expect to happen as a result of what God did in his life? What would you expect to be the result in your life if God were to do the same thing for you that He did for Saul?

Chapter
Eleven

A WEEK IN THE LIFE
OF JOHN DOE

I will conclude Section I on justification with a story that I'm sure you will immediately recognize is as made up as were the stories of the football coach and Baby Mike. We will call this story "A Week in the Life of John Doe." Below is a diagram of that week. If you look carefully at each end of the week, you will see that the diagram includes the day before the week begins and the day after it ends:

S	S	M	T	W	T	F	S	S

Unfortunately, John Doe has a problem. He has a terrible temper. When he goes into a rage, his feelings erupt like a volcano. On Saturday night, before the new week has even begun, John Doe becomes enraged at his wife over something she did that he didn't like, and he really lets her have it.

Actually, John Doe is a lot like me. When I get really angry, I'm always right. Have you ever noticed that in yourself? John Doe knew his wife deserved every word he'd said. It took him twenty-four hours to cool down enough to realize that he might actually be wrong. By Monday evening he knew he was wrong, but it still took him until Tuesday afternoon to come to the place he could confess to his wife. Here's how it looks on the diagram:

S	S	M	T	W	T	F	S	S

According to the theory of the Sabbath School teacher in my church in Texas, John Doe broke his relationship with Jesus the moment he lost his temper with his wife on Saturday night, and he didn't get that relationship back till the following Tuesday evening when he confessed to her. Presumably, had he died during those three days, he would have been lost. Fortunately, after Tuesday night, he's clean. Now he can rest in the assurance that if he were to die he would be saved, because he has his relationship with Jesus back.

Well, almost, but not quite, because unfortunately, John Doe has another problem. He also tells white lies now and then to stay out of trouble. On Monday afternoon his boss calls him in and says, "John, how are you doing on that project I gave you a couple of weeks ago?"

John feels mortified, because he hasn't done one thing on the project, so he pretends to have made some progress. He tells a white lie. Again, John has sinned, and this time there is no waiting period to learn that he was wrong. The moment the words are out of his mouth, he knows he's made a mistake. But it takes him till the following Thursday afternoon to get up the courage to make amends to the boss.

Let's put that sequence of events on our diagram:

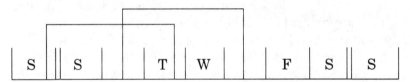

Fortunately, after confessing to the boss, John is a clean man, back in relationship with Jesus. Now he can safely die if necessary, because he would be saved.

Unfortunately, John still has a problem with his bad temper. On Thursday evening when he gets home, he blows up at the kids, and he doesn't make amends to them till Sunday morning:

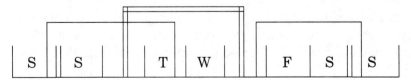

Now I want you to notice something very interesting. If John Doe breaks his relationship with Jesus every time he sins, and he doesn't get that relationship back till he confesses, then during this entire week he has had a relationship with Jesus for all of three or four hours—from the time he confessed to the boss until he blew up at the kids. Here's how that looks on our diagram:

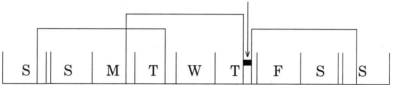

If the theology of my Sabbath School teacher in Texas is correct, then three or four hours a week in a relationship with Jesus is enough for John Doe to overcome all of his temptations and develop a character like Christ's.

Somehow that doesn't quite make sense to me.

Actually, I can prove to you that John Doe had a relationship with Jesus during this entire week. How? By the simple fact that three times during this week he sinned, three times he recognized that he'd sinned, and three times he repented and confessed. Non-Christians don't do that. Non-Christians don't care whether they sin. They sin and laugh because they got away with it.

Do you understand now why Jesus has to stick close to us between the time we sin and the time we confess that sin? For most of us, if He didn't, there'd be precious little time when we were in a relationship with Him!

I like what Jack Sequeira said in his book *Beyond Belief.* Near the end of his chapter on "Justification and Sanctification," he said, "Before concluding this chapter, we should look at some common misunderstandings about this important subject" (103). I will quote the second misunderstanding that Jack mentions and his response to it:

2. *Every time we fall or sin we become unjustified.* This is another common misunderstanding about justification. It is a monstrous teaching that has no support from the Word of God.

It is true that every time we fall into sin we misrepresent Christ and hurt Him, because even the smallest sin figured in what happened at the cross. However, God does not reject us every time we make a mistake or fall into sin. If we believe that we lose our justification in Christ each time we sin, we completely invalidate the truth of justification by faith. Such a concept is based on the idea that we are justified because of our obedience—what Christ is doing in us—and not because of what He has already accomplished for us by His doing and dying on the cross. Such an idea makes the gospel good advice instead of good news (104).

I like that way of explaining it. It helps me to understand that God loves me even when I make mistakes. As long as I *want* to overcome and am *trying* to overcome, He stays beside me—even when I *don't* overcome.

DEVOTIONAL EXERCISES
Biblical reflection on chapter 11
1. Read Romans 5:1-5. What feelings can you expect to experience when you know that God has justified you?
2. Should John Doe have experienced these feelings while he was wrestling with whether to confess to his wife and his boss?
3. After you've given your answer to question 2, answer it again, keeping in mind everything you've learned in Section I. How do you feel about that? Does this seem like the right answer? Write a paragraph reflecting on your conclusions.

Devotional study of 1 Samuel 11
1. Can you think of a time in your life when you were confronted with a threat that frightened you greatly? What did the people of Jabesh Gilead do in response to the threat of their enemies? Was this an appropriate thing to do? Is that what you did? Why or why not?
2. What evidence of God's leading do you see in the way the people of Jabesh Gilead were delivered?
3. What evidence of God's leading do you see in the way your threat was resolved?

SECTION II

How Jesus Helps Sinners
Gain the Victory
(Sanctification)

Station Break 1

We have completed Section I of this book and have started on Section II. I have organized Section II carefully so that you can more easily follow what I'm saying. However, the organization is a bit complex at best, so from time to time we will pause for a "station break" that will give us a chance to review where we've been and take a brief look at where we're going. I've also reproduced a condensed outline of Section II at the end of each station break, with an arrow pointing to where you are at that point.

You have probably already noticed the title of Section II—"How Jesus Helps Sinners Gain the Victory." Many people fear that victory is impossible for them, just as they fear that God doesn't save imperfect people. And, again, the issue isn't just theology. There's plenty of theology here, to be sure, for those who are interested in such things, but as in Section I, our primary interest is with personal experience. We Christians tend to fear that our besetting sins and addictions have such a powerful hold on us that God's promise of victory is not intended for us. For someone else, perhaps, especially the spiritual athletes among us, but "not for me," we say. That's how the *Insight* correspondent, whom I quoted in chapter 1, felt.

I want to assure every desperate sinner out there, whoever you are and wherever you are, that God's promise of victory was given *just for you*. Regardless of how discouraged you may feel about ever conquering the dragon that lurks inside you, you can overcome if you go about it right.

The purpose of Section II is to explain how to "go about it right." However, before we get into that discussion, we need to do two things. First, we need to define what character is, and second, we need to understand the relationship between sin and addiction and the role of belief in conquering them. These are the issues we will be discussing in the next two chapters.

One other point is important before concluding this station break. Four of the points for victory that I will discuss in Section II are so crucial to victory that I have called them "cardinal principles." To be sure that you spot them as you come to them, each of these cardinal principles will be clearly identified and printed in boldface type. Please watch for them, and make a special note of each one.

And now, here is where we are on the outline of Section II:

Section II: How God Helps Sinners Gain the Victory
  Station Break 1 <——
    12. Character Change
    13. Sin, Addiction, and Belief
  Part 1: Changing Our Sinful Understanding
  Part 2: Changing Our Sinful Desires
  Part 3: Changing Our Sinful Behavior
  Part 4: Final Thoughts on Victory

Chapter
Twelve

CHARACTER CHANGE

There's a saying among computer enthusiasts, "Garbage in, garbage out." They mean that if the operator puts incorrect information into the computer, he can expect to get incorrect information back out.

Suppose you're a computer operator, and you find that the computer keeps giving wrong solutions to the problems you ask it to solve. What do you do? First, you look at the data you entered. If it's correct, you check the formulas that are calculating the data to see if they are correct. You know the answers can never be correct as long as the data or the formulas you put into the computer are flawed. The wrong answer is a problem, but it's not the most basic problem. The real difficulty lies inside the computer. Once you locate the error on the inside and correct that, the computer will give you a correct answer on the outside every time.

It's the same with you and me. We can compare our character, which is inside of us, to the inside of a computer. Our behavior is the output. And, like a computer, whether our behavior is correct or incorrect—good or bad—depends on whether the programming and information in our characters are correct or incorrect.

Ellen White defines that programming quite precisely: "The thoughts and feelings combined make up the moral character" (5T, 310). We experience our thoughts and feelings on the inside, in our minds and hearts. That's why the title of this book is "Conquering the Dragon *Within*." We cannot expect to gain the victory over temptation and besetting sin merely by tinkering with our outward behavior. We must conquer sin on the *inside*. Then we will succeed in changing our behavior on the *outside*.

If character is a combination of our thoughts and feelings, then character *change* means getting a change in our thoughts and feelings. This sounds easy enough, but it's not, as we will see in a moment. We are not helpless, though. God has provided certain things we can do that make character change happen more efficiently and therefore more rapidly. We will be discussing these strategies for character change in succeeding chapters. First, however, we need to discuss three important issues that are related to character development.

Character changes slowly

It's important to understand that our character is fairly firmly fixed in our minds and emotions. That's bad news and good news at the same time. The bad news is that you can't just flip a switch in your brain to change a character defect. That's one of the significant differences between our brains and a computer. All the computer operator has to do to change the data or the formula is to type the change on the keyboard and press Enter or click the mouse, and it's done.

Character change is a much slower process.

We sometimes think of character change as a change in the direction of our life or a certain part of our life. We say, for instance, that we want to overcome our bad temper or our habit of overeating.

All a runner has to do to run the other direction is to plant a foot on the ground, turn his body, and start running back where he came from. The change takes an instant. Character change is much more like turning a battleship around in the ocean. The change begins the moment the captain turns the wheel, but a good bit of time must elapse for the change in direction to be completed. Character change can take months or even years—a wait that's frustrating, but entirely possible if we go about it right.

The good news is that our positive character traits are also firmly fixed in our minds, and neither we nor anyone else can change them with a snap of the fingers. People who feel cheerful and optimistic most of the time can usually count on staying that way.

Bad news and good news. Character changes slowly. That's the first important issue about character development that we're discussing in this chapter. Here's the second one.

Christian character change requires conversion

Did you ever buy a computer? You probably assumed that its memory was blank when you took it out of the box and put it on the desk or table in your home. However, every computer comes with certain programming built in. Without this preprogramming, the computer could not operate the software you put in it. The programming that comes with the computer when you buy it is installed by the manufacturer, and if anything goes wrong with it, only the manufacturer can repair it.

Another common assumption is that when we buy a computer, its preprogramming has been put in correctly. And, with occasional exceptions, this assumption is correct.

You and I are born with certain preprogramming built into our minds and emotions, or, to put it another way, our characters come preprogrammed to a certain extent. However, unlike the average computer, we cannot assume that the preprogramming in our characters is correct. All human beings are born with flawed characters. A number of factors can account for this, including the character traits that we inherit through the genes and chromosomes. This may be what Ellen White had in mind when she spoke about "inherited . . . tendencies to evil" (DA, 296).

However, the most significant flaw in the preprogrammed characters we receive at birth does not come through physical inheritance. It's a result of humanity's broken relationship with God. According to the Bible, every human being is born with this flaw in their preprogramming. "I was sinful at birth," David wrote, "sinful from the time my mother conceived me" (Psalm 51:5).

This problem is not God's fault, though. He created Adam and Eve "very good" (Genesis 1:31). Through the Holy Spirit dwelling in their hearts, our first parents were in union with God from the moment of their creation. Because of this, they had perfect characters on the inside.

The problem began when Adam and Eve chose to disobey God. At that time they broke their relationship with Him. The Holy Spirit left them. Another way to put it is to say that they died spiritually.

The children that were born to Adam and Eve had physical life only. Spiritually, they, too, were born dead. And every other human being since then, with the exception of Christ, has been born spiritually dead.[1] Paul had this spiritual death in mind when he told the believers in Ephesus that before their conversion they were "dead in [their] transgressions and sins" (Ephesians 2:1).

If a flaw should develop in the preprogramming that came with your computer when you bought it, you would have to send it back to the manufacturer or an authorized repair center. It's crucial to understand that the same is true of our spiritual defects. We are powerless, by ourselves, to change the preprogramming we're born with. Only God, our "Manufacturer," can do it. The Bible calls this change "being born again" (John 3:3). We are doomed to produce flawed behavior on the outside until God fixes us on the inside by reinstalling His Holy Spirit in our minds and hearts. This is one of the primary means God uses to help us change our thoughts and feelings.

Some people make the mistake of assuming that once God changes them on the inside through conversion, their characters will output totally good behavior. They insist that Christians who continue to sin after conversion have not been truly converted. We have already seen that instant victory over all sin is a myth. It doesn't happen. And the idea that a Christian who sins has not been truly converted is a cruel myth that easily throws sincerely religious people into deep depression.

The reason why the new birth doesn't work instant character perfection is simple enough. The entrance of the Holy Spirit in our hearts is not like turning on a light switch that instantly dispels all darkness throughout the room. It's more like dropping some yeast into a lump of dough. The yeast penetrates slowly, and it has to be kneaded in. As the yeast spreads through the dough, each part that it touches is changed, causing it to rise.

That's how the Holy Spirit works in our lives. The Holy Spirit is a principle of life that God drops into our minds and hearts, and as time goes on, the Spirit touches various parts of our characters—our inherited and cultivated tendencies to evil—and changes them. The change that the Holy Spirit brings about in our hearts when we first accept Christ is only the first step in Christian character development. The molding of our habits and our behavior is an ongoing process that follows.

Secular authors have described many techniques for changing habits and attitudes, and often these can be helpful to the Christian who is trying to develop his or her character. I will have more to say about this in future chapters. But by themselves, secular behavior-modification methods are not the character development that the Bible talks about. Christian character development begins with the life principle that the Holy Spirit drops into the heart at conversion, and it continues as day after day that principle softens the hard spots and smooths the rough places in our characters.

We need to keep in mind one important difference between yeast and the new birth, though. A small bit of yeast dropped into the dough one time will penetrate the entire lump. However, we can't just drop the Holy Spirit into our lives once when we are first converted and be done with it. We must have more of the Holy Spirit each day. The Holy Spirit is a Person, and conversion is an ongoing relationship with Him. This is the general conversion that I spoke about in an earlier chapter.

The Holy Spirit can also change us in specific ways. We each have character defects that cause us to make mistakes. Sometimes these defects cause us to sin. As the Holy Spirit comes in touch with first one and then another of these defects, He molds and changes them to perfection.

These defects may be inherited. For example, some children seem to be born aggressive, while others are born shy. In tiny "doses," these traits may not be flaws, but exaggerated shyness or aggression can cause untold havoc in a person's life. Other character defects are cultivated. We sometimes call our cultivated character traits "habits"—behaviors that we have repeated often enough that we do them without thinking.

Changing our flawed character traits takes much longer than the time it took to instill them in the first place. This is true of both inherited and cultivated character traits. Character change also requires conscious effort on our part. Often the effort we put forth to change our flawed character traits is painful, sometimes intensely so. Kneading the dough to spread the yeast throughout the entire lump is a lot of work. In the same way, it takes a lot of hard work on our part to spread the Holy Spirit throughout our character defects so that He can change them. That's why character change cannot be the basis of our salvation. If it were, salvation would be by works.

Faith and works

We need to settle an important theological question before getting into the third important issue about character development that I want to talk to you about in this chapter. Some people feel very uncomfortable with any discussion of Christians putting forth effort to develop character. "Human effort is works," they say, "but Christians are saved by grace, not works."

The fear that emphasizing works and human effort compromises the gospel stems from a misunderstanding of the purpose of works and personal effort in the life of the Christian. Here are two principles that resolve this confusion:

**The purpose of faith is salvation.
The purpose of effort is character development.**

It is crucial that Christians understand the difference between these two. Those who don't understand the difference risk trying to save themselves on the one hand and excusing sin on the other. Once Christians understand that the effort they put forth to develop character is not the basis of their salvation, they are free to put forth the most strenuous efforts to do good works without compromising the gospel. And, as we've already seen, they are also free to understand that God does not reject them when their efforts to produce good works fail. If God were to break His relationship with us every time we made a mistake, then our salvation would depend on our maintaining good works.

God is actually very pleased with our good works. Let people "see your good works," Jesus said, so that they may "glorify your Father which is in heaven" (Matthew 5:16, KJV). And Paul wrote, "We are God's workmanship, created in Christ Jesus to do good works" (Ephesians 2:10).

Did you see that? Paul said God created you and me for good works! One of the major purposes of our existence is good works. And Jesus said that when we do those good works, we give glory to God. Another way to put it is to say that a balanced Christian character gives glory to God, because good works on the outside can only arise from a character that has been transformed on the inside. So away with the false notion that good works compromise the gospel! The gospel is what makes it possible for people to do good works. Without the gospel, you and I and every human being on earth would be destined to a life of sin and bad works. With the gospel, we can continually output works that give glory to God and make the world a better place to live.

Since our good works are pleasing to God, and since those good works stem from what we are like on the inside, it follows that God places a high premium on what you and I are like on the inside. Our character is very important to Him. He is waiting anxiously to help you and me conquer the dragon within. The rest of this book is about how we can cooperate with God to develop a character that will produce increasingly good behavior.

This discussion of faith and works leads us into the final important issue about character development. This issue is especially significant, because it is also the outline around which most of the rest of this book is organized.

God's part and our part

It's crucial to understand that while it's impossible for us to develop a good character without God's help, He does not do all the work for us. He leaves some things for you and me to do, and if we don't do them, we will not develop a strong character.

That's how it is in other areas of life. God makes seeds that can sprout and grow, and He brings the sunshine and the rain that activate the life in the seed. But the farmer has to till the soil, plant the seeds, and keep out the weeds. The seeds cannot grow until God does His part, but all of God's efforts will not bring a harvest until human effort is introduced into the process.

The same is true in spiritual matters, including character development. God will do certain things for us that make character change possible. However, He has planned other things for you and me to do, and it is impossible for us to develop a character in harmony with His will until our effort is introduced into the process.

The fact that we can't *do* God's part, however, does not mean that we should ignore it. While you and I can't *do* His part in our character transformation, we must *understand* it, for if we don't, we may try to do God's part ourselves. We must understand His part so we can leave it to Him. And in order to cooperate the most effectively with Him, we must also have a very clear understanding of our part. Christians who understand God's part and their part, and who leave God's part to Him and put forth vigorous efforts at doing their part, will experience dramatic, and often very rapid, character change.

I have good news for *Insight*'s correspondent. You don't have to go on living in defeat day after day. You do need to understand that victory won't come instantly, but you also need to know that *it will come.*

In addition to understanding God's part and our part in character development, it's also important that we understand the areas of life in which we need to change. Character development requires that we experience change in three ways. We need a change in:

Our sinful understanding
Our sinful desires
Our sinful behavior

It is crucial that we understand the difference between God's part and our part in each of these three areas. I have prepared a chart to help you keep it all straight as we work our way through the rest of this book:

Change Needed	God's Part	Our Part
In Our Sinful **Understanding**		
In Our Sinful **Desires**		
In Our Sinful **Behavior**		

Those who have read my book *The Crisis of the End Time* will recognize some similarities and some differences between this chart and the one in chapter 7 of *Crisis*—the chapter titled "Preparing for the Close of Probation." Many people have told me they found that chapter very helpful in overcoming temptation. I hope the rest of this book will be equally helpful to you—and more so.

However, before we get into the question of how to experience a change in our sinful understanding, let's take a closer look at addiction and sin and the role of faith in conquering them.

---

[1]There may be exceptions to this general statement. The Bible says that John the Baptist was "filled with the Holy Spirit even from birth" (Luke 1:15). Was this an exception to the general rule that all babies are born spiritually dead, or can all godly parents give birth to children whose lives are under the influence of the Holy Spirit? The Bible doesn't address that question.

DEVOTIONAL EXERCISES

Biblical reflection on chapter 12
1. Read Romans 1:8-32, and make a list of all the places where Paul directly or indirectly suggests that wicked people experience evil on the inside—in their thoughts and feelings. If you have time, do the same thing for chapters 2 and 3:1-18.
2. Read Hebrews 8:10 and Romans 2:14, 15. What relationship, if any, do you see between these verses and the new birth that Jesus spoke about in John 3:3-8?
3. Can a person who claims to be a Christian know for sure that he or she has been converted? Answer this question using the texts in question 2.

Devotional study of 1 Samuel 12
1. Why did God bring a severe thunderstorm on the occasion of Samuel's speech in verses 1-15?
2. Why did the people repent of having asked for a king in verse 19, when only a short time before they had demanded a king and refused to listen when Samuel remonstrated with them? (See chapter 8:4-22.)
3. Was the people's relationship to God any different in chapter 8 from what it was in chapter 12? Was God's relationship to them any different? Were they more saved in chapter 8, less so, or the same as in chapter 11?

Chapter
Thirteen

ADDICTION, SIN, AND BELIEF

During August 1994, the *Adventist Review* ran a series of three articles called "Adventists and Family Crisis." According to authors Fred Kasischke and Audrey Johnson, Adventist families experience the same dysfunction as families in the general population. The study was limited to families in the Southeastern California Conference, and the authors were guarded in extrapolating their findings to Adventist families nationwide. Nevertheless, their conclusion that "family crises are [not] unique to those living in southern California" (*Adventist Review*, 18 August 1994, 17) seems reasonable.

Specifically, the survey found that 30 percent of those Seventh-day Adventists interviewed had been physically abused at home before the age of eighteen, 43 percent were emotionally abused, and 16 percent experienced sexual abuse or incest. In addition, 37 percent had lived with an alcohol or drug abuser, 7 percent had attempted suicide, and 3 percent were or had been practicing homosexuals.

While it is likely that some of this abuse was inflicted by a non-Adventist parent or relative, we must acknowledge that a significant number of Seventh-day Adventists have been and are abusive in various ways. This is another way of saying that a significant number of Seventh-day Adventists are severely addicted, since that is the condition under which abuse nearly always happens. The Kasischke/Johnson study does not report on addictions such as sex (other than incest), work, food, etc. However, Seventh-day Adventists need to get their heads out of the sand and recognize that these addictions exist in our church right now and have for a long, long time.

106

I do not wish to condemn, though. Abusive people *must* be called to account, and there is a time and a place for the church to do that. But the purpose of this book is to offer hope to addicted people. I am going to assume that the majority of those who are addicted and who abuse feel terribly guilty and wish they could find a way out. I want to show you the way out. In this chapter I will discuss three issues with you. First, we will talk about the nature of addiction, including some of the more common addictions that afflict the human race, especially in North America. Second, we will look at the relationship between addiction and the biblical teaching about sin. And third, we will discuss what I consider to be the addict's and sinner's most powerful tool for recovery—belief.

What is addiction?

To be addicted means to be a slave to a destructive habit. The addict cannot say No to the behavior to which he or she is addicted. Some well-meaning Christians wonder why the addict doesn't "just say No." They do not understand that the addict is driven by compulsive, obsessive emotions. Saying No is not a choice. Countless alcoholics have tried saying No, and sometimes they succeed for a few months or even a few years, but in the long run, they nearly always go back to their drinking. Very few will succeed in long-term recovery if they are depending for victory on their own ability to say No to their addiction.

The concept of addiction first arose in relation to alcoholism. Today we speak of "chemical addiction," which includes addiction to narcotics, tobacco, and caffeine, as well as to alcohol. These substances introduce chemicals into the body that the body becomes accustomed to and eventually demands.

We now know that human beings can become enslaved to a large number of obsessive-compulsive behaviors. The responses manifested by these people are so similar to the responses of chemically addicted people that it is common today to speak of them as addicts also. To put it another way, anyone who is a slave to any behavior, who cannot say No to that behavior, is an addict.

Addicts are the victims of intense emotional pain. They do not understand this pain, though. They just know that they feel awful. Suddenly, one day they discover something that causes them to feel good, and they latch onto it the way a drowning man grasps a life preserver. They are so desperate to feel good that anything will do, regardless of how destructive or evil they may know the behavior or substance to be.

There's a horrible deception going on here. The addict *thinks* he's found a solution to his problem, but he hasn't. The behavior that feels so good has merely anesthetized the pain. It has not done a thing to treat the cause of the pain. It's like taking aspirin for the pain caused by cancer.

Some addictions—chemical, sexual, food, etc.—cause the addict to feel horribly guilty, which only adds to the pain he's trying to anesthetize. The increased pain requires more of the addictive behavior to anesthetize the pain, yet each additional behavior creates more shame and pain to be anesthetized!

It's a vicious cycle that builds on itself, like a snowball rolling down a hill. Among the ultimate consequences of this process are disease, breakup of the family, bankruptcy, imprisonment, and in extreme cases, death.

Others looking on from the outside can observe the addict sliding deeper into a horrible pit, and with their logical brains they ask, "Why can't he or she 'just say No'?" They don't understand that the addict's emotions have taken charge of his life, and he can't "just say No." That's the slavery. "Those who have never passed through such an experience," wrote Ellen White, "cannot know the almost overmastering power of appetite or the fierceness of the conflict between habits of self-indulgence and the determination to be temperate in all things" (MH, 173).

This was the problem of the alcohol and cocaine addict whose story I shared with you in chapter 7. This was the problem of *Insight*'s correspondent in chapter 1. This is the problem of all those Christians who wonder, Has God abandoned me because I did it the ten thousandth time? And the answer, of course, is No. God has not abandoned you. God does not demand perfect obedience before He will accept the addict and work with him to deliver him from his addiction. All those who claim that instant victory is possible do not understand the power of addiction. All those who claim that God cannot save people who are in ongoing sin have no idea how long and intense the battle for recovery from addiction is or how discouraged the addict is who believes

God will not accept him fully into His grace until he has completely overcome the addiction.

But enough of that part of the problem, which we dealt with in Section I. Let's get back to our investigation of addiction. Let's look at some typical addictions—not the traditional chemical ones, but addictions that you may never have realized were addictions.

Food. Food addictions range from overeating habits such as snacking between meals to bulimia and anorexia. One of the characteristics of any addiction is fear of losing the "supply." Full-blown food addicts such as bulimics are terrified of leaving home very far or for very long lest they lose the easy access to food that they have at home. Bulimics do not eat for nourishment. They eat to anesthetize the intense emotional pain they are suffering. Because three meals a day is not enough "medication," bulimics will eat and then throw up (purge) so they can eat again. A full-blown bulimic may eat and purge as many as fifteen or twenty times in a single day!

Anorexia is another serious eating disorder, but it is not a food addiction as such. Anorexics are actually control addicts. Usually they feel out of control in other areas of their lives, and food is one area they can control. They gain great satisfaction out of knowing that they have been able to abstain from food. In extreme cases, anorexics will literally starve themselves to death— all the while feeling "good" that they have such wonderful self-control!

If your food problem is overeating—saying No at potlucks, abstaining between meals, etc.—the principles I discuss in this book will probably be enough to help you deal with the problem. If you are a full-blown bulimic or anorexic, you can benefit from what I say in this book, but you also *must* have the kind of professional help that only an addiction-recovery center can offer.

Sexual addiction. There are several kinds and degrees of sexual addiction. Some people are addicted to the pleasure of the sexual experience itself. Sexual arousal and orgasm provide temporary relief from their emotional pain, and they can't say No to sexual desire. Full-blown sexual addicts engage in deviant behavior such as illegal massage parlors or exposing themselves to women on the street. For these, the thrill of living dangerously is often as much a way of medicating the pain as the sex itself.[1]

You may think that problems such as bulimia and full-blown sexual addiction do not happen among Seventh-day Adventist Christians. Don't kid yourself! Fortunately, help is available for such people, but they need more than this book can offer. In addition to professional help with addiction recovery, a full-blown sexual addict needs every bit of help that Sexaholics Anonymous can offer.

Work addiction. This is probably the most common addiction in America and other Western nations today and one of the most difficult to identify and treat. And the reason is simple: Our society rewards it. Bosses love those people who are so "committed" that they will put in sixty to eighty hours a week on the job—especially salaried people who don't get paid time-and-a-half! Employers promote workaholics and give them bonuses and pay raises.

Some workaholics may not overwork on the job, but they are constantly on the go at home. They can't just relax and enjoy life. Even on a vacation trip they are obsessed about jamming as many activities as possible into the itinerary! The whole family comes home more exhausted than when they left.

Caretaking. The caretaker feels responsible for everyone else's problems. If someone in the church calls at 9:30 on Friday night and says, "My Aunt Mary came to visit; can you teach my Sabbath School class tomorrow?" the caretaker feels responsible for that person's problem and says Yes. If someone in the church is in a financial bind, the caretaker gives them money. If a poor family just moved into town, they'll put them up with room and board for a week.

All of us should help people in need. Jesus said that's one of the things His people will do as they await His second coming (see Matthew 25:31-46). The difference between the normal person and the caretaker is in the extent to which they help others and in their reason for doing it. Caretakers will drop everything and run every time they encounter someone with a need. They feel so super-responsible for everyone else's needs that they will neglect their health, their finances, and their families' needs to take care of other people's needs. But the issue is not really helping people. Like the work addict, the issue is keeping busy to cover up their own emotional pain.

People in the care*giving* professions often become care*takers*. Because they are expected to be sympathetic and helpful, pastors in particular find it easy to fall into a caretaking addiction.

Shopping addicts. Some people medicate their emotional pain by shopping. They experience such a thrill every time they make a purchase that they can't say No, especially if it's "on sale." But saving money is not the issue with shopping addicts, proudly though they may announce each discounted purchase. The real issue is to keep busy shopping so they don't have to think about their pain. These people will often run up huge charge accounts and use up their full line of credit on several credit cards before bankruptcy forces them to face reality.

Relationship addicts. The relationship addict finds his or her whole meaning in life through relationships with people. Romantic relationships are the most common form—or perhaps I should say, the most noticeable form. There are at least two kinds. The first flits from one relationship to another to another. The person who cheats on his or her spouse through multiple affairs is probably a relationship addict. Sex is not really the issue in most of these cases. It's using the relationship to medicate the pain.

The other form of relationship addiction is the person, whether married or single, who stays in an abusive relationship. The woman with this kind of relationship addiction will allow a man to abuse her in the most vicious way. She may call the police when the violence becomes life-threatening but refuse to press charges when they arrive. Or she'll seek the aid of a women's shelter for a few days and then return to her husband. Why? Because for all its abuse, the relationship medicates her emotional pain.

Control. Control addicts find their emotional satisfaction through getting their own way. They are devastated when they can't have their way, especially in relationships with those who are closest to them. The family, the church, and those they work with on the job are especially likely to experience the control addict's disease.

Some of these addicts use anger to get their way. They discover early in life that when they get mad enough, people will yield to them. Others control through guilt manipulation, whining, and nagging. They discover that if they can wear people down enough, they'll eventually get their way. Most of us can recognize that these excessive efforts to control others are offensive and very damaging to relationships, but damaged relationships don't matter to control addicts. What does matter is the emotional payoff they get when someone finally gives in to their demands.

Religious addiction. The most difficult of all addictions for religious people to recognize is religious addiction. Like food, sex, work, helping people, and relationships, religion is good. It plays an important role in our lives.

Religion addicts are super-religious and often super-conscientious. They may attend church faithfully every day, or they may read their Bible far more than most people would consider normal for a healthy Christian experience. If you are very active in your religious faith, you may wonder how to tell whether you are a religious addict or a normal person to whom religion is very important. One of the best ways to check on this is to examine the amount of guilt you experience when you say No. If you can't skip a day of Bible study or absent yourself from church even one Sabbath without feeling profound guilt, you are probably using religion to medicate your pain.

Religious addiction often arises out of warped ideas about God. Religious addicts study their Bibles and attend church to please God, as though these activities will make them worthy of God's acceptance. Theologically, Christians call this "righteousness by works." But the real issue is not religion or being religious. It's making religiosity the source of one's self-esteem.

Addiction and sin[2]

Is addiction sin? Christians have no difficulty identifying food and sexual addictions as sin. Relationship addictions that lead a married person into multiple affairs also are easily labeled sin. Most of us would probably be willing to call shopping addiction that creates major overextension of one's finances a sin. But what about caretaking or control or religion? Can religion be a sin?

Yes, if it leads to an unbalanced life. All of the addictions I described in detail in the preceding few pages are activities that in themselves are normal. They only become addictions when we carry them to excess. Ellen White said, "It is carrying that which is lawful to excess that makes it a grievous sin" (TSB, 115). This principle applies to any activity, regardless of how good it may be in itself, when it is carried to excess. Christ predicted that at His second coming He would reject many religious people who claimed to have prophesied in His name and in His name to have driven out demons and performed many miracles (see Matthew 7:21-23). Why? Not because the things these people did were wrong in themselves, but because they did them for the wrong motives.

Even though the Bible does not use the term *addiction*, some of the descriptions it gives of sin match what we today understand about addiction. One of the best examples of this is the passage in Romans 7:14-25 in which Paul expresses his great frustration over his lack of victory. "What I want to do I do not do," he said, "but what I hate I do. . . . What a wretched man I am!" (verses 15, 24). Paul was speaking of sin in this passage, but he was describing the condition we today call addiction.

The Bible also refers to sin as slavery. In Romans 6:16 Paul said:

Don't you know that when you offer yourselves to someone to obey him as slaves, you are slaves to the one whom you obey?—whether you are slaves to sin, which leads to death, or to obedience, which leads to righteousness?

A slave has no choice but to do what his master says. The sinner also has no choice but to do what his "master" says. The sinner's master is his desires. When He created us, God intended that our minds should rule over our desires. But when desire gains the upper hand, our minds lose their control over our lives.

That's the addict's problem. He has no choice but to do what his desires dictate that he shall do. Paul spoke of this when he said, "Therefore do not let sin reign in your mortal body so that you obey its *evil desires*" (Romans 6:12); "For when we were controlled by the sinful nature, the *sinful passions* aroused by the law were at work in our bodies, so that we bore fruit for death" (Romans 7:5).

I italicized the relevant words in each passage—*evil desires* and *sinful passions*. Human emotions are a powerhouse. When they are under the control of reason, they can be a power for good in the world. However, when reason loses control and emotion takes over, the power of emotion becomes terribly destructive. Once reason gives over its control to emotion, emotion becomes a dictator, and reason is powerless to regain control by itself.

That's sin. That's addiction.

The Bible speaks of a sinful nature, "the old man," that must be destroyed (Romans 6:6, KJV). Addiction is an expression of that sinful nature. But God has the answer for our sinful nature. He has the cure for all addiction.

Belief

Addicts nearly always feel a profound amount of guilt and fear and often of anger. These emotions are both the cause of the addiction and its result. Fear, shame, and anger cause the pain that the addict is trying to medicate, yet his obsessive-compulsive behavior only deepens the fear and shame. It's a vicious cycle. Most addicts who realize that they are addicts understand exactly what the apostle Paul meant when he exclaimed, "What a wretched man I am! Who will rescue me from this body of death!"

Earlier in this book I called your attention to the following statement by Ellen White, in which she described addiction even though she didn't use the term. This time I would like you to notice the concluding sentence in the paragraph, which I have italicized:

> You desire to give yourself to Him, but you are weak in moral power, in slavery to doubt, and controlled by the habits of your life of sin. Your promises and resolutions are like ropes of sand. You cannot control your thoughts, your impulses, your affections. *The knowledge of your broken promises and forfeited pledges weakens your confidence in your own sincerity, and causes you to feel that God cannot accept you* (SC, 47).

The addict who wants out feels desperate. After repeated unsuccessful efforts to escape from his addiction, he comes to the conclusion that for him victory is impossible, and that's why he feels that God cannot accept him.

If you feel that way about your addiction, then the lesson above all spiritual lessons that you need to learn is that *victory is possible for you*. There *is* a way out. If you haven't found it yet, then you still do not understand God's plan for your escape. The good news is that you have some wonderful discoveries ahead.

I do not want you to think that the way out is easy. I am only assuring you that it is possible *if you believe that it's possible.*

In the station break a couple of chapters back, I mentioned that I will be sharing with you four cardinal principles to victory over sin. Here is the first one:

CARDINAL PRINCIPLE 1
Victory is possible for those who believe that it is.

This principle lies at the foundation of the second step of the Twelve Steps of Alcoholics Anonymous:

Step 2
Came to believe that a power greater than ourselves could restore us to sanity.

I have learned that I can conquer any defect in my life, as long as I believe that I can and keep asking God to help me understand the defect and the best strategies for overcoming it. I may not know how I'm going to overcome it when I first become aware of it, but I know that God will show me the way out. And because I believe He will, He always does.

In an earlier chapter we discovered that justification is available to those who *believe.* Now I want to tell you that victory—sanctification—is also possible to those who *believe.* Regardless of how discouraged you may have been about the possibility of conquering your besetting sin before you began reading this chapter, I want you to say to yourself over and over again, Victory *is* possible for me. You cannot do it alone, but with God's help you can. God's promises are always conditional on faith. If you believe that victory is possible for you, then it is.

When I follow His leading, victory always happens. Slowly sometimes. But it always does.

The dragon within is a defeated foe already!

---

[1]The majority of sex addicts are men, but some women suffer from this addiction too.

[2]Some Christians have questioned whether the concept of addiction as sin is biblically sound, I have responded to this concern in Appendix F. Appendix C responds to concerns some Christians have expressed about the Twelve-Step program for recovery from addiction.

DEVOTIONAL EXERCISES

Biblical reflection on chapter 13

1. Read Romans 6. What does it mean to be a slave to righteousness? If slavery to sin is addiction, is there a difference between slavery to sin and slavery to righteousness? Write a paragraph explaining your answer.
2. What evidence do you find in chapter 6 that victory comes to those who believe it is possible?
3. Why does Paul not stress faith or belief as a condition for sanctification in Romans 6 to 8 the way he stresses faith as a condition for receiving justification in chapters 3 to 5? Is faith less of an essential element for victory than it is for forgiveness?

Devotional study of 1 Samuel 13

1. What does the news of Saul's attack against the Philistines as it is reported in verse 4 suggest about the attitude of the Israelites toward their enemies? What was the people's attitude in verse 7? What does this suggest about the possibility that they would be victorious?
2. In verse 11, what problem did Saul tell Samuel he was trying to solve? Rewrite verses 7 to 12, giving an imaginary account of how Saul might have responded to this problem more appropriately and gotten better results.
3. Compare the issue of faith for victory in the biblical reflection questions 2 and 3 with the issue of faith that is suggested in 1 Samuel 13.

SECTION II
Part 1
Changing Our Sinful
Understanding

Chapter
Fourteen

God's Part:
SHOW US OUR SINFUL UNDERSTANDING

Baruch Goldstein woke up early on the morning of February 25, 1994. He dressed quickly, picked up an assault rifle, and left the house. By 5:30 he had arrived at the Ibrahim Mosque in the town of Hebron in Israel. A Muslim guard blocked the entrance, but Goldstein clubbed him in the shoulder with his rifle and rushed into the mosque. For the next ten minutes, he fired into the Palestinian worshipers. When it was over, thirty people were dead, and scores lay wounded. Goldstein himself was beaten to death on the spot by enraged Palestinians. In the confusion that followed, several more people were either trampled to death or killed by Israeli soldiers who were uncertain what was going on.

I would like to ask one question: What was the cause of this ghastly deed? Psychologists will no doubt argue that point for months if not years, but the Bible is clear. The cause was sin in Goldstein's heart, and it doesn't take a Christian to understand that. *Time* magazine said it well: Goldstein was a man "so full of hate he repeatedly threatened to do precisely what he did that Friday morning: kill as many Arabs as possible to settle 'his people's' scores" (*Time*, 7 March 1994, 52).

Amazing as it may seem to you and me, though, if we could ask him, Goldstein would tell us that his motives were totally righteous and his actions were absolutely justified.

It's always that way with sin. It *seems* so right.

Ask the Serbs. Ask the IRA. Ask the apartheid diehards and their militant black opponents in South Africa. They'll all tell you they are *right*.

Ask Paul Hill, who gunned down an abortion doctor and his companion in Pensacola, Florida. Ask Hugh Heffner, the editor of *Playboy* magazine. Ask the man who cheated on his income tax. They'll all tell you they are *right*.

Ask the alcoholic. Ask the man who yells at his wife, the woman who nags her husband. Ask the church member who gossips about the preacher. Ask the Christian who criticizes people who eat the "wrong" food and wear the "wrong" clothes. They'll all tell you they are *right*.

Sin always seems *so right*. And it's the same whether you're a mass murderer or a legalistic Christian. Most of us, when we're doing wrong, think we're doing right.

Sin caused Lucifer to rebel against God in heaven. Sin caused Adam and Eve's expulsion from the Garden of Eden. Sin caused God to destroy the world with a flood several hundred years later. The history of our world is the history of sin and its devastating effects.

Jesus died on the cross to save you and me from *sin*. If we are ever to be saved, we must understand *sin*. It's not enough to understand sin as a principle. It's not enough to recognize the sins of others. *The key issue for you and me is to see our own sin in the light in which God sees it*. We must understand our own wrong thoughts and feelings. Understanding them won't save us, but we cannot be saved until we do.

Those last two sentences were so crucial to your victory over sin and addiction that I want to boldface them for you:

The key issue for you and me is to see our own sin in the light in which God sees it. We must understand our own wrong thoughts and feelings, and we cannot be saved until we do.

You see, sin is self-deceiving. That's why Goldstein thought he was right and could not understand that what he did was so terribly wrong. It's easy for you and me to recognize the evil of Goldstein's ghastly deed, but the principle involved in his big sin and your and my little sins is the same. In fact, our "little sins" are more deadly than Goldstein's, because we tend to think that because they are small they are insignificant.

The question is, How can we take sin seriously when the wrong things we do seem so right? And the answer is simple: We can't.

If we are ever going to recognize our own sins, someone must intervene from the outside to show us what's wrong with our lives.

So where does that help come from? Again, the answer is simplicity itself. The help we need to understand the truth about our sins comes from God, and from Him alone.

God's part in helping us to understand our sin

When Jesus was eight days old, His parents took Him to the temple in Jerusalem to dedicate Him to the Lord. Shortly after arriving at the temple, Joseph and Mary met two prophets—Anna and Simeon. Simeon took Jesus in his arms, and the words he said to His mother Mary have everything to do with God's part in helping us to understand our sin. "This child is destined to cause the falling and rising again of many in Israel," Simeon said, "and to be a sign that will be spoken against, *so that the thoughts of many hearts will be revealed*" (Luke 2:34, 35).

To whom, I ask, does God want to reveal the thoughts of many hearts? To the angels in heaven? To the preacher? To the board of elders? Of course not! God wants to reveal the thoughts of many hearts to the hearts themselves. He wants to reveal the thoughts of your heart to you, and He wants to reveal the thoughts of my heart to me.

Jesus revealed sin by His teaching, and He revealed righteousness by His teaching and His example. But teaching and example are not enough. Many people have read about Jesus' words and His life without making the application to their own lives. Information about right and wrong will not change us. Something has to happen inside of us. The Agent that actually works on our hearts to help us understand sin is the Holy Spirit. Jesus said, "When he, the Spirit of truth, comes, he will guide you into all truth" (John 16:13). Part of what the Spirit will reveal to us is the truth about our sins. Jesus said that the Spirit "will convict the world of guilt in regard to sin" (verse 8). This is God's part in helping us to get a change in our sinful understanding, and it's time we put it on our chart:

Change Needed	God's Part	Our Part
In Our Sinful **Understanding**	**CONVICTION: SHOW US OUR SINS**	
In Our Sinful **Desires**		
In Our Sinful **Behavior**		

The part of sin that we most need to understand

When they talk about sin, Christians typically think of the wrong things they *do*: swearing, overeating, reading pornography, watching violent television programs, etc. These are sinful behaviors, and every Christian should stop doing them. Don't ever let anyone talk you out of putting forth your best efforts to stop sinful behavior. Later in this book, I will offer some specific suggestions that can make stopping your wrong behavior easier.

However, wrong behavior is not the root of the problem. It's like the difference between a symptom and the disease. When you go to the doctor complaining of a sore throat, aching muscles, and a fever, he'll tell you that you have strep throat. You could stay home and take Tylenol pills, but as everyone knows, you would be dealing with the symptoms, not the real cause of the problem. The ideal treatment for strep throat is to take an antibiotic that will kill the germ that's causing it.

Important as it is to deal with sin at the behavior level, that is merely treating the symptom. To treat the disease, we must get into the mind and heart. Sin is both behavior and the motive that prompts it, and motive is the disease. Motive is the real source of the problem. The part of sin we most need to understand, then, is the motive that lies behind the behavior.

The reason we tend to emphasize behavior rather than motive is that behavior is visible, while motive is way out of sight. Suppose, for example, that you see me place a tithe envelope in the offering plate. You would be inclined to think that I was a very good person indeed. But God, who reads my heart, may know that the offering was prompted by pride or that in the very act of giving, I was wishing I could spend the money on clothes.

Jesus made it clear that the foundation of the sin problem is in the heart. "What comes out of a man is what makes him 'unclean,'" He said. "For from within, out of men's hearts, come evil thoughts, sexual immorality, theft, murder, adultery, greed, malice, deceit, lewdness, envy, slander, arrogance, and folly. All these evils come from inside and make a man 'unclean'" (Mark 7:20-23).

So we especially need insight into our wrong motives, and God is anxious to help us understand them. Ellen White said:

> To men whom God designs shall fill responsible positions, He in mercy reveals their hidden defects, that they may look within and examine critically the complicated emotions and exercises of their own hearts, and detect that which is wrong. . . . The Lord in His providence brings men where He can test their moral powers and reveal their motives of action. . . . God would have His servants become acquainted with the moral machinery of their own hearts (CCh, 54, 55).

In order to truly understand our sins, then, *we must understand our motives.* And this is where we especially need the Holy Spirit's help. Even if the motive is quite obviously wrong, as in the case of rage or jealousy, our emotions usually fool us into thinking that our feelings are entirely justified. Only the Holy Spirit can help us to understand that our motives are wrong.

Fortunately, the Holy Spirit is always taking the initiative to show us the things in our lives that are wrong. This is one of the few parts of salvation for which He does not require our cooperation before He will act. And it's a good thing, because if God didn't take the initiative to convict us of our sins, it would never occur to us to ask, and we would be eternally locked into them.

Shame, fear, and anger

The most basic of all evil motives is selfishness. Ellen White said that when Adam and Eve sinned, "selfishness took the place of love" (SC, 17). Every other wrong motive springs from selfishness.

However, *selfishness* is a rather nebulous term. I don't know about you, but it's rather rare that I stop and think, *I'm feeling selfish right now.* Part of the reason, I suspect, is that selfishness doesn't come on strong like some of our other feelings. I'd like to mention three wrong motives that spring from selfishness, which seem to have an especially strong hold on us humans: shame, fear, and anger. These three motives are a major source of our dysfunction and sin. Anyone who learns to recognize these feelings has gone a long way toward understanding the sin in his or her life.

Shame, fear, and anger originated early in the history of the human race. Shame has an especially interesting story behind it. According to Genesis 2:25, Adam and Eve "were both naked, and they felt no shame." Notice, however, that as soon as they sinned, they felt shame. The Bible doesn't use the word *shame* in the story, but from what they did, we know that's how they felt: "They realized they were naked; so they sewed fig leaves together and made coverings for themselves" (Genesis 3:7). Thus began the history of shame in our world.

Fear also began that day. When God came to visit Adam and Eve, they ran from Him and hid among the trees in the garden. When God found them, He asked why they had fled, and Adam said, "I heard you in the garden, and I was afraid because I was naked; so I hid" (verse 10).

Adam and Eve did not choose to be ashamed and afraid. They did not press a button on their heads that turned these feelings on in their brains. They did not say to themselves, "It's time to start feeling shame and fear." These emotions simply happened to them. They were an inevitable result of their sin. Adam and Eve could no more have stopped themselves from feeling shame and fear right then than they could have stopped themselves from being alive.

It's crucial to understand that these negative emotions are just as inevitable for you and me as they were for Adam and Eve. We cannot stop them by ourselves.

I'm going to guess that anger also showed up immediately after Adam and Eve sinned. Eve must have felt angry when her husband pushed all the blame for their sin onto her. She didn't say so, though. Instead of talking about her anger, Eve stuffed it. She denied it and passed on the blame for what happened to the snake. To this day, that's a typical human response to anger.

The first mention of anger in the Bible came a few years later when Cain and Abel got mixed up in a fight over whose sacrifice was more acceptable to God. The Bible says that when God rejected Cain's sacrifice, he was "very angry"—so angry, as we all know, that he murdered his brother (Genesis 4:7).

The good part about shame, fear, and anger

The reason why these negative emotions are so inevitable will probably surprise you. We cannot escape from them, because God built them into our minds when He created us. It's the same with food and sex. You and I don't have to make an effort to feel hungry. Most of us don't have to try feeling sexual. These emotions arise within us naturally, because God built them into our bodies when He created us, along with the capacity to feel shame, fear, and anger.

You can probably accept the idea that fear is a normal emotion, but most of us have grown up thinking that anger is a wrong emotion, and shame, if not wrong, is at least undesirable. However, when we use them the way God intended, these emotions are good.

Let's begin with fear, since it's the easiest one to understand. What happens when you get too close to a one thousand–foot cliff? If you have a normal fear of heights, your heart starts to beat harder, and the closer you get the harder it pounds. By the time you're two inches from the edge, your heart feels like it has climbed out of your chest into your throat!

What would you feel if I were to grab your hand and push it toward a hot stove? What would you feel if I gave you a shove onto a busy highway or into the cage of an angry lion?

You'd feel fear, of course!

Fear is a healthy emotion. It protects us from physical harm. Under normal circumstances, as soon as we are safe, our fear subsides. Fear is healthy as long as we experience it in small doses, as long as we use it properly to protect ourselves. It only becomes unhealthy when we allow it to go on and on and on. If you were to stand two inches from that one thousand–foot cliff all day every day, you'd probably die of a heart attack before a week was up.

Shame is also a healthy emotion in small doses. God gave us the capacity to feel shame so we could protect ourselves from getting into moral harm. Shame keeps us acting decent around other people. For example, the Ten Commandments tell me that it's wrong for me to make love to a woman other than my wife, and shame makes me *want* to keep my hands to myself when I'm around other women. I'd feel horribly ashamed if a woman were to slap me in the face for being fresh, so I behave properly.

What about anger? Isn't that always bad? If it is, then God must be at least as bad as we humans are. The Bible says that He "rebukes [the kings of the earth] in his anger and terrifies them with his wrath" (Psalm 2:5). "Who can endure his fierce anger?" asks Nahum (chapter 1:6), and Hosea tells us that His anger burns against those who worship idols (chapter 8:5). Over and over the Bible tells us that God is "slow to anger" (see, for example, Exodus 34:6; Psalm 86:15; Joel 2:13; Nahum 1:3), which means that *He does have the capacity to feel anger.* When He made you and me in His image, He gave us the capacity to feel the same anger that He Himself can experience.

"But that's righteous indignation!" you protest.

Exactly. That's the point. By whatever name you choose to call it, there is a form of anger that is not bad—that is, in fact, very healthy and appropriate. I can prove that to you. I can get you to feeling profound righteous indignation by the time you're through reading the next paragraph.

Saddam Hussein is famous, among other things, for his mistreatment of the Kurdish population in Iraq. You may not have known how horribly he mistreats them, though. When Kurdish parents resist the efforts of his soldiers to subdue them, the soldiers gouge out the eyes of their children.

Now, how do you feel? I hope profoundly angry.

Yet a Kurdish family cat would have slept right through an abusive situation like that. Why? Because cats don't have the capacity to feel anger over child abuse. You and I feel angry because God built into us the capacity to feel anger, and when the circumstances are right, we don't even have to try to feel it. It's as automatic as hunger five hours after the last meal.

Anger is the response we feel anytime we see injustice, whether it is done to ourselves or to others. God gave us the capacity to feel angry so we could protect ourselves and others from abuse and injustice.

Some people have told me that it's OK to feel anger over injustice to others, but we should not feel angry over injustice done to ourselves.

Really, now?

Suppose you are waiting in the checkout line at the grocery store with a gallon of milk in one hand and a ten-dollar bill in the other. Suddenly, the person in front of you turns around, snatches the money from your hand, and dashes out of the store. Would you just smile and say, "He must need that money—I'll let him have it"? I hope you'd feel angry, because you should. Anger would make you chase the person down and try to retrieve your money. Anger would make you take down the license number on his car and report him to the police.

If your spouse abuses your child, you should feel angry. If your spouse abuses *you*, you should feel angry. Abuse is wrong and must be stopped, regardless of whether it's done to yourself or someone else. It's a serious mistake to suppose that you can allow people to get away with abuse simply because you are the victim. If you allow abuse against yourself to go unchecked, someone else will suffer next.

Much of the sin in our world arises out of the improper use of shame, fear, and anger. These powerful emotions lie at the foundation of all addiction. That's why it's so important that we understand how to use them properly. Unfortunately, most of us use one or more of them improperly much of the time, thinking that we are using them properly. That was Baruch Goldstein's problem. He thought he was using his anger appropriately. It never occurred to him that he was being horribly abusive.

Earlier in this chapter, I explained that wrong behavior is merely a symptom. Motive is the real cause of our sin. Shame, fear, and anger are among the most powerful of the motives that cause us to sin. God built these emotions into us when He made us so that we would have the tools to protect ourselves from harm. Unfortunately, the underlying selfishness of our sinful natures causes us to use these emotions to profoundly abuse ourselves and others—and to think we are right in doing so!

Much of our effort to break away from sin must go into learning the right way to deal with these emotions. But before we can deal with them properly, we have to *understand* them. God's part is to show us our sins—all of them, including our dysfunctional shame, fear, and anger.

But what about our part in getting a change in our sinful understanding? That's what the next three chapters are about.

DEVOTIONAL EXERCISES

Biblical reflection on chapter 14

1. Read 1 Corinthians 1, then write a paragraph describing the flaw in the Corinthian Christians' understanding.
2. Have you ever seen this flaw in a church you attended? If so, write a paragraph or two describing the situation and especially any flaw in your own attitude that may have contributed to the problem.
3. Read 1 Corinthians 2, and write a paragraph or two explaining Paul's solution to the Corinthian Christians' sinful understanding. How would you apply Paul's solution to the situation in the church that you described in question 2? Especially ask yourself how to apply Paul's solution to whatever part you may have had in the problem.

Devotional study of 1 Samuel 14

1. Compare chapter 14 with chapter 13. What is the difference between these two chapters with respect to the attitude of the people in each one?
2. Compare the attitude of Saul's army toward the enemy in chapter 13 with their attitude in chapter 14:15-23. What made the difference?
3. Write a paragraph reflecting on the power of faith as it relates to victory. If you have time, write another paragraph applying these thoughts to any enemies who cause you anxiety.

Chapter

Fifteen

Our Part: 1
ASK FOR HELP WITH OUR SINFUL UNDERSTANDING

In the spring of 1993, my wife Lois and I spent three weeks vacationing in China. United Airlines flew us across the Pacific Ocean to Hong Kong in late April, and after a weekend catching up from jet lag, we took a train to the city of Guangzhou (pronounced Guan-jo, the modern name for Canton). We spent our time in Hong Kong with friends, but once we arrived in China, we were totally on our own. We were in a foreign land without the slightest idea how to so much as count to ten in the local language.

On one occasion we tried buying a train ticket using our best sign language and two words of Chinese. After half an hour of waving her arms and jabbering what to us was gibberish, the agent threw up her hands and walked out!

You and I are embarked on a journey through a country that is far more foreign than China was to a couple of green Americans. The country we are journeying through is our minds.

Now, isn't that amazing? Our brain, the place where we've lived twenty-four hours a day since we were born, is foreign territory! But it's true.

The maze
Our sin-contaminated minds are like a giant maze, and we're blindfolded, stumbling around, trying to figure our way out. The odd thing is, though, that we've stumbled around in this maze for so long (all our lives!) that it seems normal to be there. We have no idea we're lost, and even if we did, we wouldn't know the way out. Some of us wouldn't even want out. We need help!

The first thing we need help with is our sinful understanding.

God is the One who convicts us of sin, but there are three things you and I can do to cooperate with Him, which we will be discussing in this chapter and the two that follow. The first thing we can do is to *ask* Him to change our sinful understanding. We can ask Him to convict us of sin, especially our own sins. Let's put this on our chart, and then I'll explain more about it:

Change Needed	God's Part	Our Part
In Our Sinful **Understanding**	Conviction: Show us our sins	**ASK FOR IT**
In Our Sinful **Desires**		
In Our Sinful **Behavior**		

Please pay careful attention to what I say next, because I will refer to it frequently in succeeding chapters. We need to ask God for two kinds of help with our sinful understanding:

1. We need help understanding that we're in the maze. That is, we need help understanding that we are sinners.
2. We need help understanding how to get out of the maze. That is, we need help understanding the right strategies for overcoming our sins.

Each of these is crucial to our recovery from the disease of sin and addiction. Let's examine them in greater detail so you will understand exactly what I mean by them.

Understanding that we're in the maze
Many people have no idea they are even in the maze. They think they're getting along fine, and they'll thank you not to bother them with all that Bible and morality stuff. Before we can have any desire to get out of the maze, we need to recognize that we are trapped in it.

Salvation involves, among other things, coming to the realization that our lives are flawed and that we need help getting them back in order. Until we realize that something's wrong with us, we aren't going to try to fix it.

I'm assuming that everyone reading this book is a Christian, and therefore you have some awareness that you are in the maze. You have some awareness of your sins. Yet even the best of us does not understand how deeply into the maze we are. All of us have defects in our characters that we know nothing about, and all of us need a better understanding of the sins we *do* know about. If you are struggling with food, anger, sex, or some other compulsive behavior, ask God to help you understand more about how that temptation works in your mind.

Any time we talk about asking God for something, we're talking about prayer. Below are several simple prayers you can say to ask for His help with your sinful understanding:

- Lord, please show me the flaws in my character that I'm not aware of.
- Lord, please help me understand why I yield to (name the temptation).
- Lord, help me understand the defects that keep me from being like Jesus.
- **And especially help me to understand my wrong motives.**

You will find similar prayers in the Bible, especially the Psalms. David said, "Search me, O God, and know my heart; test me and know my anxious thoughts. See if there is any offensive way in me, and lead me in the way everlasting" (Psalm 139:23, 24). David asked God to show him the wrong things in his life. "Show me my wrong motives and attitudes," he said, in essence. "Help me understand them, so I can deal with them."

You may think of prayers that mean more to you than the ones I just shared with you. Let God lead you to the prayers that will be most helpful to you.

Perhaps you noticed that the last prayer in the list of prayers above was printed in boldface type: "Especially help me to understand my wrong motives." I boldfaced that prayer to show that it needs to go with each of the other prayers. Motive is the foundation of all that's wrong with us, so be sure you include it, or something like it, every time.

Understanding the way out of the maze

Once we discover that we're in the maze, it's time to learn how to get out. I'm convinced that one of the main reasons Christians fail in their efforts to conquer temptation is that they don't understand the right methods for overcoming. This is as much a part of getting a change in our sinful understanding as learning what our sins are in the first place. God is anxious to teach us strategies that will make His work in our lives more effective. The starting place is to ask God for His help. Here are some prayers you can say:

- Lord, please show me what I can start doing right now that will help me to conquer (name the temptation).
- Lord, please help me to understand anything I'm doing that's hindering my efforts to overcome.
- Lord, help me to understand the principles that lead to victory.
- **And especially help me to understand the motives that are interfering with my efforts to overcome.**

Again, because sinful motives underlie all our sin problems, the boldfaced prayer at the end of the list needs to go with each of the others.

The rest of this book is about strategies that have made victory easier for me. So read with a prayer in your heart that God will call your attention to the things I say that will make victory easier for you too.

Asking for help in the end time

God's people in the end time especially need His help in developing character and overcoming sin. Ellen White points out the importance of character development in the end time in a statement you read in the Prologue:

> Those who are living upon the earth when the intercession of Christ shall cease in the sanctuary above are to stand

in the sight of a holy God without a mediator. Their robes must be spotless, their characters must be purified from sin by the blood of sprinkling. Through the grace of God and their own diligent effort they must be conquerors in the battle with evil (GC, 425).

Many Seventh-day Adventists get very worried when they read statements like that. They say to themselves, "I could never be that good. I guess I won't be ready for the close of probation and the second coming of Jesus."

I want to relieve you of that worry. If you are faithful in doing your part in character change, God guarantees to do His part and get you ready on time. Ask Him to show you your character defects. Ask Him to show you the wrong motives that prompt you to do wrong things. Here are some prayers you can say as you seek to develop a character for the end time:

- Lord, show me the things I need to know in order to be ready for the close of probation.
- Lord, show me what I need to know in order to be among the 144,000.
- Lord, show me the things I need to know in order to reflect the image of Jesus.
- **And especially help me to understand my wrong motives.**

What can you expect?

What can you expect to happen when you say the prayers I've shared with you in this chapter? Probably nothing at first. You won't hear voices in the night or see lights flashing in the sky. But don't give up. Keep saying those prayers. Keep asking for a change in your sinful understanding. Keep asking God to show you the things in your life that need correcting, and keep asking Him to show you what you can do to overcome. In due time, He *will* give you the insight you desire.

It may happen in an obvious place like church. You're listening to an inspiring sermon, and all of a sudden, the minister says something that's just what you've been asking God for.

However, these flashes of insight will often come to you in the most ordinary way and at the most ordinary times. I've had them come to me while I was on the phone talking with a friend, who all of a sudden said something that hit me between the eyes. My friend had no idea how much his words helped me, but God used them to answer my prayer and to help me understand. Sometimes my flashes of insight seem to come from nowhere. I've had them while I was walking down the hall in my home! A thought crossed my mind, and I knew God put it there.

Remember that the most important insight you're asking for is a better understanding of your motives—the feelings and desires that prompt you to do the things you wish you didn't do. Fear, shame, and anger are among the most common underlying reasons why we yield to temptation, yet often we are totally unaware of them. So ask God to help you understand the fear, shame, and anger that prompt your wrong behavior.

I need to warn you that one of God's favorite methods for helping you understand the wrong things in your life is trial and suffering. Ellen White said that "the trials of life are God's workmen, to remove the impurities and roughness from our character" (MB, 10). So don't be surprised if, after saying those prayers, difficulties start piling up in your life. Instead of complaining, say, "God, help me to use this experience to learn what I need to know in order to develop a character more like Yours."

One of the best times to pray for a better understanding of what you can do to overcome your temptations is right after you've yielded. Ask God to show you what went wrong and what you can do to avoid yielding next time. This is genuine experimental religion.

When my wife and I first began saying those prayers, we would never in our wildest imaginings have guessed one of the most important ways God had in mind to answer them for us. Now, several years later, we know, and we are very grateful. It's called The Bridge—an Adventist chemical and codependency treatment center in Bowling Green, Kentucky.

We both attended the two-week codependency treatment program at The Bridge in 1992. We have followed that up by attending at least one and sometimes two Twelve-Step meetings nearly every week since, and we have done a lot of reading on addiction and codependence. All of this has given us excellent insights into our character strengths and weaknesses. It has also provided us with some powerful tools for overcoming. We learned, for example, that the Twelve-Step method developed by Alcoholics Anonymous for gaining the victory over alcohol is an excellent tool for overcoming any character defect. Our character development has been much more rapid since we attended The Bridge and began applying the principles we learned there.

God may not lead you to The Bridge, but He will lead you to understand the sins you are unaware of, and He will show you strategies for overcoming them.

One of the things God has had to help me learn is the difference between His part and my part in the character change process. Sometimes, instead of letting God do His part, I've tried taking over and doing it for Him. It never works. Other times I've tried pushing off onto Him what I need to be doing myself, and that doesn't work either. I've found that learning to do my part and letting Him do His takes practice, and the fact that I've learned it on one temptation is no guarantee I'll understand how to do it on the next one.

I learn about my sins and the best strategies for overcoming them by asking God to show me. I'm thankful that He always answers that prayer. He does it in His time, not mine, and often the way He shows me is through my failure. But He always shows me.

DEVOTIONAL EXERCISES

Biblical reflection on chapter 15
1. Read James 1:5. What sin are you struggling with that you need wisdom to overcome? Write a prayer that claims the promise in James 1:5 and applies it to this temptation. Be sure to include a request for insight into strategies for victory that you may not have thought about before.
2. Write a paragraph describing your feelings in the past about the possibility of victory over a particular temptation. Next write a paragraph applying the lessons of verse 6 to those feelings. With these thoughts in mind, what changes or additions might you make to the prayer you wrote for question 1?

Devotional study of 1 Samuel 15

1. What difference of opinion existed between Saul and Samuel over whether Saul had obeyed God? What basic emotion caused Saul to understand the situation the way he did?

2. Write a paragraph explaining the relationship between Saul's understanding of the situation and his disobedience of God's command. If you could have advised Saul, how would you have suggested he handle his feelings? Had Saul followed your advice, how might the story have turned out differently?

3. Can you think of a time when you experienced the same basic emotion that caused Saul to understand the situation the way he did? Apply your "advice" to Saul to your own experience.

Chapter
Sixteen

Our Part: 2
TALK ABOUT OUR SINFUL UNDERSTANDING

What I share with you in this chapter may seem very strange to you. It's so strange, in fact, that some people have actually told me it's wrong. Yet it's not strange at all. You and I do it all the time. It's called talking.

Talking is one of the simplest things you and I do. And that's good news. The part God has given you and me to do in changing our sinful understanding is not terribly complicated. We do it all the time, just like we walk, breathe, and open and shut our eyes. We do these things without even thinking.

Many of us have had the mistaken idea that overcoming our sinful character traits involves some complicated process that only the spiritual athletes among us can understand. Thus it comes as quite a surprise—and as very good news—that this part of overcoming temptation is as easy as talking about it.

Before going farther, let's put talking down on our chart, and then I'll explain it to you:

Change Needed	God's Part	Our Part
In Our Sinful **Understanding**	Conviction Show us our sins	Ask for it **TALK ABOUT IT**
In Our Sinful **Desires**		
In Our Sinful **Behavior**		

So what are we supposed to talk about to get a change in our sinful understanding?

We need to talk about our character defects. If this sounds strange to you, please keep reading, because it's based on an important spiritual principle:

**Talking about our problems
helps us to understand them.**

Remember that in this part of our book we are looking for ways we can cooperate with God to get a change in our sinful *understanding*, and talking about our character defects is one of the best things we can do to make that happen.

Talking about your defects will probably seem hard to you at first, but let me assure you that it is perfectly appropriate. James said, "Confess your faults one to another, and pray one for another, that ye may be healed" (James 5:16, KJV). Some Bible translations, such as the New International Version, say, "Confess your *sins* to one another." However, the Greek word that the King James Version translates "faults" is not the usual New Testament word for sin. It means more of a stumbling or a false step. Sin is certainly included. However, our faults may include defects such as inappropriate fear, shame, and anger that cause us to do sinful things, but that are not in themselves sinful.

Alcoholics Anonymous incorporates the principle of talking about character defects in the fifth of its Twelve Steps:

Step 5:
Admitted to God, to ourselves, and to another human being the exact nature of our wrongs.

Let me repeat the reason why you should talk about your character defects: *Talking about your character defects will help you to understand them.* Anytime you struggle to put ideas into words, you clarify those ideas in your mind. Every teacher will tell you that he or she learns more from teaching the lesson than the students do from hearing it. Talking about your character defects is a powerful way to understand them better, which will enhance your ability to deal with them.

You obviously need to be careful whom you talk to. You should look for someone with the following characteristics:

1. A person who is a strong Christian.
2. A person you can trust to keep your conversation strictly confidential.
3. A person who will accept you and not express shock at what you say.
4. A person who will mostly listen and not give advice.
5. A person who has been in recovery for some time.
6. A person of the same sex as yourself.

These characteristics of a person to confide in are so important that I'd like to discuss them with you a bit more in detail.

Choose a strong Christian. Galatians 6:1 explains why you should choose a strong Christian. Paul says, "Brothers, if someone is caught in a sin, you who are spiritual should restore him gently. *But watch yourselves, or you also may be tempted.*" When one person talks to another about his or her temptations, there is always the possibility that the one doing the counseling will be tempted by the account of the other person's sins. Notice that Paul does not say Christians should avoid counseling with those who have fallen into sin, but that only strong Christians should do this.

Choose someone you can trust. The reason for choosing someone you can trust to keep your conversation confidential is obvious enough. You don't want your problems spread all over the church or all over the neighborhood. Don't assume that because someone is a close friend he or she will make the best counselor. Someone with whom you are less emotionally involved is often a better choice.

Choose someone who will accept you. There's also a good reason for choosing someone who will accept you and not express shock at what you share. Baring your soul to another human being is difficult enough without the added burden of that person's condemning you. On the other hand, neither do you want someone who will pat you on the back and tell you that what you did isn't so bad after all. Either extreme will lessen and perhaps destroy the effectiveness of this exercise.

Choose someone who will listen without giving advice. If you expect advice from the person you talk to, you are talking to him or her for the wrong reason. The purpose of this exercise is not finding out what someone else thinks you ought to do. It's a way of discovering for yourself what you ought to do. Talking about your problems helps *you* to understand them, and when you understand what's going on in your life, you'll be in a much better position to figure out your own answers.

Choose a person who has been in recovery. You will obtain the greatest amount of help if you can choose someone who has been in recovery for some time already. One of the best ways to find such a person is to attend a Twelve-Step meeting such as Alcoholics Anonymous for a few months. In due time, you will recognize who makes comments that are most helpful to you. That is probably a good person to choose.

Choose a person of the same sex as yourself. Anytime you share personal information with another person, you engage them in a very intimate conversation. It's crucial that this intimacy remain nonromantic. This is especially true if the issues you need to talk about involve sex or marriage problems. Discussing these issues with a person of the opposite sex is almost guaranteed sooner or later to lead to romantic involvement, and the last thing you need stacked on top of all your other problems is the guilt of an inappropriate romance or sexual relationship. The safest rule is to choose someone to talk to who is the same sex as yourself.

In the Twelve-Step program, the person the addict talks to is called a "sponsor." Each addict is encouraged to find a sponsor.

Some people wonder whether a spouse would make a good sponsor. The answer is No. Ideally, you and your spouse will be completely honest with each other, and you may be as fully aware of the issues in each other's lives as your sponsors are. But often conflicts with your spouse will be the very issues you need to discuss with a sponsor. Even if you and your husband or wife get along perfectly well and are fully aware of each other's issues, it is best not to put on your spouse the responsibility of being your sponsor. A sponsor may need to confront you or give advice in ways that it would be difficult for your spouse to do without controlling the relationship, or at least appearing to control the relationship.

Other ways of talking

There are two other ways of talking that can be equally as effective in providing the insight you are looking for as talking to another individual.

Talking in a group. One of the best is sharing in a small support group that is committed to confidentiality. Some of my best insights have come in this way, not only from discussing my own issues but from listening to others discuss theirs. Often, someone else's experience will give me just the insight or the hope that I need to cope with my own issues.

Group talk is the primary method of therapy that is used by The Bridge in Bowling Green, Kentucky. During their co-dependency treatment program, fifteen to twenty people interact under the direction of two therapists several hours a day for two weeks. The three-month chemical dependency program uses the same method, but with a smaller group.

You may wonder how to find a group in which you can talk confidentially. One of the best places to start is with Alcoholics Anonymous. AA has two types of meetings—open and closed. Closed meetings are for alcoholics only, but anyone is welcome at an open AA meeting. Neither I nor my wife is an alcoholic, but we have attended AA meetings frequently in the last couple of years, and we have found them to be extremely helpful. Alanon—a meeting for the relatives and friends of alcoholics—is also helpful, and you will be welcome whether or not you have a relative who is an alcoholic.

During the last twenty to thirty years, the Twelve-Step plan for recovery has been applied to a wide variety of addictions. Today there are Twelve-Step groups for sexual addicts, love and relationship addicts, drug addicts, eating addicts, and gambling addicts, to name a few.

Some people feel that the church is an ideal organization to sponsor these small groups. Many churches make their facilities available for groups such as Alcoholics Anonymous, Overeaters Anonymous, and Sexaholics Anonymous. Churches often find it difficult to initiate these support groups for their own members, because the trust and confidentiality that anonymity provides are more difficult to establish where the group members know each other and are often together in other settings. However, churches can establish support groups for their own members when the members of the group are willing to commit themselves never to reveal outside the group who attends or what is discussed. In the winter of 1993, my wife and I started a Christian Twelve-Step support group in our church in Caldwell, Idaho, and we've attended nearly every week since. It's been an extremely beneficial experience.

I encourage you to look for a group in which you can talk about the issues that especially trouble you. If there is a Twelve-Step group in your area for your type of addiction, by all means try it out first. Appendix C lists the major Twelve-Step groups in North America with the address and telephone number for the national headquarters of each one. Also, you can call the AA service center nearest you for information on their groups, and any hospital that operates a drug and alcohol recovery program can give you a list of all the Twelve-Step groups in your area.

Shop around as you search for a group. Groups differ in their effectiveness, and one that is good for someone else may not be right for you.

You should by all means avoid those groups in which the members major on griping and complaining about their problems with very little discussion about healthy ways to cope. Look, instead, for a group in which you feel that you are getting personal help, even if all you do is listen to others talking about their issues.

What do you do if there is no group near your home for your particular area of need? You can try a couple of things. One is to attend a group that deals with a wide variety of problems, such as Codependents Anonymous or Emotions Anonymous. Even if these groups are not available to you, you can find help, because Alcoholics Anonymous groups are everywhere. I doubt there is a place in North America where you could not find an AA group within a few miles of your home.

The other thing you might consider is starting a group that focuses on your area of need. Generally speaking, it is wise not to start a support group yourself until you have been a part of a successful group for several months. Attend AA meetings to learn how it's done, and then start your group. Appendix D gives suggestions for starting a support group.

Writing. Another good person to talk to about your problems is yourself, and the best way to do that is by writing. This is also called "journaling." I have found writing to be a powerful way to gain insight into the issues that trouble me. Many years ago, when I first got out of seminary and began my ministerial internship, I felt depressed much of the time. I can still remember spending a lot of time writing about my feelings. Today, I have almost entirely overcome the tendency to become depressed, and I believe that writing about my feelings was one of the important steps I took to cope with them. And writing just happens to be easier to do than talking to another person!

Objections to talking about personal problems

I would like to discuss with you two objections that occasionally come up in the seminars in which I have suggested talking about one's character defects as a way to gain insight into them.

The Catholic confessional. Some Adventists object to the idea of discussing their problems with another person or with a group of people on the grounds that this is the same thing as the Catholic confessional. However, there is a world of difference between the Catholic confessional and what I am recommending.

Catholics are obligated to confess the darkest secrets of their hearts to a priest as a way to gain the assurance of forgiveness and salvation. I am recommending that you talk to a friend as a way to gain insight into the issues you struggle with. In a future chapter, I will mention one other powerful benefit that you will gain from talking about your character defects.

Ellen White. Another objection that some have raised to talking with others about character defects is based on statements by Ellen White such as the following one:

> I have been shown that many, many confessions should never be spoken in the hearing of mortals; for the result is that which the limited judgment of finite beings does not anticipate. Seeds of evil are scattered in the minds and hearts of those who hear, and when they are under temptation, these seeds will spring up and bear fruit, and the same sad experience will be repeated.
>
> For, think the tempted ones, these sins cannot be grievous; for did not those who have made confession, Christians

of long standing, do these very things? Thus the open confession in the church of these secret sins will prove a savor of death rather than of life (5T, 645).

Before using this statement to conclude that it would be wrong for you to ever talk to another human being about your character defects and sins, please consider the following points:

- Ellen White is talking about open confession in church. This is very clear from the last sentence, and it is especially clear from the context in the chapter where the statement appears.
- The problem as Ellen White describes it is not that talking to someone about our sins and character defects is a mistake, but that we should avoid talking to people who are weak in the faith and would be spiritually unprepared to handle the information we share with them. Paul said exactly the same thing in Galatians 6:1.
- Ellen White did not say that it is wrong to talk about our sins with others, but that in some instances this is inappropriate, especially in a public forum such as a church meeting.

A biblical basis

This is an appropriate point in our discussion to look at the biblical foundation for my recommendation that you talk to someone about your character defects. Some people believe that Christians should never discuss a sin or a character defect with anyone but God. However, it is very clear from the Bible that Christians have a responsibility to discuss such things with each other.

Jesus said that Christians must seek the lost sheep (see Luke 15:3-7). Lost sheep sometimes need to be told that they are lost, and sometimes they need to be shown how they are lost. In 1 Corinthians 5, Paul told the church to confront a man who was living in an immoral relationship. Jesus gave the same advice in Matthew 18:15-20. A brother who feels that he has been wronged by someone else in the church should go to that person and try to settle the problem.

A page or two back, I mentioned Galatians 6:1, where Paul says, "Brothers, if someone is caught in a sin, you who are spiritual should restore him gently." And James said that "whoever turns a sinner from the error of his way will save him from death and cover a multitude of sins" (James 5:19, 20).

In each of these examples, it is the loyal Christian who is to seek out the one in error. *God's people are responsible to approach those who are caught in sin and try to help them.* It is their duty to do everything in their power to restore them. We have a greater responsibility to seek the lost than they have to seek us. And when we do approach the lost, one of the things we must discuss with them is their sin. Often, we must discuss particular sins with them. That's what Paul meant when he said that if someone is caught in a sin, the spiritually strong members of the church should restore him or her. That's what James meant when he said that Christians should restore sinners from the error of their ways.

So the notion that Christians should never discuss specific sins with each other is simply not found in the Bible. To the contrary, the Bible *commands* Christians to discuss sin with each other.

All I am suggesting in this chapter is that the Christian who is seeking to live a more perfect life turn the initiative around. Instead of waiting for the spiritual members of the church to come to you, you should go to the spiritual members of the church and say, "I need help. Will you talk to me?"

First John 1:6-9 provides excellent biblical support for the importance of sharing our character defects with other Christians, though it may not seem to do so at first glance. Here is what that passage says:

> If we claim to have fellowship with him yet walk in the darkness, we lie and do not live by the truth. But if we walk in the light, as he is in the light, we have fellowship with one another, and the blood of Jesus, his Son, purifies us from all sin.
>
> If we claim to be without sin, we deceive ourselves and the truth is not in us. If we confess our sins, he is faithful and just and will forgive us our sins and purify us from all unrighteousness.

The first thing to notice about this passage is that from beginning to end it focuses on honesty and denial, which we will discuss in chapter 18. The very first sentence talks about people who claim to have fellowship with God but live like the world. That's denial. On the other hand, those who walk in the light, who are honest, have fellowship with each other. Notice that those who are in denial claim to have fellowship with God, whereas those who are honest actually do have fellowship with each other.

In this context, what does it mean to be honest? If the fellowship of those who are honest is with each other, then it means that they are honest with each other. They don't claim to be sinless. They are not afraid to let others see their character defects. They can relax about the fact that they are less than perfect.

Let's apply that in a practical way, shall we? Have you ever attended a church testimony service? What do the people say? They all stand up and praise God for the miracles He's performed on their behalf and the victories He's given them over sin.

When was the last time you saw someone stand up in church and testify that she or he was struggling with a bad temper or the temptation to shoplift?

I don't mean that we should never praise God for His goodness during a testimony service. But if that's *all* we do, what are we saying to discouraged people who may be present that day? They may think, *The people in this church sure do have it all together. My life is such a mess. I guess I'm not such a good Christian after all.*

Neither do I mean that we should unload every secret sin on the church. We read Ellen White's warning against that a few pages back. But the Bible does say that we should "carry each other's burdens" (Galatians 6:2), and a wise sharing of certain character defects in a testimony service or during a Sabbath School class is one way to do that.

John concludes the passage I quoted above with the familiar words of verse 9: "If we confess our sins . . ." This verse certainly means that we should confess our sins to God and those people we have wronged. However, in the context of honesty and fellowship with one another in the previous verses, I believe John is advising us to be open with each other about our character defects, even when we have not wronged each other. After all, the text does not say, "If we confess our sins to God and the people we have wronged." It says, simply, "If we confess our sins . . ."

And what is the result when we confess our sins? God, the people we have wronged, and indeed the whole church offer their acceptance and forgiveness, and the cleansing process goes on. Forgiveness and cleansing are available to those who are honest. They cannot be present in the lives of people who refuse to be open and honest with each other. Honesty about our human frailty is the basis for fellowship, and it is the basis for both forgiveness (justification) and cleansing (sanctification).

I suspect the idea that it is wrong for Christians to discuss their sins with one another arises more out of our shame than it does out of Bible principle. We feel embarrassed to expose our imperfections to other people. Our resort to Bible principle as a reason for not doing so is simply a cover for our shame. Unfortunately, if we wait too long to expose our imperfections to others, the error may become so obvious that they will feel compelled to come to us about the problem, and our embarrassment will be even greater, because then we will have been "caught."

A personal example

The very day that I was writing this chapter, my wife and I received a telephone call that illustrates perfectly what I'm trying to explain to you.

For several years we have been acquainted with a woman in the western part of the United States whom I will call Jennifer. Jennifer has a love and relationship addiction. She is involved in a highly addictive relationship with a man whom we will call George. George and Jennifer have known each other for several years and are involved sexually, even though they have never married. They fight constantly. She keeps calling us up and telling us how hurt she feels by the cruel things he says and does, and, listening to just her side of the story, we can tell that he feels equally hurt by what she says and does to him.

We have encouraged Jennifer repeatedly to break off the relationship with George, and she has vowed as repeatedly to do so, but the next day or the next week she goes back to see him. She cannot leave George alone, and he cannot leave her alone. Even though we have never met George, in our opinion, he is as addicted to the relationship as she is.

We encouraged Jennifer to enroll in a codependence and addiction treatment program, and eventually she did so at a center near her home. She stayed at the treatment center for about a month and gained a great deal of help.

About halfway through the program, she called us up, and among other things, she complained about the fact that nearly all the women in her group ignored her. "I want so badly to have a close relationship with another woman," she said, "but they all avoid me. It really hurts."

Jennifer went on about this for several minutes, and suddenly it dawned on me that she was talking about her addiction. So I stopped her right in the middle of a sentence. "Jennifer," I said, "what is your basic addiction?"

She said, "Love."

I said, "What else?"

She thought a moment, and then she said, "Relationships."

"Exactly," I replied. "And what you've been telling me about your relationship with women is part of the same addiction." I explained to Jennifer that the basic problem was not just George, but the fact that her self-esteem was based on relationships period.

Jennifer paused for a moment, and then very quietly she said, "You know, I'd never thought of that. I think you're right."

The point is that by calling my wife and me and talking, Jennifer gained a new insight into the extent of her addiction. I've experienced the same thing myself after talking with another person about my character defects. Jennifer is absolutely committed to recovery, and I am convinced that the insight she gained through talking to my wife and me that day will help her to progress more rapidly in her recovery.

Talking about our character defects *does* give insight. Often victory is virtually impossible without the insights that come through talking with another person or a group.

So talk about it. Share your burden with someone you can trust to help you bear it. I've tried it. It works. I recommend it.

DEVOTIONAL EXERCISES

Biblical reflection on chapter 16

1. Read John 4. Make a list of the spiritual insights that the woman at the well gained through her conversation with Jesus. In what ways was her sinful understanding changed?
2. Review the verses in the section "A biblical basis" that are given in support of talking to someone about your character defects. Next, think of someone who comes as close as possible to meeting the criteria for a "sponsor" (see page 138), and ask that person if he or she is willing to listen while you talk about a character defect. After you have done this, write a page or two describing the experience in light of these verses.

Devotional study of 1 Samuel 16

1. Why do you think Jesse had not invited his youngest son to attend the sacrifice? What was God's view of this situation?
2. God clearly guided Samuel in his evaluation of Jesse's sons. How can you and I obtain God's guidance in evaluating people today so that we make wise decisions?
3. What term in common use today would you use to describe Saul's mental health problem?
4. As you reflect on what you have learned about Saul's earlier life, what basic emotion lay behind his problem? What might he have done earlier in his life that would have kept his mental condition from deteriorating to this point?

Chapter

Seventeen

Our Part: 3
SEARCH FOR OUR SINFUL UNDERSTANDING

Thomas Edison was America's most prolific inventor. His two most famous inventions are the phonograph and the electric light bulb. He also transformed the entertainment industry with his motion picture projector.

Edison was still in his twenties when, in 1876, he established a $40,000 research laboratory in Menlo Park, New Jersey. Twenty skilled technicians joined him in this venture. Eleven years later he moved to West Orange, New Jersey, where he built a research laboratory ten times larger than the first one. His West Orange facility was eventually surrounded by manufacturing plants employing some five thousand people!

Edison was an inveterate learner. At the young age of ten he read an elementary physical science book, and as a young man he read every scientific journal that he could get his hands on. When he was twenty-one, he read Michael Faraday's *Experimental Researches in Electricity* without stopping and then performed every one of the experiments that Faraday described!

This is the attitude that you and I need to have toward our character development. Edison craved scientific learning. We need to crave spiritual learning. Edison soaked up information about science like a sponge. We need to be sponges of spiritual information. Edison spent millions of dollars for scientific research. How much do you and I spend for spiritual research?

While it's not in the Bible, the old saying that "God helps those who help themselves" holds a lot of truth. After we've asked Him to reveal our character defects and how to change them, search for the information. Let's put this aspect of our part in changing our sinful understanding on the chart, and then talk about it.

Change Needed	God's Part	Our Part
In Our Sinful **Understanding**	Conviction: Show us our sins	Ask for it
		Talk about it
		SEARCH FOR IT
In Our Sinful **Desires**		
In Our Sinful **Behavior**		

Solomon said, "If you call out for insight and cry aloud for understanding, and if you look for it as for silver and search for it as for hidden treasure, then you will understand the fear of the Lord and find the knowledge of God" (Proverbs 2:3-5).

People who become rich through their own efforts spend most of their time learning about money and how to make it. Some people who play the stock market spend fifteen hours a day at it! Is it any wonder they succeed?

Solomon said that if we will search for spiritual insight the way rich people search for economic insight, we will get it. Please fix this principle firmly in your mind:

**Knowledge about spiritual issues
comes to those who search for it.**

When you ask God to give you insight into your sinful understanding, you are doing spiritual research. When you talk to others as a way of gaining insight into your sinful understanding, you are doing spiritual research. Everything we discussed in the previous two chapters was spiritual research. In this chapter, we will focus on research in the more traditional sense. I'd like to suggest three places you and I can do this spiritual research.

The Bible

The most obvious place to begin is with the Bible. The author of Hebrews wrote that "the word of God is living and active. Sharper than any double-edged sword, it penetrates even to dividing soul and spirit, joints and marrow; *it judges the thoughts and attitudes of the heart"* (Hebrews 4:12).

That's exactly what you and I need! We are not looking just for insight into our wrong behavior. Far more importantly, we are looking for insight into our wrong attitudes, motives, and desires. So the Bible is a significant research tool for Christians!

Paul told Timothy that "all Scripture . . . is profitable for teaching, rebuking, correcting, and training in righteousness" (2 Timothy 3:16). Again, the Bible provides exactly what we need. It points out our character defects, corrects our errors, and trains us in the way we should go.

It's extremely important that you understand exactly how to do biblical research for insight into your character defects. It's called a *devotional life.* This kind of Bible research is best understood when we contrast it with more traditional Bible study for doctrine and technical information. The purpose of technical research is to learn what the Bible says about such teachings as the Sabbath, the state of the dead, healthful living, etc. During the early years of the Adventist Church, our pioneers were very good at this kind of biblical research, and many of us still are. However, by itself, such research tends to be a sterile exercise of the intellect. The pioneers were very good at defining "the truth" in terms of doctrine, but spiritually, they were, as Ellen White put it, "as dry as the hills of Gilboa" (RH, 11 March 1890).

Devotional research means reading the Bible for what it says to you and me about our daily life, about our spiritual struggles, and about how to deal with the temptations that we face.

Devotional research is best done in a quiet place at a time when you know that you will not be interrupted. Fifteen minutes is enough, but half an hour to an hour is better. For me, the early-morning hours are ideal. In the evening I usually find myself so rushed trying to cram a few more things into the day that when I finally collapse in bed I'm too tired to spend much time with the Bible. I may feel sleepy when I first wake up in the morning, but usually my mind will clear up in a few minutes. And, with the entire day to work on my agenda, I tend not to obsess so much about everything else I have to do.

I usually get up in time to spend an hour on personal devotions, though occasionally I have only a half-hour. I try to divide the time equally between Bible study and prayer. This is not a hard and fast rule, though. Sometimes I will spend most of the time praying or reading the Bible.

I like to choose a book of the Bible and read it through slowly. Each day, before I begin, I ask God to use the passage I will read that day to help me understand my spiritual strengths and weaknesses and the areas of my life that especially need attention. God answers that prayer. I don't mean that every single day I come away with a startling new insight, but usually I find a helpful thought. And, as time goes on, my insight into my spiritual strengths and weaknesses grows.

An excellent way that I have discovered to study the Bible for insight is to write as I study. I find that I get much more out of a Bible passage by journaling. Sometimes I get so engrossed in writing about a Bible passage that I spend an entire hour on one or two verses! That tends to be a problem as well as a help, though. Reading through an entire book of the Bible at the rate of an hour every verse or two takes an enormous amount of time. Consequently, I often read and meditate without writing.

Seventh-day Adventists believe that Ellen White was inspired in the same way the Bible writers were. Most of us have great confidence in the spiritual value of what she said, and I share that confidence. Some of my best insights into my character and the principles by which character changes have come from Ellen White. I urge you to make her writings a part of your daily devotional life, especially such deeply spiritual works as *Christ's Object Lessons*, *The Desire of Ages*, and *The Ministry of Healing*.

Please do not think that devotional study is everything, and doctrinal or technical study is unimportant. Often the deeply spiritual lessons of the Bible come to us while we are doing careful technical study.

For example, for two or three months now, I have been studying Paul's letter to the Romans, and at the present time, I am working on chapters 6 to 8, which deal with sanctification. I knew as I got into these chapters that they contained excellent counsel on how to gain the victory over sin, but much of it was confusing to me because of Paul's seemingly contradictory statements about law. His marriage analogy in chapter 7:1-6 was especially problematic. I spent several weeks doing a careful study of Paul's discussion of law, slavery versus freedom, and Spirit versus letter. Now that I am through, his spiritual lessons are much more clear, and I have found that they are very practical.

I believe each Christian should spend some time in doctrinal study. If what Seventh-day Adventists believe about the future is true, the day is coming when each of us will have to testify to what we believe before the enemies of the truth. Doctrinal study may not seem all that important, but if you aren't doing it now, a day is coming when you will wish you had. Each of us needs to obtain a solid understanding of the biblical basis for our beliefs.

However, devotional study is especially useful for getting insight into our sins and the strategies for overcoming them. In some cases, technical study is necessary to break through an obscure passage; but for the most part, devotional study means reading, praying, and meditating. The devotional exercises at the end of each chapter will help you do this kind of Bible study.

Books, tapes, and seminars on recovery

Recovery is a fairly new term in mental health circles. It means recovery from addiction and codependence. A whole recovery movement has developed in North America during the last twenty to thirty years, complete with a wide array of literature, audio and video tapes, seminars, and treatment centers. The origin of this movement is the Twelve Steps for recovery from alcoholism that were developed by Alcoholics Anonymous. Much of the contemporary material on recovery is an invaluable aid for Christians who want to conquer temptation.

Seventh-day Adventist material. At the time I am writing this book (1994), Seventh-day Adventists are just beginning to get involved in the recovery movement. I know of two books that have been published by a denominational publishing house in this area. One is Carol Cannon's *Never Good Enough: Growing Up Imperfect in a "Perfect" Family*, published in 1993 by Pacific Press. Carol gives an excellent explanation of codependence and addiction. *Too Much Is Never Enough,* by Gaylen Larson, was published by Pacific Press in 1992. It explains a variety of addictive behaviors that most people never associate with addiction.

The general Christian market. A wide range of books, tapes, and videos on recovery is available. I suggest that you go to a

Christian bookstore and ask to see their section on recovery. Then look for books that deal with your problem. Appendix E lists many of the Christian books that are available.

The secular market. The secular market also has excellent resources for people in recovery. Occasionally, when I bring this up in my seminars, someone will raise a hand and ask about the danger of Christians reading secular authors for help with overcoming temptation.

It's important to understand that most of these authors approach the question of recovery from a strictly humanistic point of view. They tend to talk about addiction and codependence rather than sin. They tend to emphasize early childhood abuse rather than sin as the major cause of addiction and codependence, and they emphasize human strategies such as counseling and group therapy rather than divine grace for recovery.

On the other side of the question, Christians need to understand that there is a great deal of truth in what the world has learned about addiction, codependence, and recovery.

Some people will object that all we need is the Bible and, for Seventh-day Adventists, the writings of Ellen White. That's like the doctor telling the cancer patient to go home and pray. As I study the Bible and the writings of Ellen White carefully, I find in them the same principles of addiction and codependence that are in the Christian and secular books I have read on recovery. Generally speaking, there is no contradiction between the Christian understanding of sin and the secular understanding of addiction and codependence. They use different language and focus on different aspects of the problem. But all addiction is sin.

For myself, this combination of secular theory with biblical theory has meant a dramatic improvement in my success with overcoming temptation. Today, I understand much better than I did even two years ago what is happening inside me when I'm tempted, and I understand much better what to do about it. When I put into practice the things I have learned, I overcome my character defects. Some temptations that bothered me for years are almost no problem at all anymore. I still believe the same theology of sin that I held before I got into recovery, but combining that theology with codependence and addiction theory yielded a more effective strategy for dealing with sinful behavior.

Recently I received a letter from a woman who attended one of my seminars in the midwest:

> While our son Edgar [not his real name] was away at boarding school, he developed anorexia-bulimia. It was a devastating experience for my husband and me and his sister, as we all love Edgar. So that is how I began my journey into secular books. I had to understand *how and why this could have happened to our family*.
>
> Reading these books opened up a whole new world. I read everything I could get my hands on. I literally went "underground" for six months, studying and taking notes, and every time I found something significant I would write it down. In due time all the basic principles of the Spirit of Prophecy and the Bible began to make more sense. How thankful I am that I had God's Word and the Spirit of Prophecy, for they helped me so much. But some of us need more help.
>
> I clung to the rock of stability Jesus Christ and hung on to His hand tighter than ever before. My heart was full of gratitude for His saving grace.

I would like you to notice two things this woman said about reading secular books. First, she said that she clung to Jesus "tighter than ever before" during this time. And second, she said that as she read these books, "in due time all the basic principles of the Spirit of Prophecy and the Bible began to make more sense."

I have discovered exactly the same thing. I used to puzzle over the meaning of certain statements Paul made in Romans, especially chapters 6, 7, and 8. Then, after about two years of intense study of addiction and codependence theory, I returned to a study of these chapters, and they were like an open window. *For the first time in my life, I understood what Paul was talking about!*

The woman who wrote the letter to me said, "How thankful I am that I had God's Word and the Spirit of Prophecy, for they helped me so much. *But some of us need more help.*"

How true! And that help is out there for us—in the world, if you please—if we will only go after it with a prayer that God will help us to recognize any false principles we may run across.

Unfortunately, some of us think that all knowledge about the human mind and emotions is to be found in the Bible and the writings of Ellen White. We think that if it doesn't come off the presses of our denominational publishing houses, it can't be fit to read. That, in my opinion, is a very proud, arrogant attitude that we must get rid of if we are to make significant progress in recovery from our addictions and besetting sins.

The truth is that the Bible and Ellen White can't possibly contain all knowledge. There is so much more available to those who will search for it with a prayer for guidance.

So I urge you to read these secular books. Read everything you can get your hands on that explains addiction and codependence. Once you have a good understanding of these principles, then read books and listen to tapes that discuss your area of temptation. Appendix E lists books on addiction and recovery.

Daily life

The third major area where Christians can search for insight into their sinful understanding is in their daily life. Ellen White is very clear on this point:

> If [God's people] would make the actions of each day a subject of careful thought and deliberate review, with the object to become acquainted with their own habits of life, they would better know themselves. By a close scrutiny of their daily life under all circumstances they would know their own motives, the principles that actuate them. This daily review of our acts, to see whether conscience approves or condemns, is necessary for all who wish to arrive at the perfection of Christian character (2T, 512).

Please notice in particular that last sentence: "This daily review of our acts . . . is necessary for all who wish to arrive at the perfection of Christian character." Adventists who are trying to be "good enough" for the close of probation need to pay careful attention to this advice.

The Twelve Steps of Alcoholics Anonymous also encourage addicts to search their daily lives. Two of the Twelve Steps speak very specifically about it:

Step 4
Made a fearless and searching moral inventory of ourselves.

Step 10
Continued to take personal inventory, and when we were
wrong, promptly admitted it.

How does a Christian go about searching his or her daily life?
One of the best aids that I have found for doing this is a book
called *The Twelve Steps: A Spiritual Journey*, published by Recovery Publications in San Diego, California.

This is a workbook with questions and lines for writing answers. It is a Christian application of the Twelve Steps. There is
a chapter on each of the Steps, and each chapter alternates between Bible verses that illuminate the Steps and questions that
help the reader to reflect on his or her personal life.

This is not a book that you will rush through. It took me a year
to work my way through it the first time. I usually meditated on
two or three questions each morning, along with the Bible reading and praying that I was doing in my devotional hour. The questions helped me think about areas of my life that I would never
have thought to examine on my own. I highly recommend this
book to anyone who is serious about victory over sin.

A summary of what we have learned thus far
This concludes our discussion of the three things you and I can
do to work with God in getting a change in our sinful understanding. Let's review briefly what we have learned.

It is impossible to overcome sin and temptation until we
understand it and realize that it is destroying us. God has a part
in changing our sinful understanding, and we have a part. God
has the only accurate view of sin, and His part is to convict us. It
is utterly impossible for human beings to understand sin in the
light in which God views it without the aid of the Holy Spirit.

However, we can cooperate with God in three important ways.
First, we can *ask* God to change our defective thinking about sin.
This gives Him permission to convict us. We need His help to
understand both our sins and the strategies for overcoming them.

Second, *talking* is a powerful way to increase our understanding of our sins and the strategies for overcoming them. We should talk to others in recovery, especially Christians, about our character defects. Talking can be one on one or in groups, and "talking" to ourselves by writing is also helpful.

Third, we need to go in *search* of a change in our sinful understanding. Our search should begin with the Bible, and for Seventh-day Adventists, the writings of Ellen White. We can also read books, listen to tapes, and watch videos that discuss addiction and recovery. And we should search our lives each day.

We are almost ready to begin our discussion of strategies for overcoming temptation. But first we need to discuss one additional aspect of getting a change in our sinful understanding.

DEVOTIONAL EXERCISES

Biblical reflection on chapter 17
1. Read Psalm 139. How would you feel about another human being knowing as much about you as God does? How do you feel about God knowing this much about you?
2. What verses in this chapter suggest God's willingness to reveal to us what He knows about us? Make a list of at least three things you will do in the next few days to search for God's understanding about your life, especially your attitudes and motives. A week from now, write a paragraph about the insights you gained.

Devotional study of 1 Samuel 17
1. Write a paragraph or two describing David's character as it is described in this chapter.
2. What made the difference between the attitude of the Israelite army as a whole toward Goliath and David's attitude?
3. Write a paragraph describing how you think David felt as he walked toward Goliath armed with only a sling. Have you ever felt that way in the face of danger? Have you ever felt the opposite in the face of danger?
4. What made it possible for David to feel the way he did about confronting Goliath? How can you apply this lesson to your attitude in the face of danger?

Chapter
Eighteen

HONESTY AND DENIAL

Tobacco was much in the news in the United States during April 1994. The chief executive officers of five of America's largest tobacco companies testified before Congress. The issue was twofold: Does tobacco cause addiction, and does it cause disease? Predictably, the five tobacco executives denied any relationship whatsoever between tobacco and either addiction or disease.

However, in recent years the scientific evidence for a link between smoking and disease has become so overwhelming that denying the relationship makes about as much sense as joining the Flat Earth Society. And as for addiction, during the congressional hearings on tobacco, two scientists testified before a House Subcommittee that they had found hints during the early 1980s that nicotine may be addictive, but their company, Philip Morris, Inc., suppressed the evidence and shut down their laboratory. Yet the chief executives of Philip Morris and the other tobacco companies told Congress that tobacco was not addictive!

How can rational, intelligent human beings be so blind? How can they so blatantly deny the obvious?

The answer is simple: Selfishness. Self-interest.

The same issue of my newspaper that reported the uncovering of evidence of nicotine's addictive potential during the early 1980s also ran a story about Aldrich and Rosario Ames, the husband-wife team who were arrested in 1994 on a charge of spying for the Soviet Union. Government officials called the case "the most damaging spy case in the history of this country." Yet at his sentencing hearing Ames said, "I do not believe that our nation's interests have been noticeably damaged by my acts."

The margin of difference between Ames's view of his deeds and the government's view is as wide as the Pacific Ocean and about as deep. How can two people look at the same set of facts and draw such enormously differing opinions? This is especially puzzling in view of an interview Ames held with reporters in a small prison conference room during April. According to the news story, Ames "spoke concisely and with apparent reflection, as if he had carefully considered and ordered his words." How can a man who appears that rational be so blind to the consequences of his acts?

Again, the answer is simple: Selfishness. Self-interest. We all want to see ourselves in the best possible light. The worst criminals, even while admitting their crimes, will often claim that they did nothing wrong. And we all shake our heads and wonder how people can be so oblivious to reality.

How, indeed! We're all blind! We all rationalize our misdeeds. It began in Eden when Adam said, "The woman you put here with me—she gave me some fruit from the tree, and I ate it" (Genesis 3:11). Adam denied responsibility for his disobedience by pushing the blame onto his wife, and she pushed the blame for her disobedience onto the snake. When God confronted Cain with the murder he had committed, he replied, "Am I my brother's keeper?" (Genesis 4:9).

The problem is that even when caught in the most blatant iniquity, we all want to look good. We want to think well of ourselves, and we want others to think well of us. So we reinterpret our misdeeds to make them seem less evil.

And it's just non-Christians who do this. Not at all.

Several years ago, when I was a pastor in Texas, a woman whom I'll call Andrea came to me weeping because another woman whom we'll call Donna was spreading a story about her around the church. I asked Donna where she got the information about Andrea, and she said her twin sister Shirley had told her. When I questioned Shirley, she said, "I never called Donna about a thing."

I was a little surprised at this apparent inconsistency between the two women's stories until, on further investigation, it turned out that Shirley had indeed never phoned Donna. On this particular occasion, Donna had phoned Shirley!

When I pointed out the deception to Shirley, she shrugged and said, "Oh, I didn't really think it was all that wrong."

At the time, Shirley and her husband happened to be members of a conferencewide group that was trying to get rid of the conference president. I found it most interesting that one of their main charges against the president was dishonesty, and Shirley was particularly vocal about the charge!

There's a name for Shirley's behavior and that of Aldrich Ames and the five tobacco executives. It's called:

Denial

You and I have to be aware of denial if we're ever going to get a change in our sinful understanding. It would be nice to suppose that getting a change in our sinful understanding was a simple matter of finding out the facts about good and evil. Unfortunately, it's not. If it were, even Baruch Goldstein would agree that his mass murder at the Ibrahim Mosque in Hebron was wrong. The real barrier to understanding the sinfulness of our behavior is denial, which is prompted by our selfishness. In order to get a change in our sinful understanding, we have to break out of denial.

"Christian" denial

"I'd never deny anything as obvious as Shirley's dishonesty," you say. "I'd never sell government secrets to Russia or tell Congress that there was no relationship between tobacco and disease. And I'd certainly not deny the evil of mass murder."

I'm relieved!

But the fact that you wouldn't deny such obvious evils is all the more reason why you should watch out for your own denial. If the human propensity for denial is so strong that intelligent humans will deny these indisputable sins, then surely those of us who are guilty of lesser "crimes" need to be on guard!

The truth is that every human being is in denial, including every Christian on the face of the earth. I discovered this in myself when I went to The Bridge. I've never used alcohol, and I've always felt quite horrified at alcoholics who beat their wives and yell at their kids and deprive their families of food and clothing to feed their addiction. Why couldn't they realize the damage they were doing to their families and just stop?

Thus it came as quite a shock, a day or two after arriving at

The Bridge, to be told that I was an addict and that my addiction had damaged my family just as much as if I were an alcoholic! To use Carol Cannon's words, I was the Big "A" in my family.

Come on, folks, let's get real! Me, Marvin Moore, a preacher and an editor, the Big "A"—an addict?

Now do you understand how easy denial is?

My chief addiction is work. Workaholism, they call it. And, unfortunately, my addiction happens to be very respectable. Bosses love it. And the church is sometimes one of the worst offenders. Some administrators put tremendous pressure on pastors to reach goals, and church members expect the preacher to be on call twenty-four hours a day.

"But I can't be a work addict," you say. "I love my work!"

True enough. The alcoholic loves his bottle too, and the heroin addict loves his needle.

When our work is so "important" that we have to neglect our families to get it all done, then we are abusing our families even if the boss is the conference president. And until those of us who are work addicts understand that, we are in denial.

Some of the worst condemnations Jesus ever pronounced were against addicts. The people who fail to make it into His kingdom, He said, will be those who refuse to feed the hungry, take care of the sick, and visit people in prison (see Matthew 25:41-46). He didn't call these people addicts, to be sure, but why did they abuse others? Might it be that they failed to help people because they were too busy—in some cases too busy doing God's work—to be caring, helping Christians?

Matthew 7:22 makes me think that this may indeed be the case. Jesus warned, "Many will say in that day, 'Lord, Lord, did we not prophesy in your name, and in your name drive out demons, and perform many miracles?' Then I will tell them plainly, 'I never knew you. Away from me, you evildoers!'" Here are people who were so busy doing the Lord's work that they failed to develop a relationship with Jesus. What better way is there to do that than to abuse Him in the person of His needy people? What better way is there for parents to abuse the very people they ought to love the most—their children—than with their work addiction?

The worst of all addictions is religious addiction, and the most deadly form of abuse is the spiritual abuse that arises from religious addiction. And no form of denial is more difficult for God to break through than religious addiction, for the religion addict is utterly convinced from his interpretation of Scripture that he's right and everyone else is wrong.

Many religion addicts form themselves into groups, and they give their groups names so everyone can know who they are. Not that they intend these names to proclaim to the world that they are addicts. No, no! They want to call attention to how religious they are. That's the denial. They think they are so good, and they want the world to know how good they are, when all along they are abusing people with their religious addiction. One such group at Jesus' time called themselves Pharisees. Notice the religious abuse that Jesus said they heaped on innocent people:

> Woe to you, teachers of the law and Pharisees, you hypocrites! You shut the kingdom of heaven in men's faces. You yourselves do not enter, nor will you let those enter who are trying to. . . .
>
> You travel over land and sea to win a single convert, and when he becomes one, you make him twice as much a son of hell as you are. . . .
>
> You give a tenth of your spices—mint, dill and cumin. But you have neglected the more important matters of the law—justice, mercy and faithfulness (Matthew 23:13-15, 23).

Control is another powerful addiction that is extremely difficult for its victims to recognize. Control addiction is simply the need to get one's way all the time or to always be right. One of the best ways to recognize a control addiction is to ask yourself, "How do I react when I don't get my way? What is my response to people who disagree with me?"

Control addicts have a number of strategies for getting their way. Some get what they want with anger. "What the blankety-blank do you think you're doing, anyway?"

Others are more subtle. They use shame (also called guilt manipulation) to get their way: "If you loved me, you'd do such and such," or, "You surely wouldn't want people to think you'd neglect your family, would you?" Some people even use religion to manipulate others into doing what they want. "The Bible says to obey your parents," or, "God says that wives are supposed to submit to their husbands." Yet if you were to ask these people whether they were addicts, they would almost certainly recoil in horror. Even if you were to explain the facts to them the way I've explained them in this book, most would justify their behavior.

That's denial.

Some Adventists are addicted in the more traditional ways such as to alcohol and drugs. This problem is far more widespread in the church than most people realize, as are sexual addiction, food addiction, and anger addiction. And we are just as likely to deny having these addictions as we are to deny that we are work, religion, or control addicts.

Alcoholic Adventists will tell you that the Bible doesn't condemn drinking. It just warns against getting drunk. Sexaholic Adventists will tell you that a little pornography never hurt anyone. Adventist food addicts are just cleaning up the leftovers, and the anger addicts among us are telling it like it is, albeit in no uncertain terms. "Christian" pedophiles justify their behavior by rationalizing that they are helping children to learn about sex!

Some people in the church will feel horrified that I should bring up such sins. Don't I realize that I'm dragging the good name of the church in the mud?

These people are just raising the denial from the personal level to the corporate level. It's not enough to deny their own sins. They have to deny everyone else's so their church can look good. Oddly enough, that's an addiction too. It's called perfectionism. Perfectionists can be very difficult to live with, especially those who are also addicted to control. Not only do these people have to live "perfect" lives themselves, but they make life miserable for anyone who doesn't live up to their perception of perfection.

Honesty and repentance

Many words have an opposite. The opposite of *hot*, for example, is *cold*. The opposite of *long* is *short,* and the opposite of *dry* is *wet*. There's also a word for the opposite of *denial*. It's called:

Honesty

Our goal is honesty—to break out of our denial and frankly admit, "I'm wrong." My purpose in this book, and especially in this chapter, is to help you understand how important it is to acknowledge our faults and wrong feelings and bring them out into the open. There's something liberating about looking at our feelings and attitudes and honestly admitting them. Fear goes away.

There's another name for honesty in the recovery sense. It's called:

Repentance

You and I *must* have God's help to repent. We cannot make this change in our sinful understanding on our own. We can understand that we have cheated and lusted without God's help, but we cannot understand the evil of these behaviors and the attitudes behind them without His help. The Holy Spirit must convict each of us, telling us the things that are wrong about our lives and encouraging us to live the right way. Repentance means that we say, "God, You're right."

That's honesty.

You and I must experience this change in our sinful understanding before God can begin changing us to be like Jesus on the inside. That's why a change in our sinful understanding heads the list of changes we must experience in order to gain the victory over temptation and sin. To put it another way, a change in our sinful understanding is the foundation of sanctification.

Honesty is so important that I have included it among the four cardinal principles that are keys to victory over temptation:

CARDINAL PRINCIPLE 2
To gain the victory, you must get honest with yourself and with God.

Repentance and justification

Repentance—God's change in our sinful understanding—is the foundation of sanctification. In an earlier chapter, I said that repentance is the condition for receiving justification. Thus repentance is the link between justification and sanctification. Until you and I break out of our denial and get honest with ourselves and God, He cannot justify us. He cannot save us. When we do get honest He can justify us and begin sanctifying us.

When Jesus justifies us—when He makes up for our deficiencies with His own divine merit—He's simply saying, "I'm going to treat you as though you really had overcome the sins you honestly want to overcome." God does not require that we actually have overcome our character defects before He will accept us and justify us. But He does require that we break out of our denial and honestly repent of them.[1]

Whenever we do this, we have truly begun to experience a change in our sinful understanding. We are on the way to conquering the dragon within.

---

[1]When we truly repent of the sins we do know about, God treats those we don't know about with the same justifying grace.

DEVOTIONAL EXERCISES

Biblical reflection on chapter 18

1. Read Psalm 51, which David wrote after Nathan confronted him about his sin of murdering Uriah and taking Bathsheba for himself. Which verses speak to you the most powerfully about the genuineness of David's repentance?
2. Review 1 Samuel 15. Both David and Saul were confronted by prophets about their sins. Write a paragraph about each man's response. Keep in mind the issues of honesty and denial and repentance that we discussed in this chapter.

Devotional study of 1 Samuel 18

1. What shared character traits drew David and Jonathan into such a close friendship? (See 1 Samuel 14 and 17.)
2. Were Saul's feelings toward David in verses 8 and 12 understandable? Were they justified?
3. What strategy did Saul devise for dealing with David? Write a paragraph that explains how Saul's strategy arose out of his feelings and why this was an inappropriate way for him to deal with them. What would have been a better way?
4. Can you think of a situation in your life in which you had feelings similar to Saul's? Write a paragraph about your response. If it was inappropriate, what might you have done differently?

SECTION II
Part 2
*Changing Our Sinful
Desires*

Station Break 2

We have now completed our discussion of how to change our sinful understanding. This is the first of the three major changes we must experience in order to develop a character like Christ's and be ready for the close of probation.

We are now ready to talk about the second of these major changes—changing our sinful desires. This is where the work of actual character change begins. Once again, God has a part, and we have a part. We cannot do His part, and He will not do our part. But we must give Him permission to do His part in our lives, and we must actively engage in our part. We are not truly repentant unless we have committed ourselves to the change process. Our efforts may not always succeed, but we must put ourselves on God's side in spite of our failures and be willing to do whatever it takes to be like Jesus. That's what Ellen White had in mind when she said, "When it is in the heart to obey God, when efforts are put forth to this end . . ." (SM, 1:382).

Here is an abbreviated summary pointing out where we are now:

Section II: How Jesus Helps Sinners Gain the Victory
  Part 1: Changing Our Sinful Understanding
  Part 2: Changing Our Sinful Desires
  Station Break 2 <———
     19. God's Part: Change Our Sinful Desires
     20. Our Part: Ask for Help With Our Sinful Desires
     21. Our Part: Talk About Our Sinful Desires
     22. Our Part: Surrender Our Sinful Desires

  Part 3: Changing Our Sinful Behavior
  Part 4: Final Thoughts on Victory

Chapter
Nineteen

God's Part:
CHANGE OUR SINFUL DESIRES

The following letter to the editor appeared on page 2 of the May 26, 1994, issue of the *Adventist Review*:

I am presently completing my tenth year of a 99-year sentence for a first offense of having oral sex with a child under 14. I make no excuses for what I did. I know now that what I did was wrong and hurtful, but at that time I didn't. I did not make a conscientious [sic.] decision that "I'm going to be a child molester." I have been sexually attracted to children (girls only) for as long as I can remember, my first encounter at age 6 being with my 6-year-old "girlfriend" across the street.

I have been a Seventh-day Adventist for about nine years now. I realize that sex with children is sin. I have tried to change, but found that I cannot do so; my mind is willing, but my flesh is weak (Matt. 26:41), and I find myself repeating Paul when he said, "For the good that I would I do not: but the evil which I would not, that I do" (Rom. 7:19).

Our sin is no worse than any other (James 2:10). We need help, love, and acceptance just like any other, not the loathing and rejection that we now receive. I need help too. Where do *I* turn? God hasn't answered, and neither has humanity.

This letter and the one from *Insight* that I quoted in chapter 1 are identical in one important way: The writers of both letters are pleading for victory over temptation, and neither had found it as of the time he or she wrote. *Insight*'s correspondent was the most dramatic: "I'm all for 'victory to victory,' but HOW?" The child molester frankly acknowledged, "I realize that sex with children is sin. I have tried to change, but found that I cannot do so."

In the previous several chapters, I explained how Christians can experience a change in their sinful understanding that will lead to genuine repentance for sin. But *Insight's* correspondent understands his or her sin very well. So does the child molester. Both of them have clearly repented. Both are begging for deliverance. And where has their pleading gotten them? So far, nowhere. Thus, while there can be no victory without insight, unless we also experience victory, insight into our sinful condition only torments us with guilt. In this chapter we're going to begin our search for victory. I will begin by sharing a simple diagram with you:

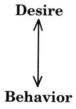

Desire

Behavior

The point of this diagram is that both our desires and our behavior are involved in victory over sin, and they are related. I illustrated this relationship by putting an arrow between them that points both up and down. Our character change will be much more rapid and our victory over sin will be much more complete when we understand this relationship.

I suspect that for all their sincerity, both *Insight's* correspondent and the child molester failed to understand the relationship between desire and behavior, and as a result, their strategy for character development and conquering sin was flawed. They were doing certain things backward. In this chapter, we will begin looking at the principles for a balanced relationship between desire and behavior, and much of the rest of the book will clarify these principles even further.

The real issue is character change

Imagine you have a tree that is producing sinful fruit. Naturally, you don't like this sinful fruit, so even before it's ripe, you pick it all off. "Now there's no sinful fruit on the tree," you say.

True enough. But the sinful fruit is not the problem. The problem is the sinful tree. To change the fruit, you have to change the whole tree. Otherwise, the next fruit-growing season, the tree will produce more sinful fruit.

One of the major problems with those who are struggling with a besetting sin, I suspect, is that they have the wrong goal in mind. They think their goal is to stop *doing* a particular sin. That's true, of course, but I'd like to suggest that the real goal is character change. Genuine victory over sin happens as a result of character change. Until character changes, we may stop *doing* a particular sin, but we have not really *conquered* it.

Several chapters back, I shared with you Ellen White's simple definition of character: "The thoughts and feelings combined make up the moral character" (5T, 310). A sinful character is made up of wrong thoughts and feelings, and a virtuous character is made up of right thoughts and feelings. Obviously, changing our character requires changes in both our thoughts and our feelings.

In Part 1, called "Getting a Change in Our Sinful Understanding," we talked about how to get a change in our sinful thoughts. In Part 2, which we are starting with this chapter, we will be discussing how to get a change in our sinful desires. Two principles are involved.

Desire must change first

Suppose you were to hire a contractor to build a house for you, and after examining the blueprint, he said, "We'll start with the roof. When that's done, we'll put up the walls, and then we'll pour the foundation."

That's silly, you say. How can anyone put the roof on a house that hasn't got walls and a foundation?

Precisely. No builder is going to ignore the roof. The house isn't complete till it's on and shingled. But the roof is not where the builder begins. He starts with the foundation.

It's the same with character development and victory over sin. Ellen White understood this. "There are many who try to reform by correcting this or that bad habit," she said, "and they hope in this way to become Christians, but they are beginning in the wrong place. *Our first work is with the heart*" (COL, 97, emphasis added).

Ellen White did not say we should ignore our wrong behavior.

She only said it's a mistake to begin there. "Our first work," she said, "is with the heart"—our evil motives, purposes, and desires.

We humans tend to label as sin the part that we can see, which is the behavior. We think we have to stop *doing* wrong things. And we think when we've quit *doing* wrong things we've gotten the victory over sin. But we can't stop *doing* wrong things until we stop *wanting* wrong things. We have to overcome the evil *desire* before we can expect to overcome the wrong *behavior*. This insight provides us with a crucial strategy for conquering sin:

> **We must begin with the**
> **evil desire, not the**
> **evil behavior.**

I do not mean to minimize the importance of changing our sinful behavior. We are coming to that, I assure you. But evil desire is the foundation of the problem, not the other way around. Until we understand this principle and apply it, we will be continually frustrated in our efforts to overcome sin.

I suspect this explains a lot of the frustration that *Insight's* correspondent and the child molester were experiencing. The child molester said: "I realize that sex with children is sin. I have tried to change, but found that I cannot." He was trying to stop the behavior. But his problem goes much deeper than that. He needs a change in the desire that produces the behavior.

We cannot change our own desires

Now I want to share with you one of the most important principles in this entire book:

> **We are absolutely powerless**
> **to change our evil desires.**

Ellen White made this point emphatically:

It is impossible for us, of ourselves, to escape from the pit of sin in which we are sunken. Our hearts are evil, and we cannot change them (SC, 18).

The key point here is that *we cannot change our evil hearts*. An evil heart is made up of evil motives, purposes, and desires, and we cannot change those evil desires.

Next, Ellen White said:

Education, culture, the exercise of the will, human effort, all have their proper sphere, but here they are powerless. They may produce an outward correctness of behavior, but they cannot change the heart; they cannot purify the springs of life (SC, 18).

Please notice the word *powerless* tucked in the middle of Ellen White's statement: "Education, culture, the exercise of the will, [and] human effort . . . are *powerless*" to "change the heart." This does not mean that education, culture, the exercise of the will, and human effort have nothing to do with living a good life in society or even with a successful Christian experience. Ellen White assures us that these "may produce an outward correctness of behavior." I'm glad that even in a sinful world, most people treat each other decently.

But suppose that with some good education, a touch of Emily Post, and a lot of hard work you manage to live a good life as far as the world is concerned, but you still have evil desires. Have you overcome your sins?

No.

Why? Because sin is more than wrong behavior. It is also the *desire* for wrong behavior. Jesus made this clear in the Sermon on the Mount when He said that murder is more than killing people. It's hating them. Adultery is more than a man and woman engaging in unlawful sexual intercourse. It's lust. The real sin, Jesus said, happens in the heart. But right here is where we run into a brick wall. For we are powerless to change our evil desires.

Alcoholics Anonymous recognizes this principle. Notice what the very first step of the Twelve Steps says:

Step 1
We admitted that we were *powerless* over alcohol—that our lives had become unmanageable (emphasis added).

What is your cherished sin? Is it TV, food, losing your temper, inappropriate sexual behavior, spending money you don't have? Plug it into that first step: "I admitted I was powerless over television." "I admitted I was powerless over food." "I admitted I was powerless over my temper." "I admitted I was powerless over sex." "I admitted I was powerless over money." And on and on.

Alcoholics Anonymous publishes a book called *The Twelve Steps and the Twelve Traditions*—they call it *The Twelve and Twelve* for short. I found the following statement in this book. Please notice especially the words I have italicized:

> Our sponsors declared that we were the victims of a mental *obsession* so subtly powerful that *no amount of human will power could break it* (22).

Did you see the word *obsession*? An obsession is a desire that you can't make go away. Your willpower cannot make it go away.

Two monks were walking down a dusty road one day—a young man and an older man—when they came to a river. At that very moment, a beautiful young woman approached the river. "Sirs," she said, "could you help me get across the river?"

"Of course," said the older monk, and he picked her up in his arms and carried her across. The younger monk followed. When they reached the other side, the older monk set the young woman down, and she went her way and they went theirs.

For two days, the monks walked along, but the younger man was deep in thought, so they said very little. At the end of the second day, the young monk broke the silence. "Sir," he said, "don't you think it was dangerous for you to carry that young woman across the river? She was very beautiful, sir. Just think what a temptation that could have been to lust."

The older monk replied, "Young man, I carried that woman across the river. You have carried her for the past two days."

That's an obsession, and obsession is the foundation of all addiction and cherished sin.

Did you ever lie in bed half the night wide awake thinking about what you were going to do or say the next time you saw the person who abused you the day before? That's an obsession. Did you ever spend half the day thinking about food? That's an obsession. Did you ever lie awake at night all tensed up with sexual desire, clutching the sheets to keep from doing something wrong? That's an obsession.

And that's the desire that your will is incapable of changing.

God must change our desires

Fortunately, when Ellen White said that we are powerless to change our own hearts and the evil desires that spring from them, she did not stop there. In the very next paragraph, she told us what *will* work:

> The Saviour said, "Except a man be born from above," unless he shall receive a new heart, new desires, purposes, and motives, leading to a new life, "he cannot see the kingdom of God." John 3:3, margin (SC, 18).

Let's analyze that statement a bit. Ellen White began with Jesus' statement about the new birth: "Except a man be born from above." But she broke into the middle of Jesus' sentence and inserted her own understanding of what the new birth means: "Unless he shall receive a new heart, new desires, purposes, and motives, leading to a new life." Then she completed Jesus' thought: "he cannot see the kingdom of God."

Notice that a new heart involves "new *desires*, purposes, and motives."

New desires. That's the very thing we're talking about in this chapter! God's part in helping us to get a change in our sinful desires is to give us the new birth. And this new birth instills new desires, purposes, and motives that will lead to a life of victory—the very victory that our child molester and *Insight's* correspondent and you and I so desperately want!

Buried in this short paragraph from *Steps to Christ* is another word—a key word for you and me to understand, because it explains the difference between God's part and our part in getting a change in our sinful desires. The word I have in mind is:

Receive

Did you ever *receive* a letter? How did it happen? What did you do? "Well," you say, "I went to the mailbox and opened it up, and inside was this letter that someone had sent me."

Good explanation! You took from the mailbox a letter that *someone had sent you*. You didn't write the letter yourself. You didn't put it in an envelope, paste a stamp in the upper right corner, and drop it in the mail. Oh no. Someone else did all that. They *sent* the letter. You *received* it.

If I want to receive something, I can't reach out and grab it. I can *get* it by grabbing it, but I can't *receive* it that way. The only thing I can do to receive an object is to hold out my hand. Someone else has to put it there.

Ellen White said that you and I must *receive* new desires. We can't reach inside our minds, twist our sinful desires around, and make them right. We cannot inject new desires into our own hearts. That's precisely where we are so powerless. All we can do is "hold out our hands" and *receive* new desires. God has to put them there. That's His part.

As we have seen, God's part is called the *new birth*. Paul said, "Do not be conformed any longer to the pattern of this world, but *be transformed by the renewing of your mind*" (Romans 12:2). Transforming the mind is another way of describing the new birth.

Over and over, with a variety of illustrations and analogies, the Bible tells us that God works a spiritual change on the inside of people who invite Him into their lives, and that spiritual change reorients their desires, purposes, and motives so that the things they once loved they now hate, and the things they once hated they now love. And when that happens, victory over sin is easy. The struggle is over, because they no longer want to sin.

I find it extremely significant that Alcoholics Anonymous has discovered this very same principle. Here's another statement from *The Twelve and Twelve*:

> Who cares to admit complete defeat? Practically no one, of course. Every natural instinct cries out against the idea of personal powerlessness. It is truly awful to admit, glass in hand, that we have warped our minds into such an obsession for destructive drinking that *only an act of Providence can remove it from us* (21, emphasis added).

Now you know why Alcoholics Anonymous is so successful in

getting addicts off the bottle. They recognize the foundational principle that the basis of alcoholism is an obsession for alcohol that the addict's willpower is totally inadequate to change. *Only God can remove it.*

It's time now to put God's part in helping us to get a change in our sinful desires on the diagram:

Change Needed	God's Part	Our Part
In Our Sinful **Understanding**	Conviction: Show us Our sins	Ask for it Talk about it Search for it
In Our Sinful **Desires**	**CONVERSION: CHANGE OUR DESIRES**	
In Our Sinful **Behavior**		

A word of caution

I need to give you one important word of caution: Do not expect that God will give you an instantaneous, permanent change in your evil desires. I do not mean that God *couldn't* change your desires instantly or even that He will *never* do so. At times, He clearly does. We've all heard, for example, about the smoker who threw away his cigarettes and never wanted another one. However, for every smoker who throws away his cigarettes and never wants another one, I can show you a hundred who struggled for a year or five years before they finally gained the victory.

Many people have had the experience of one particular temptation leaving them instantly, but no one has all of his or her temptations removed at once. Usually God allows us to struggle with our temptations, and they fade slowly.

Why does God deliver some people from a particular temptation instantly, while others have to struggle with the same issue for months or years? I wish I knew the answer to that question. The best explanation I can give is another question: Why does God heal some people from cancer instantly, while the majority of cancer victims have to run the gamut of surgery, radiation therapy, and chemical therapy to get well? I don't know. Maybe

He'll explain it to us someday when we all get to heaven.

Unhealthy emotions

Some emotions we struggle with are not sinful in themselves, but they can easily lead to sinful behavior. I am thinking in particular of shame and fear, which we discussed in an earlier chapter. Each of these emotions is healthy in moderation. The problem comes when they become excessive. Allow me to explain.

Shame. Shame keeps us from going out in public without any clothes on. It reminds us to behave respectfully around other people. Healthy shame also leads us to feel guilty when we've done something that is genuinely wrong.

However, shame can also be unhealthy. I will mention three forms of diseased shame. First, unhealthy shame is the foundation of all feelings of worthlessness—the notion that everyone else is better than I am. Much of the depression from which we suffer stems from shame.

Second, unhealthy shame often shows up as misplaced guilt. Misplaced guilt leads us to believe that certain things are wrong, when, in fact, they are not wrong at all. For example, some people experience mild to extreme feelings of guilt over sex within marriage, when the Bible is very clear that God invented sex and gave it to the human race both for procreation and enjoyment.

A third form of unhealthy shame is the lack of shame. People who have no shame are often obnoxious. They offend people without realizing that they have violated the rules of social propriety. This is sinful, even though we don't usually think of it that way. Actually, these people may be suffering from shame that is so intense the only way they can handle it is to deny it. Their obnoxious behavior is a way to prove to themselves that they are OK.

Fear. Fear is healthy when it keeps us from touching a hot stove or jumping out in front of a big Mack truck. It is unhealthy when it causes us to avoid doing what we are perfectly capable of doing. The case of the one-talent man in Jesus' parable of the talents is a good example. He said to his master, "I buried your talent because I was *afraid*" (Matthew 25:25). Fear is also unhealthy when we bury it deep in our psyches as an underlying anxiety that we cannot explain but always feel.

Even though shame and fear may not be sinful in the more

traditional sense of the word *sin*, both usually lie near the foundation of addiction. The addict nearly always feels intense shame over his obsessive/compulsive behavior and wishes desperately that he could stop. Many addicts take extreme precautions to hide their addiction because of the shame they would feel if the world were to find out.

Fear in addiction takes two contradictory forms. The addict is desperately afraid that he *won't* get his "fix" (alcohol, sex, TV, ad infinitum). On the other hand, because he knows he'll feel so guilty about it, he's also desperately afraid that he *will* end up "doing it." So he clenches his fists and grits his teeth in the vain hope that he won't do it, all the while wishing desperately that he could. And, sooner or later, he always does.

Often guilt and fear get so mixed together in our heads that it's difficult for us to tell one from the other. Much of the depression that we humans experience is a combination of shame and fear, often mixed up with anger and a few other unhealthy emotions. Usually we cannot explain these feelings. We cannot distinguish between the shame, the fear, and the anger. All we know is that we feel horrible, so we call it depression.

We feel ashamed and afraid of our addictions, wishing we could control them and failing to realize that this very shame and fear are what drive our addictions. It is crucial to understand that we almost certainly will not conquer our more traditional sins until we can get rid of the shame and the fear that lie behind them.

We must also understand that *we can no more rid ourselves of unhealthy shame and fear than we can rid ourselves of any other sinful feelings and desires.* We must allow God to remove our unhealthy shame and fear. We cannot do it alone.

The good news

And now I have some wonderful news to share with you. When God removes the desire for your cherished sin, victory will be easy, because you no longer want the sin. So make it your goal, not so much to stop *doing* wrong things as to stop *wanting* wrong things. Peter had this in mind when he said:

> His divine power has given us everything we need for life
> and godliness. . . . He has given us his very great and pre-

cious promises, so that through them you may participate in the divine nature [conversion] and escape the corruption in the world caused by evil desires (2 Peter 1:3, 4).

This principle—that you and I are powerless to change our own desires; that God must change them for us—is one of your most important keys for conquering the dragon within.

DEVOTIONAL EXERCISES

Biblical reflection on chapter 19
1. Read James 1:13-15. Write a paragraph describing a time in your life when a wrong desire led you into sin. Be as specific as possible in describing the desire or feeling and why it was wrong. What might you have done to deal with it more appropriately?
2. Read the parable of the talents in Matthew 25:14-30. What was the difference in the feelings experienced by the first two men and the third man?
3. Think of a time in your life when you felt like the first two men and another time when you felt like the third man. Did these attitudes have any influence on the success or lack of success in your life at that time?
4. Write a paragraph analyzing the moral quality (sinfulness) of the third man's attitude.

Devotional study of 1 Samuel 19
1. Was Saul's attitude toward David justified? What name do we today give to such attitudes?
2. In light of the present chapter in this book, what was the real solution to Saul's problem? What should he have done?
3. How did Saul deal with his feelings? How might he have dealt with them more appropriately?
4. Of the three basic emotions discussed so far in this book— shame, fear, and anger—which ones are most evident in Saul's attitude toward David? Have you ever felt this way toward someone? Write a paragraph or two applying your answer to question 3 to yourself in that situation.

Chapter
Twenty

Our Part: 1
ASK FOR HELP WITH OUR SINFUL DESIRES

Let's talk some more about that building project I mentioned in the previous chapter. Suppose you want to build a beautiful mansion for your family to live in, but you have no skills in construction. You can't even drive a straight nail or paint a straight line! Fortunately, you have a friend who is the best building contractor in the area. He has said he'll be glad to put up your house for you, and he won't even charge you for labor and materials. Wonderful! Please introduce me to your friend.

So do you just sit around and wait for your friend to start? Of course not. Kind though his offer may be, there are still some things you have to do. You must furnish the blueprint, choose your colors and fixtures, and sign a contract.

As a first step in conquering our sins, God promises to change our sinful desires. We are totally incapable of doing that. Our minds and our willpower are not equal to the task.

So do we just sit back and let Him take over? Of course not. You and I still have a part. God has provided certain ways for us to cooperate with Him in the construction of our character. If we don't do our part, He can't do His.

Lest you think I've started talking about righteousness by works, let me remind you of my explanation in an earlier chapter that our works are ineffective only in the area of justification, which is the basis of our salvation. Human effort has a crucial role in sanctification, and that's why sanctification can never be the basis of our salvation. Sanctification is what we're talking about right now, and in this chapter and the three that follow, we're going to look at our part in changing our sinful desires.

The addict is a slave

Let's begin by looking at a statement by Ellen White from *Steps to Christ*, page 47:

> You desire to give yourself to Him, but you are weak in moral power, in slavery to doubt, and controlled by the habits of your life of sin. Your promises and resolutions are like ropes of sand. You cannot control your thoughts, your impulses, your affections.

We've seen that statement before in this book, but let's analyze it again. Though Ellen White does not use the word *addiction* here, she is clearly describing that condition. She says, "You desire to give yourself to Him, but you are weak in moral power, in *slavery* to doubt, and *controlled* by the habits of your life of sin." An addict is *controlled* by his sinful habits. He has no choice about whether to "do it." That's the *slavery*. A slave is under the control of his master. He has no choice. Paul described this condition in Romans 6:20 when he said to the Christians in Rome, "You were *slaves* to sin." And in chapter 7:5 he said, "When we were *controlled* by the sinful nature, the sinful passions . . . were at work in our bodies, so that we bore fruit for death."

Ellen White goes on to say, "Your promises and resolutions are like ropes of sand." An addict will vow "never to do it again," but five minutes later, he'll be back at it. I met a woman in California who told me that her addiction was shoplifting. "I could stand in front of a store before going in and absolutely determine to pay for everything," she said. "But when I came out, there would be something in my purse that I *hadn't* paid for."

Ellen White concluded the statement above by saying, "You cannot control your thoughts, your impulses, your affections." That's an addict. If an addict feels like it, he has no choice but to do it. Saying No is not an option. Paul was describing addiction in Romans 7:14-25 when he said, "What I want to do I do not do, but what I hate I do" (verse 15).

In the seminars I conduct in churches, I sometimes ask all the addicts in the congregation to please raise their hands. Usually a few brave souls will sneak their hands into the air. Then I say, "Now I'd like everyone to raise a hand." After a bit of coaxing, when I can tell that nearly all the hands are in the air, I say, "Now I'm looking at the hands of all the addicts here today."

Everyone chuckles, of course, but it's true. We tend to think of addicts as alcoholics, druggies, and maybe sexaholics. But the truth is that *every one of us is an addict.* This becomes more apparent when we understand that Ellen White's expression "cherished sin" is another way of saying addiction.

Another way to put it is to say, as I pointed out in the previous chapter, that we are powerless over our cherished sins and addictions. We humans want to think we are in charge. "I can handle my alcohol," says the alcoholic as he reaches for the bottle. "Just one more bite, and then I'll stop," says the food addict as she reaches for another piece of cake. "Just one more program," says the TV addict as he switches channels. We hate to admit our powerlessness. But there is no victory till we do and ask God to do for us what we cannot do for ourselves.

I got a dramatic firsthand lesson about this when I was a pastor in Texas. A young woman started attending church, and immediately the "chemistry" hit me. I loved my wife deeply, and I wasn't about to compromise our relationship by getting into an affair. But that didn't settle down the chemistry. I asked God to help me, and the chemistry subsided, but a month or two later, it came back, so I prayed, and the problem went away again. Predictably it returned, though, so I prayed again. By the time I had gone back and forth like this four or five times, I was feeling exasperated at my crazy emotions.

One day after church, I was walking out to my car, and I glanced over and saw this young woman walking to her car. Suddenly, the chemistry hit again—harder this time than ever. I felt profoundly frustrated. I got in my car, backed out of my parking space, and headed toward the street. As I approached the street, I banged the steering wheel and cried out, "Lord, I'm powerless to get rid of these feelings! Can You please help me? I can't do anything about them."

The chemistry left, and it never came back. That young woman stayed in the church for a couple more years, and I saw her repeatedly in church services and on committees, but never again did the chemistry bother me. I did not realize at the time why my prayer worked that last time when it had not worked before, but

I do now. Only when I came to the point of admitting my powerlessness over my obsession could God really deal with my emotions. Alcoholics Anonymous calls this "hitting bottom." By whatever name it is called, I have discovered that until you and I admit our powerlessness over our besetting sins, we cannot overcome them.

Using the will to escape addiction

Fortunately, both the apostle Paul and Ellen White assure us that there is a way out of addiction. "Who will deliver me from this body of death?" Paul asked, and he gave the answer: "Thanks be to God—through Jesus Christ our Lord." In other words, Jesus is the way out. This is especially true in the sense that He removes our sinful desires and replaces them with good ones, as we discussed in the previous chapter.

Ellen White's explanation of the way out applies to our part, and her explanation will probably surprise you:

> You need not despair. What you need to understand is the true force of the will. This is the governing power in the nature of man, the power of decision, or of choice. *Everything depends on the right action of the will* (SC, 47, emphasis added).

The surprise is in the last sentence of Ellen White's statement, because it seems so contradictory to one we discussed earlier. On page 18 of *Steps to Christ,* she says that "the will [is] . . . powerless [to] change the heart," while on page 47 she says that "everything depends on the right action of the will."

So which way is it? Does the will have a role to play in overcoming our addictions and sins, or doesn't it? I found the answer to this question in the word *right*. "Everything," she said, "depends on the *right* action of the will." In other words, there is a right way and a wrong way to use the will. If we understand the right way, we will succeed in overcoming our besetting sins. If we don't understand the right way, we will fail.

I'd like to carry this principle a step farther. The diagram below illustrates my point. You will recognize it from the previous chapter, but with the addition of *Right Use of the Will*:

Desire

Right Use of the Will

Behavior

Notice that an arrow points up from *Right Use of the Will* to *Desire*, and another points down from *Right Use of the Will* to *Behavior*. There is a right way to use our will as we seek a change in our desires, and there is a right way to use the will in changing our behavior. It's crucial to understand that these two ways are very different. Unfortunately, one of the most common problems among Christians is to switch these two. They apply to their sinful desires the willpower strategies they ought to be using on their sinful behavior and vice versa. I won't say that this never works, but it's like driving a car on four flat tires.

The two ways to use the will are determination and choice. Let's define each one.

Determination. Some people, reading Ellen White's statement that "everything depends on the right action of the will," will no doubt say, "I'll just clench my fists a little tighter, grit my teeth a little harder, say No a little louder, and I won't do it."

I'll grant you it's possible to keep from *doing* wrong things that way, at least for a time. But that's a miserable way to live, and it's exactly what the ropes of sand are made out of. Eventually we give in and do it. There's another way to use the will properly to get a change in our sinful desires.

Choice. Choice means to look at two or more options and select one. And this is the use of the will that Ellen White had in mind in the statement above. The will, she said, "is the governing power in the nature of man, the power of decision, or of *choice*."

We cannot change our own desires by determination—that is, by gritting our teeth and clenching our fists and commanding the wrong desires to go away. But we can change our desires by making the proper choice. The question is, What is that choice? On the answer to that question rests our victory over sin.

Making the right choice

Once we admit our powerlessness, we are ready to let God do for us what we cannot do for ourselves by our willpower or any other method. We must *choose* to say the following prayer:

**Lord, please remove my desire for this sin,
and replace it with a desire for what is right.**

Let's put the first part of our part in getting a change in our sinful desires on our chart:

Change Needed	God's Part	Our Part
In Our Sinful **Understanding**	Conviction: Show us Our sins	Ask for it
		Talk about it
		Search for it
In Our Sinful **Desires**	Conversion: Change our desires	**ASK FOR IT**
In Our Sinful **Behavior**		

That prayer—"Lord, please remove my desire for this sin, and replace it with a desire for what is right"—is so simple you could teach it to a five-year-old. However, choosing to say it is one of the hardest things you will ever do.

Why? Because you have to say it when you least want to. You have to ask God to remove your anger when you want nothing worse than to punch your enemy in the nose. You have to ask Him to remove your gluttony just when you can't wait to binge on food. You have to ask Him to remove your lust at the very moment when your eyes are yearning to read that pornographic magazine or watch that pornographic video.

It isn't so hard asking God to remove the desire during your morning and evening devotions when it isn't burning inside you. But an hour later, when passion is white hot, the last thing you want is God to take away what you love. You want to do it first, then you'll be *glad* for God to remove the desire! But there will be no victory until you start asking God to remove the desire *before* you engage in the cherished sinful behavior.

In *The Crisis of the End Time* I told the story of Gary, who was a member of my church in Texas several years ago. I'm repeating it here because it is an excellent example of how hard it is to choose to ask God to remove our wrong desires and give us new ones. However, this time I'm going to call him Charlie, because that's his real name, and I have his permission to use his name.

Charlie came to me one day and said, "Pastor, I need help."

I said, "What's the problem?"

"I drink coffee," Charlie said. "I know it's wrong to drink coffee, Pastor, and I've been asking God to help me quit. But I love coffee. Every morning when I go out to the kitchen, I have to brew up my coffee, or the day doesn't go right. But I really would like to stop. Can you help me?"

At the time Charlie came to me, I understood the principles for overcoming temptation that I am sharing with you in this book. Charlie loved coffee—the desire; but he was asking God to help him stop drinking coffee—the behavior. So I said, "Charlie, you're saying the wrong prayer. If you'll say the right prayer, you'll start overcoming your temptation to drink coffee."

"Oh, Pastor, what is the right prayer?" Charlie said as he leaned forward in his chair.

"Tomorrow morning when you come out to the kitchen," I said, "instead of saying, 'Lord, help me not to *drink* coffee today,' you need to say, 'Lord, help me not to *want* coffee today.' "

Charlie looked at me kind of funny, and then he looked at the floor, and then he looked back at me, and he said, "But, Pastor, if I did that, I might not get my coffee."

You smile, but that's exactly the conflict you and I go through at the moment our sinful desire is the hottest. We have to ask God to kill the evil desire at the moment we are desperate to enjoy it. Ellen White described this struggle in graphic language:

Darling, cherished idols will have to be given up, the sins that have been indulged in, even if it comes as close as the plucking out of the right eye, or cutting off the right arm. Arouse, force your way through the very armies of hell that oppose your passage (PC, 345).

Did you see that? Victory over temptation will sometimes seem like plucking out an eye or cutting off an arm. Tough stuff! People who think that victory over sin is a matter of sitting back and enjoying the ride while Jesus converts them and changes their desires are not going to get very far in conquering the dragon within! Yes, Jesus has to change our desires, and yes, when the desire is gone, victory will be easy. *But we have to ask Him before the desire is gone.* We have to ask Him to change the desire while it's still yelling and screaming at us. That's the tough part. That's the "plucking out the eye and cutting off the arm" part.

Do you recall my mentioning earlier that I would share with you a cardinal principle for character development in each of the three parts of the section on victory? Here is the one for the part on getting a change in our sinful desires:

CARDINAL PRINCIPLE 3
Ask God to remove the desire for sin when you want nothing more than to enjoy it and act on it.

There are two things you cannot do with your willpower and one that you can. Here are the two you cannot do:

1. You cannot change your own wrong desires.
2. You cannot refuse permanently to act on a wrong desire as long as the desire is around. If you want it, eventually you will do it.

The one thing we can do is this:

We must *choose* to ask God to change our desires. That choice we can make.

Some people reading this book will find it impossible to choose to pray for help at the moment of white-hot temptation. If that is your problem, you still have a choice. Say a "backup" prayer at a time when the desire is not so strong. Ask God at a time when the temptation is not white hot to give you the courage to say the prayer when it *is* white hot. An excellent time to say this backup prayer is during your morning and evening devotions. If you haven't already established a regular devotional hour, this is a good time to start. A daily devotional time should be a major strategy in your life if you are serious about victory over besetting sin.

Emotions fade gradually

I must warn you again, though, of one thing: Don't expect the desire to fade the moment you say that prayer. Emotions fade gradually.

I had a vivid illustration of this back in 1993. I had a seminar beginning on Friday night in Tennessee, but I failed to calculate correctly the time to leave my house for the airport on Friday morning. I pulled out of my driveway thirty minutes too late, but I was halfway to the Boise airport before I realized my mistake. When I did, my heart leapt into my throat, and my knuckles turned white on the steering wheel. I'm sure my bloodstream was 50 percent adrenaline by the time I boarded the plane. I was one huge, raw nerve. I sank down in my seat by the window, weak with relief, just as the flight attendant closed the door. I was so pumped up that my emotions didn't settle down till the plane touched down in Denver! I experienced a first-class example that day of the law that *our emotions fade gradually*.

So when you say, "Lord, please remove my desire for this sin," don't be surprised if the desire stays around for an hour or even a day before it begins to subside.

Unfortunately, many people fall into what I call "desperation praying" when God doesn't change their desires immediately. Desperation praying is when you say, "Lord, please remove my desire for this sin. Please, Lord, remove this sinful desire. Oh, Lord, please. *Please, God, I beg of You, take it away!* **Oh, God, please. PLEASE, GOD, TAKE IT AWAY!**" Pretty soon, you're screaming at God.

You may be ever so sincere, but all you're doing is obsessing in your prayer. You are pumping up the very desire you want to kill. Your prayer is making your addiction worse rather than better. *And the dragon is rejoicing!* He loves desperation prayers, because he knows that he has already conquered.

The proper way to pray is to say, "Lord, please remove my desire for this sin, and replace it with a desire for what is right," and then go about your business, trusting that in His time He will remove the evil desire. Don't worry about the fact that it stays around a while—even if it stays around all day. Say the prayer every now and then, and keep going about your activities. Eventually, the desire will fade.

The key to victory is to acknowledge your powerlessness over every sinful desire and negative emotion, and ask God to change it for you. You must choose to ask Him, regardless of how painful the choice may be. God will understand if you have to start with a backup prayer that's easier. Eventually, you will be able to say that prayer at the moment of strongest temptation. When that happens, you will be on the way to real character change and victory over your cherished sins and addictions.

And you will be on the way to conquering the dragon within!

DEVOTIONAL EXERCISES

Biblical reflection on chapter 20

1. Read Matthew 7:7-12. Name some of the "good gifts" that God wants to give to His children. Keep the topic of this chapter in mind as you make your list.
2. Make a list of the wrong desires you would like God to change in your life. Draw a circle around the one you would most like Him to change.
3. Is faith implied in Matthew 7:7-12? Answer this question by writing a paragraph about it.
4. Follow Jesus' instruction in verse 7 with respect to the item you circled in question 2. As you do this, apply what you learned in the answer to question 3.

Devotional study of 1 Samuel 20

1. How did honesty in expressing their true feelings to each other contribute to the strong friendship between David and Jonathan? Write a paragraph discussing this matter.
2. Verse 30 says that Saul was angry at Jonathan. What was the cause of his anger? Was it justified?
3. Verse 34 says that Jonathan was angry. What was the cause of his anger? Was it justified?
4. Write a paragraph discussing the relative merits of Saul's and Jonathan's anger.

Chapter
Twenty-one

Our Part: 2
TALK ABOUT
OUR SINFUL DESIRES

My wife and I have known Gerald for several years. Gerald is addicted to fast sports cars. He keeps trading in his cars every few months, usually at quite a loss. And he keeps adding all kinds of expensive accessories to each car in order to make it more powerful or more attractive. He justifies all of these purchases with the excuse that they are "necessary."

At the time Gerald came to my wife and me for help, his wife had left him out of sheer panic over his financial irresponsibility, and his creditors were closing in. Gerald initially came to us to talk about his failed marriage, but it quickly became evident that finances were the real problem. As we talked, my wife and I realized that Gerald was addicted to sports cars and could not say No to spending money on them. We recommended that he seek professional help for his problem, and he actually went to a treatment center.

Gerald returned enthusiastic about what he had learned. As we talked to him, we could tell that he had gained a lot of insight into the issues he was dealing with. But, as with any addict, understanding the pain doesn't make it any less painful. And, as is always the case with addiction, except where God works a miracle, healing takes time, which means that the pain doesn't go away immediately. There are still times when Gerald thinks he's going crazy over his mixed-up emotions about sports cars. He wants to drive one but knows he can't—if he wants to get well.

That's the disease.

And every addict understands Gerald's pain perfectly, regardless of the nature of the addiction, because the process is always the same. Whatever your "fix" is, you are desperate to have it, but you know you can't.

It's the same with cherished sin. Which is why cherished sin is simply another name for addiction. Sin gives a slightly different connotation to the problem that is very important. We should always call sin by its right name, and we should never excuse it by saying, "Oh, well, it's just an addiction." However, I've found that it helps to think of my cherished sins as addictions. Victory comes easier when I treat them with the methods addicts use to deal with addiction. Some people think addiction and sin are mutually exclusive terms, but I prefer to think of them as different models of the same spiritual disease, each of which offers its own special help for recovery.

But back to our story about Gerald. My wife and I have encouraged him to deal with his pain using the concepts for recovery offered by addiction theory, one of the most important of which is to call a sponsor on a regular basis and talk. My wife and I have made ourselves available whenever Gerald needs to talk. He calls quite often, and it's working. Sometimes Gerald doesn't think so, but my wife and I know that it is. Slowly but surely, Gerald is healing from his disease. And, as with physical disease, it's no less a miracle because it's slow.

Why have I shared this story with you? Because it illustrates so well the point that I want to make in this chapter: Talking about our sinful desires is a powerful tool for changing them.

Why, you may ask, should talking make such a difference in changing our sinful desires? I found at least a partial answer to that question in a book called *The Twelve Steps: A Spiritual Journey* that I mentioned several chapters back:

> Just as the healing of a physical disease can only begin when we acknowledge the disease, so the spiritual healing of our obsessive/compulsive behavior begins when we acknowledge the existence of the problem (9).

So what does this have to do with talking as a way to change our sinful desires?

We take a powerful step toward acknowledging the existence of our problems when we open up to another human being and admit our wrong desires, *and only when we get honest can God change our sinful desires.*

Alcoholics Anonymous recognizes the importance of this principle. Notice the fifth step of the Twelve Steps:

Step 5

Admitted to God, to ourselves, and to another human being the exact nature of our wrongs.

If you want God to remove your wrong desires, one of the most effective things you can do is to find someone who is willing to listen, and tell that person about them. This strategy for conquering temptation is so effective that I have included it as one of the major things you and I can do to get a change in our sinful desires. So let's put it on our chart:

Change Needed	God's Part	Our Part
In Our Sinful **Understanding**	Conviction: Show us Our sins	Ask for it Talk about it Search for it
In Our Sinful **Desires**	Conversion: Change our desires	Ask for it **TALK ABOUT IT**
In Our Sinful **Behavior**		

But who should I talk to? you may ask. I'll grant you that finding the right person to talk to can be a problem, but it is not an impossible one.

In chapter 16, I pointed out that the Twelve-Step program recommends that each addict get a sponsor with whom he can talk about the defects in his character and the crises in his life. If you are serious about overcoming your besetting sin, I urge you to find someone you can talk to about your wrong desires. I have given recommendations for finding such a sponsor in chapter 16.

What should you tell your sponsor? A good place to begin is to do the fourth and fifth steps of the Twelve Steps of Alcoholics Anonymous:

Step 4
Made a fearless and searching moral inventory of ourselves.

Step 5
Admitted to ourselves, to God, and to another human being the exact nature of our wrongs.

A "fearless and searching moral inventory" will include the defects in your character, but it should also include your strong points. One way to do a fourth step is to draw a line down the middle of a sheet of paper and put the word *Strengths* over the left column and the word *Weaknesses* over the right column. It is especially important to write your character weaknesses on the paper rather than specific examples of the wrong behavior in your life that arise out of those character traits, because character defects are the foundation of the problem. Your sheet might look something like this:

Strengths	**Weaknesses**
1. I enjoy completing one task before going on to another.	1. Sometimes I get irritated when I don't get my way.
2. I like to keep a clean house (or an orderly workplace).	2. I have a hard time dealing with my sexual impulses.
3. I like good music.	3. Sometimes I eat too much.
4. I am usually willing to be honest about my defects.	4. I feel inferior to other people much of the time.

Probably the hardest part about sharing your character weaknesses with another person, if you've never done so before, is "taking the plunge" the first time. I can assure you that if you do it regularly, you will begin to experience a great sense of freedom—even before you have conquered the defects you talk about. In due time you will come to the place that when you spot a defect, you will *want* to talk about it.

The freedom you will experience from talking about your defects is in the honesty, not the victory. But the wonderful part is that with the honesty comes the victory! Why? Because honesty is the same thing as repentance. When we honestly admit our wrong desires and repent of them, we give God permission to change them.

In addition to a sponsor, you should make a point of sharing your character defects in a small group. One of the best places for this kind of sharing is a Twelve-Step group. For many years, only alcoholics had a Twelve-Step meeting for their addiction. However, today, the Twelve-Step concept has proliferated to many addictions, including Overeaters Anonymous, Sexaholics Anonymous, and Gamblers Anonymous. There's even one called Workaholics Anonymous, though the members tend to be so busy working they often have difficulty finding the time to attend! Chapter 16 and Appendix C also give several suggestions for finding a Twelve-Step group.

A woman raised her hand during a seminar that I conducted in the southern part of the United States in the summer of 1994. "Why can't we just talk to God about our defects?" she asked.

"Because you can't look God in the eye while you're talking to Him," I replied.

In order to get a change in our sinful desires, we have to break out of our denial over them. Admitting our character defects to another human being whom we can see with our eyes and hear with our ears is a powerful way to do that. Also, most of us realize that God already knows all about our defects, so telling Him about them is no big deal. But telling another human being is a different matter altogether, because that person does not know our defects, and telling them to him or her is a humbling experience. Telling God seems so much easier!

That's precisely why telling another *human being* is such a powerful way to break out of denial!

Talking about your sinful desires is neither a quick fix nor a cure-all. However, it will help you begin to heal. I assure you that you will find great freedom in being honest and sharing with others the defects in your character and the flaws in your desires and behavior. And as your character changes, you will increasingly experience victory over sins you may now think you could never overcome.

DEVOTIONAL EXERCISES

Biblical reflection on chapter 21

1. Read Luke 5:1-11. Why did the large catch of fish cause Peter to feel sinful? Have you ever felt sinful? What caused you to feel that way? Were Peter's feelings appropriate and healthy? Are yours? Write a paragraph discussing when it is appropriate for a Christian to feel sinful and when it is not.
2. How did Peter deal with his feelings? Why was this a good thing to do? Would this be a good way for you to deal with your feelings of sinfulness?
3. Write a paragraph discussing how you feel about sharing your character defects with another person. Include in the paragraph whether your feelings are appropriate and healthy, and if they are not, what you can do about it.

Devotional study of 1 Samuel 21

1. What feelings do you think David experienced as he and Jonathan went their separate ways (see chapter 20:42)? How did this affect his behavior when he met Ahimelech? Was David's response to Ahimelech's question appropriate? Why or why not?
2. Why did David go to the Philistine city of Gath? How did he feel when he got there, and how did he handle the situation? Reflect on the relationship between David's feelings and his behavior and the appropriateness of both. Had you been there to counsel David at this stressful time in his life, how would you have suggested he handle his feelings?
3. Write a paragraph summarizing your evaluation of David's response to his feelings in this chapter.

Chapter
Twenty-two

Our Part: 3
SURRENDER OUR
SINFUL DESIRES

Linda is addicted to her relationship with her abusive husband. She came to see my wife and me a year or two ago. "I know that I can't handle my relationship with Bill," she said, "but I'm afraid of losing him."

"Linda," I replied, "you just made an extremely insightful remark." I went on to explain that every addict is afraid of losing his or her "fix." The alcoholic is terrified that she might find herself in a situation in which she can't buy alcohol. The food addict will pack along boxes of food on a trip for fear he'll get caught where there is no food. We addicts love our "fixes." They make us feel so-o-o-o good! We can't bear the thought of being without them.

"Most women would have left Bill after the first slap on the face," I said to Linda. "But Bill can beat on you and swear at you and mop the floor with you, yet you want to go back to him. And you just told me why. Something about Bill makes you feel good, and whatever it is, you're terrified of losing it. You'd rather endure the pain than give it up."

"Pastor, I know I ought to give Bill up," Linda said in desperation. "Why can't I? What can I do to give him up?"

The answer I gave Linda that day is the one I want to share with you now: Surrender. This is the third aspect of our part in changing our sinful desires. Let's put it on our chart, and then we'll talk about it. The chart is on the next page.

One of the marks of addiction is fear of giving it up. If you feel like you'd rather die than lose the substance or behavior, then you're addicted to it. That's why it's a cherished sin. That's why you need to surrender it.

Change Needed	God's Part	Our Part
In Our Sinful **Understanding**	Conviction: Show us Our sins	Ask for it
		Talk about it
		Search for it
In Our Sinful **Desires**	Conversion: Change our desires	Ask for it
		SURRENDER IT
In Our Sinful **Behavior**		

Surrender means three things to me.

First, it means that I believe God's way is best, even though I have never experienced it. It means I trust that when He has changed my desires so I want something else instead of my cherished sin, I'll be happier, even though right now, my emotions tell me I'd die without my cherished sin.

Second, surrender means that I give God permission to remove my sinful desire. I give Him the wrong desire to change into whatever right desire He knows is best for me.

And third, surrender means that I accept the fact that giving up my cherished sin will be painful, and I accept the pain.

Here's a prayer of surrender:

Lord, it's painful, but I turn this desire over to You. It belongs to You now. Change it into whatever You see is best.

Sometimes our addictions have such a powerful hold on us that we simply cannot bring ourselves to the point of surrendering them to God. If that's where you are right now, don't give up. Try giving Him your *fear* of losing the addiction instead. I said to Linda, "Since you're having a hard time giving up Bill, turn your *fear* of losing Bill over to God. Give Him permission to remove your fear. The more He removes the fear, the less of a hindrance fear will be to surrendering Bill himself to God."

Remember, there's always a fall-back strategy for any of God's requirements that you can't bring yourself to follow. Be honest with Him. Tell Him you can't give up your addiction right now, and ask Him to show you what feeling in you is keeping you from giving it up. Then ask Him to remove *that* emotion or change it to the place where you *are* willing to follow His way. This is part of the process of developing character and overcoming sin, and God will stick close beside you. He will never leave you, as long as you are involved in the process.

Surrender is the link between getting a change in our sinful desires and getting a change in our sinful behaviors. So with this brief explanation, I will conclude our discussion of surrender, and we'll take it up again in a later chapter when we talk about how to change our sinful behavior.

DEVOTIONAL EXERCISES

Biblical reflection on chapter 22

1. Use a concordance to look up what the Gospels say about Judas. As you reflect on his life, what do you think was his besetting sin? Would you call this an addiction?
2. How might Judas's life have turned out differently had he surrendered his addiction? Reflect on how the book of Acts might have been written had Judas been one of the apostles.
3. Do you have a cherished sin? Write a paragraph or two describing what your life will be like if you surrender this sin; write another paragraph or two about what your life will be like if you don't. Pray as you write that God will help you to understand these issues correctly.

Devotional study of 1 Samuel 22

1. Did Saul think he was doing the right thing by killing the priests of the Lord? What caused him to have such a distorted view of reality? What could Saul have done to ensure that he had a healthy outlook on life?
2. Does your outlook on life seem right to you? How can you be sure that it really is?
3. Does God hold Christians responsible for their attitudes? What can you do to ensure that your outlook on life is increasingly healthy and that your behavior is appropriate? Write a paragraph or two about this.

Chapter
Twenty-three

SOME FINAL THOUGHTS ABOUT DESIRE

What I say in this chapter may be somewhat repetitious either of ideas expressed earlier in this book or that I will share with you in chapters yet to come. However, I think these things need to be said, and in this chapter I can go into greater detail. This amount of detail added to other chapters would have gotten them off track from their main purpose. In this chapter, I especially want to discuss false guilt, and we will also touch on fear near the end of the chapter.

False guilt

I pointed out in an earlier chapter that some emotions are good in themselves, but in our broken, sinful condition we easily abuse them. One of these is shame. Often, we feel guilty over things that are not sinful at all. This was a major problem in Jesus' time. The Pharisees had piled all sorts of man-made regulations onto God's requirements in the Bible, and they insisted that the people obey these as though God Himself had commanded them. The common people were suffering under an incredible load of guilt as a result—and it was all so unnecessary.

"Fortunately, we live in a more enlightened age," you say. "Adventists don't have this problem."

Spare me! It's endemic among us! I went into some detail about this in my book *The Gospel vs. Legalism*, and I suggest you read that book, especially chapter 16, if you want to understand this problem better. However, I will mention a few points here.

A major source of false guilt comes from condemnation by modern Pharisees. For example, the Bible tells us to keep the Sabbath, and it offers some general guidelines for doing so, but it leaves most of the details for us to work out in our individual relationship with God. Unfortunately, after deciding what is right for them, some people vigorously condemn anyone who does not keep the Sabbath their way. The same problem exists with the health principles given us by Ellen White, which also allow for a certain amount of leeway in their actual application. Again, the Pharisees among us see their way as the only way, and they pile incredible loads of guilt onto those of us who disagree with them.

This problem is not limited to the condemnation we receive from others. Some of us are experts at condemning ourselves. My wife and I know an Adventist woman who for years never wore a wedding ring. However, she worked in a public office, and on two or three occasions, some very fine non-Adventist men asked her for a date. They felt mortified when she informed them that she was married, and they apologized profusely. Finally, our friend decided that under the circumstances, it would be appropriate for her to wear a wedding band, so she bought a dime-store ring and put it on. Nobody in the church condemned her for it. None of her relatives said a word. But she felt terribly guilty over wearing that ring.

"It was as though God was talking to me, condemning me, and telling me to take it off," she said.

But was God really telling her this? Was the Holy Spirit talking to her through her conscience? I don't think so. Let me explain.

We tend to think of our conscience as a spot in the brain that God "touches" when we've done something wrong, causing us to feel guilty. However, I don't think God directly inspires our feelings of guilt. Again, let me explain.

Shame is a normal emotion that God gave us when He created us. Guilt is simply a form of shame. The question is, Does this shame come from God?

Yes, but only indirectly.

Jesus said that the Holy Spirit convicts us of sin (see John 16:8), but I don't think that means He pushes our shame buttons. I believe that when the Holy Spirit convicts us, He gives us *information* about our lives, nothing more. When that information contradicts what we have grown up thinking is right, our shame "kicks in," and we say that we feel guilty. If our understanding of right and wrong is in harmony with God's understanding of right and wrong, the shame we feel for violating our conscience is appropriate.

Unfortunately, most of us have grown up with a variety of warped ideas about what is right and wrong. It is always appropriate to feel guilty when we do something that is indeed wrong, but if what we thought was wrong really isn't, then the guilt we feel is not God "talking" to us. It's our misplaced shame. Yet this "guilt" *feels* exactly like the real thing.

So how can we tell the difference?

Through careful Bible study and prayer. *Our ideas of right and wrong must always be grounded in the Word of God.* The following statement by Ellen White, which I quoted earlier, has helped me understand how to set aside false ideas and adopt correct ideas of what is right and wrong:

> Real experience is a variety of careful experiments made with the mind freed from prejudice and uncontrolled by previously established opinions and habits (3T, 69).

Sometimes freeing our minds from previously established opinions and habits means a willingness to set aside our most cherished traditions about what we have *thought* all our lives was wrong or what others try to *tell* us is wrong and searching out the truth in the Bible for ourselves. If our minds are oppressed with false guilt, then we must pray that God will help us to put it away and understand the Bible for what it *really* says, not for what our warped emotions would like us to *think* it says.

Let me illustrate with anger, which is one of the most common issues over which we humans tend to interpret false guilt as real guilt. I pointed out in an earlier chapter that anger is a gift from God that we can use to protect ourselves and others from abuse and injustice. Unfortunately, many Christians—perhaps I should say most Christians—have grown up thinking that any expression of anger, especially in self-defense, is always evil. People who have never been taught how to use anger appropriately almost invariably misuse it either by lashing out with it, which is abusive to others, or by stuffing it, which is abusive to themselves. We use our anger appropriately when we simply state how we feel about what someone has done, ask them to change their behavior, and tell them how we will respond if they don't. This is called setting a boundary.

But people who grew up thinking all anger is bad will feel guilty, even when they use their anger appropriately. These people have a major lesson to *unlearn*—the falsehood that all anger is bad, and another major lesson to *learn*—that anger is healthy when it is expressed appropriately.

The point I'm making here is that *learning appropriate ways to deal with our anger includes getting rid of our inappropriate guilt feelings about anger.* And the same is true of any false guilt.

When you learn to recognize false guilt, you will find it popping up in a variety of situations. Back when I was a pastor, a woman who had a problem with food said to me one day, "Every time I eat a bite of food I feel guilty." Is it appropriate to feel guilty over *every* bite of food we eat? Of course not! Was the Holy Spirit talking to that woman when she felt guilty over eating even *one* bite of food? No! Yet I can assure you that this woman *felt* like it was the Holy Spirit speaking to her conscience. Why? Because she, along with most of us Christians, has come to associate guilt feelings with the Holy Spirit "talking to us," and we have an unbearably hard time believing it's *not* the Holy Spirit when it *feels* like the Holy Spirit.

Sex is another common source of unhealthy shame, and here the problem is often appropriate guilt carried to excess. We humans have a built-in shame about sex that is quite normal. For example, we cover the sexual parts of our bodies except in private or intimate situations. Not to do so would be highly abusive. Unfortunately, when we misbehave sexually, our normal sense of sexual shame that is very appropriate often piles on top of our legitimate guilt, causing us to feel far more guilty than we do with most other forms of wrongdoing. In God's eyes, sexual wrongdoing is less evil than pride, yet we feel far more guilt over it!

One day my wife and I were visiting with a woman from New York City who shared with us an interesting form of misplaced guilt. We'll call her Rita. Rita's church put on a social one Saturday night, and one of the people who attended was a young man who had recently revealed to his family and friends that he was a homosexual. He brought his homosexual companion with him to the social, and Rita was standing near the door when the two young men entered. Because his family and hers were good friends, she was suddenly confronted with deciding just how she should relate to her friend and his companion. Prior to his announcement of his homosexuality, she would have welcomed both of them to the social with a warm hug. Rita decided that their homosexual orientation did not change the fact that they were human beings for whom Christ died, so she welcomed both of them just as she would have had she not known "the facts."

"The next day I felt horribly depressed," Rita said. "It took me most of the day to figure out why, but I finally realized that my depression was caused by a profound sense of shame that I had welcomed these young men to our church's social."

My wife and I asked Rita why she felt such shame over welcoming her homosexual friends, and she said, "Because I felt that by welcoming them I was approving of their lifestyle."

Shades of the Pharisees! Refusing to make sinners feel welcome lest we appear to approve of their lifestyle! I used to be amazed that the Pharisees would condemn Jesus for eating with tax collectors and sinners (see Luke 15:1). Rita's story helps me to understand why: misplaced shame, false guilt. The problem of the Pharisees is alive and well in today's Christian community, including the Adventist community.

Now do you understand why it's important that we deal with inappropriate shame? Not only is it eating the heart and soul out of our own lives; it may be causing us to abuse the very people for whom Christ died! And the truth is that until we get rid of the inappropriate shame and false guilt in our lives, we aren't going to make much progress in overcoming our cherished sins and addictions.

Fear

Another emotion that we must deal with in our recovery from cherished sin and addiction is fear. The addict is faced with a bitter paradox. On the one hand, he loves his "fix" and is terribly afraid he *won't* get to indulge in it. For example, some alcoholics are so afraid of being without their liquor that they hide bottles of the stuff all over the house. Many bulimics are terrified of traveling long distances lest they be caught in a situation in which they can't eat and purge.

On the other hand, the addict is terribly afraid that he *will* indulge in his addiction and feel an overwhelming sense of guilt as a result. So he beats himself back and forth, afraid he'll get it and afraid he won't. He clenches his fists and grits his teeth to keep from doing it so he won't feel guilty, but his fear of not getting it finally wins out, and he does it again. The profound guilt from doing it drives him to vow never to do it again, yet he's terrified he may *not* get to do it. So around and around he goes, his fears jerking him two ways.

Much of the obsession that drives our addictions is this fear that's pulling us and pushing us at the same time. I am convinced that addicts will overcome their addiction much more easily when they can identify their shame and the fear associated with it and learn to deal with these issues along with the addiction itself.

The question is, How do we deal with these powerful emotions? The answer is simple. We take them through the process I've outlined in this book. We start by seeking a change in our understanding of these feelings, using the strategies I suggested in Part 1—"Changing Our Sinful Understanding." Then we go through Part 2—"Changing Our Sinful Desires." Finally, we apply these lessons to our behavior, using the strategies you'll read in Part 3—"Changing Our Sinful Behavior."

Another excellent way to deal with our inappropriate shame and fear is to take them through the Twelve Steps. One of the best ways I can recommend for you to do that is to purchase the workbook *The Twelve Steps: A Spiritual Journey,* and work your way through it, giving special attention to these unhealthy emotions. Another way to deal with inappropriate shame and fear is to open up and talk about them in a Twelve-Step meeting. Talk to a sponsor about them. Talk to God about them, and ask Him to remove them. This is honesty, and honesty is always one of the best ways to overcome our sins and the unhealthy emotions that cause them.

I cannot overemphasize that, important as it is to identify our actual sinful desires such as lust, jealousy, and gluttony (to name a few) and ask God to deal with them, we must also ask Him to deal with the shame and fear that so often lie behind these desires and may actually be driving them.

This is essential for everyone who is serious about conquering the dragon within.

DEVOTIONAL EXERCISES

Biblical reflection on chapter 23

1. Read Matthew 12:1-8. Given the religious tradition about the Sabbath that they grew up with, how do you think the disciples felt when the Pharisees condemned them for picking grain and eating it on the Sabbath?
2. Analyze Jesus' response to the Pharisees. On what authority did He base His argument? Was "human reason" a part of the process He went through to deal with this false guilt?
3. Identify an issue over which you have tended to feel false guilt. Do you feel guilty over this matter, even though you know in your head that it's not wrong? Do you feel as though the Holy Spirit is "talking" to you, even though you know in your rational mind that He's not?
4. Write out a strategy for overcoming these feelings based on what you have learned so far in this book.

Devotional study of 1 Samuel 23

1. What did David do in response to the fear that his men felt over going to Keilah? How did he respond to the threat that the people of Keilah might hand him and his men over to Saul?
2. How can you be sure of God's guidance in your life when you feel afraid?
3. What other source of help for dealing with his fear came to David? (See verses 15-18.) How can you avail yourself of this source of help for dealing with your fears?

SECTION II

Part 3

Changing Our Sinful Behavior

Station Break 3

We have completed our discussion of how to get a change in our sinful desires—the second of the three major changes we must experience in order to develop a character like Christ's and be ready for the close of probation. It is impossible to change our evil behavior on a permanent basis as long as we have evil desires. Clenching the fists and gritting the teeth is useless as long as we still *want* to do what's wrong.

However, we must not assume that once God has changed our evil desires, our behavior will change all by itself with no effort on our part. We must also pay very careful attention to changing our behavior, and we must use the right methods to bring about that change.

That's what we will be discussing next. The arrow on the outline below shows you where we are now. You can see that, as with a change in our sinful understanding and our sinful desires, God has a part in our behavior change, and we have a part.

Chapter
Twenty-four

God's Part:
GIVE US THE POWER

Imagine that you are at the shopping mall near your home one day, browsing through the clothing department at the JCPenney store, when you happen to come to the perfume counter. Most of the perfumes are stored inside glass cases, but a brand that is on sale is displayed on top of the counter. You spray a small amount on your wrist and sniff it.

"Nice! I think my husband will like that!" you say to yourself. "I wonder how much it is?" You turn the bottle over in your hands, looking for a price tag. "Uh-oh. Maybe not today."

The price is $75 for a single ounce!

You sniff your wrist again. "What a lovely scent! I know he'd love it! Hmmmm. I wonder who's looking?"

You glance around, and all the clerks are busy with customers.

"I know I shouldn't, but I'd *really* like to surprise him."

Before you know it, you've opened your purse and dropped the bottle inside. You glance around again to be sure no one saw you.

No one did.

You are about to close your purse when a giant hand reaches down from above and clamps around your wrist.

At first you panic, afraid that a security guard has caught you red-handed. But a quick glance around confirms that nobody is near you. Then where did that giant hand come from?

"Uh-oh again. God."

Then a voice from above says, "Put it back, sister. Put it back."

You hesitate a moment, so the giant hand forces your hand down into your purse. "Pick it up!" the voice commands.

You wrap your fingers around the offending bottle.

Slowly the giant hand pulls your wrist out of the purse and

moves it toward the counter. When your hand is over the counter, the voice says, "Let it go, sister. Let it go."

You aren't quite fast enough, and the fingers on the giant hand start squeezing your wrist. That really hurts! Unless you want to be in serious pain, you have no choice, so you let go of the bottle.

Finally, the giant hand lets go. What a relief!

Has that ever happened to you?

Of course not! God doesn't reach down from heaven and force people to stop sinning.

Now maybe you will better understand the basic principle behind changing our sinful behavior. I'll begin by stating the basic principle behind changing our sinful desires and follow it immediately with the one for changing our sinful behavior:

**Only God can change
our evil desires.**

**Only we can change
our evil behavior.**

**And He gives us the power
to do so.**

I began with evil desire because that is where we must always begin. Any time we set out to conquer a temptation—even the tiniest one—we should *always* begin with evil desire.

However, as soon as we've dealt with the desire, then we need to pay attention to the behavior. And please notice the principle:

**Only we can change
our evil behavior.**

If God were to change our evil behavior, He would have to reach down from heaven and physically force us to do or abstain from doing wrong things. But that would be forcing our will, and He won't do that. *If our behavior changes at all, it's because we change it, not God.*

This doesn't mean that God has no part in helping us to change our behavior. Not at all! His part is summarized in a short verse in Philippians 4:13. I like the King James Version's way of putting it best, so I'm going to quote it from that version:

I can do all things through Christ, which strengtheneth me.

Let's take a moment to analyze that statement. First, notice that this is a behavior statement, not a desire statement. We know that because Paul said, "I can *do*." Doing is behavior.

Who's doing it? Paul said, "*I* can do." That means you and me. Philippians 4:13 is the biblical basis for the principle that "only we can change our evil behavior."

How much of our evil behavior can we change? Paul said, "I can do *all* things." That means that it is possible for you and me to overcome every sin in our lives.

Fortunately, we are not alone, for Paul said, "I can do all things *through Christ*." Jesus is there, not to force us to behave right but to help us. That reminds me of the verse in 1 Corinthians 10:13 that says, "No temptation has seized you except what is common to man. And God will not let you be tempted beyond what you can bear. But when you are tempted, he will also provide a way out so that you can stand up under it."

Finally, Paul tells us how Jesus helps us: "I can do all things," he says, "through Christ *which strengtheneth me.*"

There it is. God's part in helping us to get a change in our sinful behavior is to give us the power not to do it. So let's put that on our chart:

Change Needed	**God's Part**	**Our Part**
In Our Sinful **Understanding**	Conviction: Show us Our sins	Ask for it
		Talk about it
		Search for it
In Our Sinful **Desires**	Conversion: Change our desires	Ask for it
		Talk about it
		Surrender it
In Our Sinful **Behavior**	**GIVE US POWER**	

God does not change our sinful desires and then tell us we are on our own to change our sinful behavior. At each step of the way, He has a plan for helping us to gain the victory over our temptations. Every one of them!

DEVOTIONAL EXERCISES

Biblical reflection on chapter 24
1. Read John 15:5, and write a few sentences comparing this verse with Philippians 4:13. What is the "fruit" that Jesus spoke about? Does Paul speak of the same thing in Philippians? What does it mean to "remain" in Jesus? How does this add to your understanding of Philippians 4:13?
2. Read John 15:1-4. What are the good and bad branches? What does "pruning" mean? How does God do this? What relationship, if any, does this have with getting a change in your sinful behavior?

Devotional study of 1 Samuel 24
1. Verse 5 says that David was "conscience-stricken for having cut off a corner of his [Saul's] robe." Was the issue in David's guilt feelings the piece of cloth, or was a larger principle involved? Write a paragraph expressing David's feelings as you understand them.
2. Write another paragraph expressing Saul's feelings as you understand them when David revealed himself to the king.
3. Was there a danger in David's revealing himself to the king? What attitude made it possible for him to take this risk? At what earlier time in his life was David able to risk his life in God's cause because of this same attitude?
4. Have you ever faced a situation that, to best handle it, required that you have David's attitude? Did you have that attitude, and did you act on it? What was the result?

Chapter

Twenty-five

Our Part: 1
ASK FOR HELP WITH OUR SINFUL BEHAVIOR

Several chapters back, I shared with you the diagram that is reproduced below, and we discussed the right way to use the will to get a change in our sinful desires. It's now time to discuss the right way to use the will to get a change in our sinful behavior:

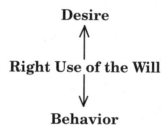

Desire

↑
|

Right Use of the Will

|
↓

Behavior

You will recall that I pointed out two ways to use the will. One is choice, and the other is determination. Choice is the appropriate method to use for getting a change in our sinful desires. We must choose to ask God to change them. Determination is the appropriate way to use our willpower to get a change in our sinful behavior. You no doubt recall that determination means clenching the fists, gritting the teeth, and saying, "I'm not going to do it." However, it's extremely important that you understand exactly what determination can and cannot do. So before I explain the proper use of determination, I would like to point out two things for which this use of the will is ineffective:

1. Determination will not work to change your sinful desires.
2. Determination will not work to bring about a *permanent* change in your sinful behavior.

If you are gritting your teeth and clenching your fists as a permanent way to control your wrong desires and keep your behavior in line with God's will, then, as I've said several times already in this book, you can forget it. It won't work. You may succeed in not "doing it" for a while, but eventually your desires will win. Even if you should succeed in being a super Christian and keep the lid clamped down on your desires permanently, that's a miserable way to live the Christian life.

If you cannot expect to use determination as a permanent way to get a change in your sinful desires, what good is determination? The principle here is so important that I'm going to boldface it for you:

Determination will work as a temporary way to control your behavior while the desire fades.

Once or twice before in this book, I've pointed out that under normal circumstances, our desires change slowly. If you're burning-up mad at someone one minute, you can't just flip a switch in your brain and be cool as a cucumber the next. God does not violate this principle when He changes our sinful desires. Here is where determination comes in. Perhaps you will more easily understand the point I'm making if I illustrate it with a diagram:

Prayer for God to remove the desire	**The desire finally fades away**
Clench the fists Grit the teeth	

Determination will work as a temporary way to control your behavior till the desire to do it fades. We sometimes call this "white knuckling it," and it has a crucial role in any effort to overcome sin and addiction.

Please don't think, though, that God leaves us totally on our own as we use the "determination" aspect of willpower to conquer our temptations. No, no! Remember that while He will not change our behavior, He is more than willing to give us the power to change our behavior. Or, to put it another way, He will give us the power to clench our fists and grit our teeth and refuse to do it.

The question is, How do we access that power? I'm sure that by now you've guessed the answer, especially if you've noticed the pattern that I've already established in discussing our part in getting a change in our sinful understanding and our sinful desires. It's called "Ask for it." Let's put it on our diagram:

Change Needed	God's Part	Our Part
In Our Sinful **Understanding**	Conviction: Show us Our sins	Ask for it
		Talk about it
		Search for it
In Our Sinful **Desires**	Conversion: Change our desires	Ask for it
		Talk about it
		Surrender it
In Our Sinful **Behavior**	Give us power	**ASK FOR IT**

A determination prayer

You remember, I'm sure, that each of the other "Ask for it" strategies I shared with you for overcoming temptation had a prayer to go with it, and so does this one. Here it is:

**Lord, please remove
the desire for this sin,**

**and please give me the power
not to do it right now.**

Notice that this prayer actually begins by asking for help with our sinful desires. There's a good reason for that. It's based on a principle stated by Ellen White that I shared with you earlier: "There are many who try to reform by correcting this or that bad habit, [but] *our first work is with the heart*" (COL, 97). The point is this:

We should never try to deal with our sinful behavior until we have done something to deal with the sinful desires that prompt it.

Even the simplest prayer for help with your sinful behavior should *always* begin with asking God to change your sinful desires. *Then* you can ask Him for help not to do it *right now*.

You will also notice that I put the "right now" part of the prayer with the behavior, not the desire. God may not remove your desires "right now," but He will give you the power not to do it "right now."

The pressure-cooker analogy

Let me share with you an illustration that I think will help to nail down the basic point of this chapter. I call it the "pressure-cooker" analogy.

Imagine that you have a pressure cooker with no rim around the edge to hold the lid on, and the lid has no clamps to hold it to the kettle. Fortunately, the kettle does have two U-shaped handles near the top that are large enough you can put a pair of padded gloves on your hands and grip the handles without getting burned. To keep the lid on the pressure cooker, you have to put your hands through the handles, bring the ball of your palm down on top of the kettle on each side, and squeeze real tight.

The kettle has split peas and an inch or so of water in it, and the burner on your stove is on. So you put on the padded gloves, pick up the pressure cooker by the handles, and set it on the hot stove. When you first bring your hands down over the lid, there is no pressure at all. However, a couple of minutes later, you begin to feel the lid pushing up against your hands. By the time another minute is up, you're having to press down on the lid to keep it on; and two minutes later, you're straining pretty hard.

As the pressure builds, you're straining so hard to hold the lid down that your hands start to tremble. You begin to feel very tired, but the pressure keeps building. Soon you're totally exhausted, straining every muscle in your body to hold that lid on; and the more tired you get, the more the pressure builds.

Suddenly, *boom!* There's split pea soup all over the ceiling.

That's how it is when you try to use determination as a

long-term strategy for "holding down the lid" on your evil behavior. The pressure from desire will eventually build to the point that you do it anyway.

Fortunately, there's a perfectly simple way to solve the problem with the pressure cooker. Just ask someone to open the valve on the lid and let some of the steam escape. *You can hold the lid down while the steam is escaping.*

The point is this. You cannot use "determination" as the *permanent* way to change your behavior, because eventually your desires will build to the point that "the lid blows off." But you can ask God to remove the pressure that your desires are creating inside of you, and with some strong determination, you can "hold the lid down" *during the time the desire is fading.*

People who try to conquer their evil behavior by determination alone are doomed to failure. But those who ask God to change their desires and give them the power not to "do it" while He is removing the desire begin to discover victory where before they had only experienced defeat.

In the spring of 1994, I received a postcard from a woman who had attended one of my seminars a few weeks earlier. I'd like to share with you what she told me:

> IT WORKS! Before when God has held me up under temptation and helped me have a way of escape, I've felt cheated sometimes because I missed the indulgence. But yesterday I said, "Take away the desire and help me hold tight until You do!" I finally realized I didn't really want to indulge. I felt He had answered my prayer. He is *so good and so able to deliver and transform us.*

Yes, it does work. As you experiment with strategies for overcoming temptation, you will find that exercising the determination part of your willpower while God is removing the desire is one of the most effective ways for conquering the dragon within.

DEVOTIONAL EXERCISES

Biblical reflection on chapter 25
1. Read Romans 8:5-8; then write a prayer asking God for power

to control your behavior. Use some of the language from this passage in your prayer.

2. What does it mean to "set" the mind on what the sinful nature desires? What does it mean to "set" the mind on what the Spirit desires? Identify an area in your life in which you are struggling to keep your mind off what the sinful nature desires and on what the Spirit desires. Write a paragraph in which you tell God exactly how you feel in this struggle. Conclude by asking Him to help you set your mind on what the Spirit desires.

3. How do you expect your answer to the questions in number 2 will affect your actions in that area?

Devotional study of 1 Samuel 25

1. Have you ever felt like Nabal did when someone asked a favor of you? Write a few sentences describing your feelings at that time. From what you have learned so far in this book, what should Nabal have done to handle his feelings appropriately?

2. Describe Abigail's feelings when she heard what her husband had done. Which do you think was strongest—fear, shame, or anger? Have you ever experienced a similar situation? Which of these three feelings was strongest in you? Are you satisfied that your response was appropriate, or would you do differently if you had a chance?

3. What feeling dominated David's mind and controlled his behavior when he received word of Nabal's discourtesy? Was this feeling understandable? Was it appropriate? Was David's behavior understandable? Was it appropriate?

4. Write a paragraph discussing how one person's feelings and behavior can influence another person's feelings and behavior. Use the story of Abigail and David to illustrate the point. If you have time, also use the encounter between David and Saul in chapter 24 as an illustration.

5. Explain the difference between David's response to Saul in chapter 24 and his response to Nabal in chapter 25. In view of the fact that the circumstances were similar, why was David's response so different? What useful lesson do you find in this for your life?

Chapter
Twenty-six

Our Part 2
TALK ABOUT OUR SINFUL BEHAVIOR

One of the toughest things I've ever done is to confess a sin. There've been times when I would rather have died than confess. You know what I mean, don't you?

But then there's the Bible to deal with: "If we *confess* our sins, he is faithful and just to forgive us our sins" (1 John 1:9, KJV). I have yet to find a way to get around that text. If we want forgiveness, we must confess.

There's also Ellen White's bold statement: "Sins that are not confessed will never be forgiven; the name of him who thus rejects the grace of God will be blotted out of the book of life" (RH, 16 December 1890).

Tough stuff.

Why?

Honesty. That's why.

God is perfectly willing—He's *anxious*—to accept you and me just as we are, character defects and all. The condition is not that we overcome all our defects. That will take a lifetime. The condition, as I've stressed already in this book, is repentance. And repentance means honesty.

God wants you and me to acknowledge our character defects. Until we honestly admit the sin that infects us and *want* out of it enough to *do* something about it, we aren't being honest, and God can't help us. And part of that honesty is acknowledging to others the ways in which our behavior has injured them. In order to overcome our wrong behavior, we must confess to others the ways in which our wrong behavior has injured them. That's why confession is so important.

Confessing the ways in which we have injured others is so important that Alcoholics Anonymous includes it in three of its Twelve Steps:

Step 8
> Made a list of all persons we had harmed, and became willing to make amends [confess] to them all.

Step 9
> Made direct amends to such people wherever possible, except when to do so would injure them or others.

Step 10
> Continued to take personal inventory and when we were wrong promptly admitted it.

The second aspect of our part in changing our sinful behavior is to "talk about it," which means confessing to others the ways in which our wrong behavior has injured them. Let's put it on our chart:

Change Needed	God's Part	Our Part
In Our Sinful **Understanding**	Conviction: Show us Our sins	Ask for it Talk about it Search for it
In Our Sinful **Desires**	Conversion: Change our desires	Ask for it Talk about it Surrender it
In Our Sinful **Behavior**	Give us power	Ask for it **TALK ABOUT IT**

Confession is a fairly straightforward matter. When we do something wrong, we acknowledge it. If I were to stop right here, I would have shared enough information with you that you could do this part of your part in getting a change in your sinful behavior quite adequately. However, over the years, people have asked me about several issues related to confession that I would like to discuss with you in the rest of this chapter.

Confession should for the right reason

The first question we can ask is, Why confess? The basic purpose of confession is to restore relationships and put them on an honest foundation. However, it is possible to confess for the wrong reason, with the wrong motive in mind. I will mention two motives you might have for confessing that would indicate you probably should not confess.

The first is when your confession would actually be a way of injuring the person you are confessing to even more. If you know that your confession will cause that individual great pain and you actually want to cause that pain, perhaps as a way to "get even," then you should not confess until your motive is right.

Second, your reason for confessing should go generally beyond the mere relief of your own guilt feelings. This is especially true if the person you have injured would be devastated by the confession. Under such circumstances, you should confess only if you can have reasonable certainty that in spite of the devastation it will cause, that person needs to know and will be benefited by knowing what you did. Usually, it is best to seek professional help, either from a pastor or a trained counselor, before confessing to someone who would be devastated by your confession.

Make confession as direct as possible

You should always confess every sin to God, and when your behavior has injured another person, under normal circumstances, you should confess to that person also. The ninth step of Alcoholics Anonymous, quoted above, gives good advice. It says, "Made *direct* amends to such people." That means you should make every effort to speak personally with the one whom you injured. If circumstances make it impossible to speak to that person even by telephone, then making amends by letter is certainly acceptable. Only under very special circumstances should you consider making amends anonymously through a third party, and then only on the advice of someone qualified to counsel you.

An example would be if you have injured another person in a way that was a serious violation of the law. Your best course in such a situation is to discuss everything with a Christian attorney who understands both the laws of your state or country and your need as a Christian to be honest with God and the person you have harmed. If you can't find a Christian attorney to consult with, you might consider asking your pastor to go with you as you visit with an attorney who is not a Christian. The attorney can advise you about the law, and with that information, your pastor can help you to think through the best approach to take from a Christian perspective.

Usually, the sooner you can confess after the injury has occurred, the better. However, in some circumstances, you may be wise to wait. An example would be the one I mentioned in the previous paragraph, in which you take the time to think through the best approach when your injury to another is a serious violation of the law.

I would also urge you to seek two kinds of professional advice before confessing a sin that the other person is unaware of and might well be devastated to learn about. First, you should seek the advice of a professional counselor, who can assist you in making the confession in a way that will be most helpful to the individual involved. And second, you should consult an attorney to find out the legal implications of making the confession.

When confession may be unwise

Should you confess to your spouse an act of adultery you committed with another person? Many Christian counselors advise against doing this. Keep in mind that your spouse will almost certainly be devastated by such a confession. If your confession is merely to relieve your own feelings of guilt, you should probably not confess. While it is true that adultery is a violation of the marriage vow, the sin was between you and the person you committed the adultery with. If an amend is to be made, that is where it should begin.

A woman once told me that she confessed an affair to her husband, and while it did not end the marriage, it damaged the marriage permanently. I asked her, if she had it to do over, whether she would confess to her husband, and she said No. Others who went through it might say, "I'm glad I confessed." This is very much a personal decision. You need to know, though, that many Christian counselors and pastors advise against confessing an affair to a spouse. You should by all means seek proper counsel before doing so.

Anytime you confess a serious wrong to a person who is unaware of what you did, you place on that individual a very heavy burden. He or she is going to have some powerful emotions to deal with. This is one of the reasons why the ninth step of Alcoholics Anonymous says, "Made direct amends to such people wherever possible, *except when to do so would injure them or others.*"

When you can't bring yourself to confess

In 1992 I gave one of my seminars at a church in Lincoln, Nebraska. After the seminar, a woman came to me and said, "Pastor, there is a sin I ought to confess, but I would rather die than to make that confession. What should I do?"

If that's how you feel about something you did that was wrong, it is very likely that what you did was quite serious. You should begin by asking yourself whether the confession needs to be made, and if it does, whether you should seek professional advice first. Remember that professional advice will never hurt you or the person you wronged, but an inappropriate confession has the potential for serious, lifelong consequences for both of you. It is better to postpone confession until you are sure that making it is appropriate, and if it is, that you will make it in the right way.

If, after proper consultation, you decide that you, indeed, should make the confession and you have decided on an appropriate way to make it, you still will probably be faced with your feelings. How do you bring yourself to confess something you'd rather die than confess?

The first thing you need to do is deal with your feelings. And there is a very simple way to do that. Tell God how you feel—that at the present time, you cannot bring yourself to confess. That's honesty, and God is always willing to work with us when we are honest. Tell Him that you are willing to confess if He can bring your feelings around to that point, and ask Him to help you with your feelings. He is as willing to change your feelings about this as He is about any other area of your imperfect emotional life.

I have mentioned several situations in which it is best to postpone confession for a time. This brings up the problem of your relationship with God during the delay. If you believe, as did my Sabbath School teacher in Texas, that your relationship with Jesus remains broken until you confess your sin, then logically the sooner you can confess, the better. However, I am convinced that God accepts your postponement of confession when there is a good reason for doing so. He is willing to accept you while you are waiting for a change in your feelings that will give you the courage to confess.

What about forgiveness?

I used to always combine my confessions with a request for forgiveness: "I did such and such that was wrong. I am sorry. Will you forgive me?" However, I have come to the conclusion that, especially where the injury I caused was serious, it is best that I not ask for forgiveness. Forgiveness is for the other person to grant, and he or she may not be emotionally prepared to grant it immediately.

The next question is whether there is something wrong with refusing to grant immediate forgiveness. God does. Shouldn't we?

I will answer that question in two ways.

First, the other person's relationship with God is not your business. It's not the issue at the moment of confession. The issue is making amends for what you did that was wrong. You have done your part by confessing, and that's as far as your responsibility goes. If the person to whom you confessed cannot grant you immediate forgiveness, that's their problem, not yours. Let them solve it their way.

Second, it's OK not to forgive immediately. If you are the person who was injured, you may have powerful feelings of anger to deal with before you can honestly say to that person, "I forgive you." It is better to withhold an expression of forgiveness until you can honestly and completely forgive than it is to say "I forgive you" when doing so would be dishonest.

"But God forgives us immediately," you say. "Shouldn't we do the same for others?"

I don't believe it is fair to compare ourselves to God in situations like this. God is much greater than we are and much more able to see the "total picture" than we. He is also holy and does not have to struggle with ingrained sinfulness. In our broken human condition and with our limited perspective on life, the healing of our wounds often takes time. It is better that we allow the wounds to heal first and deal with the forgiveness when our feelings have matured to the place where we can do so honestly.

Dealing with the guilt

Many people continue to feel guilty after they have confessed. They feel that God still cannot accept them. I will respond to that problem in two ways.

If you have confessed your sin and insofar as possible made restitution, then you have fulfilled your responsibility to that person and to God. Any "guilt" you feel beyond that point is shame, not true guilt. You need to ask God to remove it the way He does every other wrong desire.

My second response to guilt that continues after confession is to ask yourself whether your feeling is guilt or remorse. Sometimes, even after we have made all the amends possible, the other person will still have to suffer the effects of our wrongdoing. For example, if someone suffered a lifelong injury because you struck them with your car while driving under the influence of alcohol, you can confess all you want, but their disability won't go away. It's all right to feel long-term remorse for the injury you caused, but not guilt.

Restitution

Restitution means taking responsibility for the injury you caused another person and doing everything in your power to restore their circumstances to what they were before you harmed them. If it is in your power to restore, you should do so regardless of the cost to yourself. The qualification here would be that you cannot pay someone 100 percent of your income for the rest of your life or even for a part of your life, or you would have nothing left over to pay your own expenses and those of your family.

The basic purpose of confession is honesty and restored relationships. Victory over sin requires honesty, and that's why confession is so important. It makes us honest.

DEVOTIONAL EXERCISES

Biblical reflection on chapter 26

1. Read Proverbs 28:13. How many Bible characters can you think of who refused to confess their sins? How many can

you think of who did confess their sins? Write a paragraph or two explaining why confession is essential to prosperity.
2. What attitudes does confession affect that most have to do with prosperity?
3. Is there a sin you know you should confess, but you have not had the courage to do so? Write a paragraph telling how you feel about this. Do you sense any effect on your prosperity?
4. Write a prayer acknowledging to God how you feel about making this confession and asking Him to help you understand how to solve the problem.

Devotional study of 1 Samuel 26

1. Have you ever had an opportunity to take revenge on someone who had harmed you? Did you have conflicting feelings over what to do? If so, which feelings did you act on and why? On reflection, would you do the same thing if you had it to do over?
2. What indication is there in this chapter that David was afraid of Saul? Was this fear appropriate? Was David's behavior in response to this fear appropriate?
3. Compare David's response to his fear of Saul in this chapter with his response to his fear of Saul in chapter 21. Write a paragraph reflecting on the difference between these two chapters. What lesson is there here for your life?

Chapter
Twenty-seven

Our Part 3
ABSTAIN FROM OUR SINFUL BEHAVIOR

Alone.

Hot and dry. A desert.

Wild animals for companions.

And hungry. Not a bite of food anywhere.

Can you imagine what it must have been like—forty days wandering around in the Judean desert without anything to eat? And the strange thing is, He chose to do it. Well, not exactly. The Bible says that God's Spirit led Him out there (see Matthew 4:1).

So this was part of God's plan for Jesus' life!

There's a name for what Jesus did in the wilderness. It's called *abstinence.* Abstinence means to go for a long period of time without engaging in a particular behavior.

Why did God want Jesus to abstain from food? Because Adam and Eve fell on the point of appetite, and Jesus had to begin His victory over sin on the point where they lost. God wanted Jesus to endure the temptation on appetite and passion to demonstrate that you and I can also gain control of our appetites and passions. Ellen White said, "It was to break the power of appetite that in the forty days' fast in the wilderness He suffered in our behalf the severest test that humanity could endure" (MH, 333).

Jesus did more than show that victory is *possible,* though. He provided an example, showing us *how* to gain the victory. He broke the power of appetite in His life to show you and me *how* we can break the power of appetite in our lives—by abstinence.

Jesus abstained from food. You and I may have to abstain from alcohol or tobacco, sex, television, money, or (don't panic) even religion, for those of us who are addicted to religion. In order to conquer the dragon within and develop a well-balanced character, we must include abstinence among the strategies we use for overcoming our cherished sins and addictions. It's a very painful strategy, as you will see, but it is powerful. You cannot gain total victory—you cannot reach Christian perfection—without it.

Abstinence is the last of the recommendations I'm making for you and me as we cooperate with God in overcoming temptation. It's such an important strategy that I'm taking two chapters to explain it. Let's begin by putting it on our diagram:

Change Needed	God's Part	Our Part
In Our Sinful **Understanding**	Conviction: Show us Our sins	Ask for it Talk about it Search for it
In Our Sinful **Desires**	Conversion: Change our desires	Ask for it Talk about it Surrender it
In Our Sinful **Behavior**	Give us power	Ask for it Talk about it **ABSTAIN FROM IT**

The human race is consumed with passion. It's everywhere—on our television screens, in our magazines and on our billboards, and in the language on our streets. Our society does not like restraint. We don't like saying No. We much prefer the slogan, "If it feels good, do it." But if we are ever going to gain the victory over our sins and addictions, we must learn to practice abstinence.

Abstinence means that at the time when we most want to "do it," we say No instead, and then refuse to do it. And that's tough business! But it's crucial. "Who will enter in through the gates into the city?" Ellen White asked. "Not those who declare that they cannot break the force of appetite" (CDF, 169, 170).

During the initial stages of our victory over sin, we must practice abstinence by white knuckling it—gritting our teeth and clenching our fists. This is the "determination" form of willpower that we've discovered is appropriate to use on our sinful behavior. And, as we have seen, God promises to give us the power to do it. We have also seen that determination is useful only as a short-term strategy for overcoming our sinful behavior while God is removing our sinful desires. I illustrated this point in the previous chapter with a diagram. I have reproduced that diagram below with some modifications:

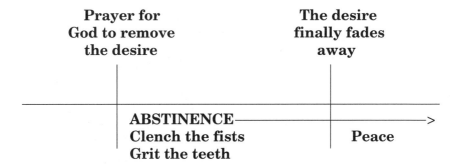

This diagram is different in two ways from the earlier one. First, it includes abstinence. Abstinence is not exclusively an exercise of the will in which we refuse to "do it." Abstinence must be preceded by a prayer for God to remove the desire. During the time you are clenching your fists and gritting your teeth and refusing to "do it," abstinence will seem like some of the worst spiritual pain you have ever endured.

The second point I want to make about the diagram above is that abstinence does not always have to mean clenching the fists and gritting the teeth. You will notice that the line from abstinence extends to the right beyond the point where the desire fades away. In other words, abstinence can also be peaceful, and it is no less abstinence because it is peaceful. In fact, peaceful abstinence should be your goal. A person with a well-balanced character isn't constantly struggling with temptation. He's learned to *enjoy* abstinence!

I am convinced that Jesus conquered temptation in the wilderness just the way you and I must conquer—initially with clenching His fists and gritting His teeth, but moving toward the peaceful form of abstinence. Jesus was not some super Conqueror who could clamp the lid on His passions forever, any more than you and I can. Jesus conquered because His desires were continually subdued by the Holy Spirit. Without God's help to subdue His desires,[1] He could no more have conquered than you and I can.

I am a bit troubled by the talk I hear in some circles about the power of God to give us the victory over temptation. I believe in the concept, to be sure. Haven't I said repeatedly in the last few chapters that God's part in helping us to change our sinful behavior is to give us the power not to do it? But listening to the way some people say it, I get the distinct impression that their concept of victory is pure clenching the fists and gritting the teeth. They do not seem to understand the importance, along with abstinence, of accessing God's power to change the desire for sin.

Please notice this principle:

Abstinence without a corresponding change in our desires is utterly unworkable and is one of the major reasons why so many Christians fail in their effort to conquer temptation.

I suspect that this is the primary cause of the frustration expressed by *Insight*'s correspondent, whom I quoted in chapter 1.

The pain of abstinence

People who are addicted to a particular substance or practice usually feel petrified of abstinence. They think they will die if they cannot get their "fix." One of the best marks of an addiction is this fear of abstinence.

For me, abstinence has at times been excruciatingly painful, especially in the early stages of overcoming a particular cherished sin or addiction. Clenching the fists and gritting the teeth seemed almost impossible to do at first.

Ellen White's comment about cutting off the arm and plucking out the eye applies as much to the difficulty of practicing abstinence as it does to asking God to remove the desire. Her statement is so important that I will quote it again:

Darling, cherished idols will have to be given up, the sins that have been indulged in, even if it comes as close as the plucking out of the right eye, or cutting off the right arm. Arouse, force your way through the very armies of hell that oppose your passage (PC, 345).

It will often seem to you that clenching your fists and gritting your teeth to abstain is like cutting off an arm or plucking out an eye. But do not give up. Keep asking God to remove the desire, and keep trying not to do it. When you fail, ask God to forgive you, and start over. You will start winning. I guarantee it. And your victories will probably begin sooner than you would at first have imagined possible.

A learned skill

Abstinence is learned, and learning is always a process. It takes time. Just as the mastery of a musical instrument requires practice day after day, so mastery of our appetites and addictions requires practice day after day. Occasionally God removes the desire immediately, but when He chooses not to, the addict must learn to overcome by practicing abstinence. And it is as unrealistic to expect perfect performance on the first try at abstinence as it is to expect perfect performance on the first try at a musical instrument. If that thought troubles you, let me remind you of some statements on this very point that I shared with you earlier in this book:

Wrong habits are not overcome by a single effort. Only through long and severe struggles is self mastered (4T, 612).

It is foolish not to anticipate relapses (*The Twelve Steps: A Spiritual Journey*, 26).

It is wise to be gentle with ourselves and remember that it took a lifetime to develop these habits. It is not realistic to expect them to disappear overnight (ibid., 90).

Victory comes through trying and learning, trying and learning. Notice that I said "trying and learning," not "trying and failing." Some people would rather say "trying and failing," and that's one way to look at it. But I find that victory comes much more easily when I think of my failures as opportunities for learning. That makes each "failure" a steppingstone toward the next victory.

I learn abstinence by reflecting on what went wrong when I failed. Often I will ask God to show me what went wrong. And often, He answers that prayer by giving me insight into my desires that will help me to be more specific in asking Him to change them. For example, I have discovered that in some instances, the reason why I was not able to overcome a particular temptation was not so much a result of the desire itself being out of control as it was shame and fear, which drove me to obsess about the desire. And obsession almost invariably leads to "doing it."

Abstaining from thoughts and mental pictures

I would like to suggest that most sin happens in the imagination before it is done by the body. For example, suppose you see a piece of cake on the counter in the kitchen. Your imagination paints a picture of that cake in your mind, and that picture arouses a desire to eat the cake. If television is your addiction, the mere fact that the hour for your favorite wrong program has arrived can stimulate a mental picture of yourself watching it. If you allow that mental picture to stay in your mind, it will overpower you, and you will almost certainly watch the program.

Because we experience our desires in our minds, it is easy to suppose that anything that's in the mind is God's domain, and we can't do anything about it. However, this is not true. Our thoughts and imaginations are behaviors, which God expects us to control. Our desires prompt the images in our minds, but the images themselves must be under the control of reason as much as the movements of our arms and legs.

Ellen White once said that "the first work of those who would reform is to purify the imagination" (CTBH, 136). That's an excellent point! I couldn't have said it better.

Reflect carefully the next time you yield to temptation, and you will almost certainly discover that your imagination was *enjoying* the sin before your body actually *did* the sin. You *must* understand that last sentence, because it provides the key to self-control of your imagination. I will say it again, and I will break the last part of it into two parts for analysis:

Reflect carefully the next time you yield to temptation, and you will almost certainly discover that:
1. Your imagination was *enjoying* the sin
2. Before your body actually *did* the sin.

Your imagination *enjoying* the sin is the desire that you are powerless to change. God must remove it from your mind for you. But the mental picture itself, which is present before your body does the sin, is a "behavior" that God leaves for you to control. He will not remove it for you.

It is imperative that you ask God to remove the *desire* for the wrong pictures in your mind before you try removing the pictures themselves. Then you must force the wrong pictures out of your mind. This is one of the most difficult and painful exercises you will ever engage in. However, I can assure you that it is *possible*. Pushing the wrong images out of your mind will get easier as time goes on, and eventually it will be no trouble at all.

A strategy for practicing abstinence

I'd like to share with you a little strategy for practicing abstinence that has worked very well for me. Ellen White said something once that states the principle on which this strategy is based:

> It is an important law of the mind—one which should not be overlooked—that when a desired object is so firmly denied as to remove all hope, the mind will soon cease to long for it and will be occupied with other pursuits. But as long as there is any hope of gaining the desired object, an effort will be made to obtain it (MCP, 2:419).

In my seminars I like to tell a little made-up story at this point. Suppose that Junior comes to his father and says, "Dad, can I have a piece of candy?"

"Hmmm. Well, son, didn't we, er, have dessert for lunch?"

"Yes, we did, Dad, but all I want is just one piece."

"Well, er, uh, Mother and I have decided that, uh, we need to be cutting back on the amount of sugar that we eat, so, uh . . ."

"Dad, I promise, I won't ask for another piece of candy all afternoon."

"Well, er, uh, son, it seems to me that, uh . . ."

"Just one piece, Dad? Please? No more all afternoon. Promise."

"Well, er, uh, do you really promise, son?"

"Yes, Dad, I promise!"

"Well, uh, I guess it will be OK, this once."

What did Ellen White say? "As long as there is any hope of gaining the desired object, an effort will be made to obtain it." I would like to rephrase that and say that as long as there is any hope of gaining the object, the desire for it will grow stronger and stronger until it is almost impossible to resist. That's what happened to Eve in the Garden of Eden. The longer she looked at the fruit, the stronger the desire for it became.

But now consider this scenario. Junior comes to his father and says, "Dad, can I have a piece of candy?"

"Of course not, son. We had dessert for lunch."

"I know, Dad, but all I want is one piece."

"Son, did you hear what I said?"

"Yes, but, Dad, I promise not to ask for any more candy . . ."

"Look, I said No, and the answer is No. Now go outside and play."

"Aw, Dad, just one piece? I won't ask for any more . . ."

"OK, I'm giving you a choice. You can go outside and play, or you can spend the rest of the afternoon upstairs in your room. Now, if I hear one more word about candy, it'll be your room for the afternoon."

"But, Dad, I promise . . ."

Dad points upstairs with one hand and to the front door with the other. "I said not one more word, or it's to your room for the rest of the afternoon. It's your choice. Which is it?"

Junior scowls and looks at the floor and walks out the front door muttering under his breath.

But I can almost guarantee you that if Dad will look outside five minutes later, he'll see Junior playing with his friends as though he had never thought about candy. Why? Because "it is an important law of the mind . . . that when a desired object is so firmly denied as to remove all hope, the mind will soon cease to long for it."

I have discovered that when I am under severe temptation, if I will say to myself, "No, no, no! You aren't going to get it right now! Stop! End of discussion!" I can program myself out of the desire just as easily as if someone else had said it to me. Eve would never have eaten the fruit if she had said No! and then turned and walked away the instant the serpent started talking to her.

A man came up to me one day after one of my seminars, and he said, "Pastor Moore, I found a text that says exactly what you told us about saying No." I asked him what text he had in mind, and he read Titus 2:11, 12:

> For the grace of God that brings salvation has appeared to all men. It teaches us to say "No" to ungodliness and worldly passions, and to live self-controlled upright and godly lives in this present age.

That's perfect! Try it. You'll discover that it *does* work.

Another cardinal principle
Abstinence is so important that I want to put it down as the last cardinal principle for victory over addiction and cherished sin:

CARDINAL PRINCIPLE 4
Practice abstinence—clench your fists and grit your teeth—when you want nothing more than to yield.

Abstinence comes last in the list of things you and I can do to cooperate with God in our effort to conquer the dragon within, but it's one of our most important strategies. It's so important that I'm taking two chapters to explain it. So keep reading.

---

[1] I am not suggesting that Jesus had sinful desires that needed changing. See the Additional Note at the end of this chapter for a comment on this point.

DEVOTIONAL EXERCISES

Biblical reflection on chapter 27
1. In 1 Peter 2:11, Peter urged his readers to "abstain from sinful desires." This chapter encourages you to abstain from evil behavior. Write a few sentences explaining the relationship between abstaining from sinful desires and abstaining from sinful behavior.
2. Think of a sin you have difficulty abstaining from. Write a

paragraph in which you tell God exactly how you feel. If anger, fear, or shame are a part of the emotional mix in your mind, explain them the best you can in your paragraph. Conclude by asking God to show you a new idea that will make abstaining easier.

Devotional study of 1 Samuel 27:1–28:2

1. Why did David decide to go live among the Philistines? Did his strategy work?

2. Write a paragraph stating the negative aspects of David's decision (reasons why it was a mistake) and another stating the positive aspects (reasons why it was a wise decision). Do you think David struggled with the issue of whether God would want him to make this move? How did he reach his decision?

3. Think of a difficult situation you have had to face, especially one that involved moral choices and conflicting feelings over what God would have you to do. Write a paragraph or two stating the reasons why you made the choice you did and whether you still think it was the best choice.

Additional Note to Chapter 27

The question of whether Christ had our sinful passions has, unfortunately, become something of a theological football in the Adventist Church during the last forty or fifty years. I am not suggesting that Jesus had sinful desires. Ellen White says that "He was a mighty petitioner, not possessing the passions of our human, fallen natures" (2T, 509). But Jesus did experience the strength of the desires that in you and me are so often out of control. On that point, Ellen White said that "He *realized* the power of appetite upon man" (AG, 164). I am satisfied to accept Ellen White's simple statements on both sides of this issue and let the matter rest there. This side of heaven, we will not understand everything about the human nature of Christ—exactly what He did and did not possess with respect to our human nature. We make a mistake to try, and it is a terrible mistake to make of these fine points of theology a test of each other's orthodoxy.

Chapter
Twenty-eight

ABSTINENCE AND SURRENDER

I heard a knock on my door one afternoon, back when I was a pastor in Keene, Texas. A student from Southwestern Adventist College greeted me when I opened the door. We'll call him Daryl.

We chatted in the front room for a few minutes, and then Daryl said, "Pastor, I've got a problem."

"What is it?" I asked.

"Sexual fantasies," he said. "If I see a young woman walking down the street in tight shorts, or if I see a lingerie ad, my mind goes in the wrong direction, and I can't stop it. Can you help me?"

Unfortunately, at the time Daryl came to me, I still did not understand the principles I've been sharing with you in this book, so I gave him a nice Christian platitude and sent him on his way. I felt frustrated, though, because I knew I hadn't helped him, and I suspect that he felt frustrated too.

Two weeks later, Daryl was back, and he was jubilant. "Pastor, it's over!" he exclaimed.

"What's over?" I asked.

"The sexual fantasies. Remember I told you how I couldn't get rid of them? Well, they're gone. I'm not troubled by them anymore."

"Wonderful, Daryl. What happened?" I asked.

"I went to see Elder Blank about my problem," Daryl said. "Do you know him?"

I nodded. Elder Blank was a pastor in a neighboring district.

"Well, he told me that I had a demon in me. Pastor, he said there's a demon for everything. There's a demon for TV, there's a demon for food and a demon for sex. There's even a demon for cancer and asthma! Pastor Blank told me that I had a demon of sex in me. He said that if I would let him lay his hands on me and cast out the demon of sex, my problem would be over."

I told Daryl that I was aware of Elder Blank's interest in a "deliverance ministry," and he continued his story. "Elder Blank laid his hands on me and prayed and cast out the demon of sex, and it's wonderful, Pastor. I haven't been troubled by sexual fantasies since. Praise the Lord!"

I told Daryl how glad I was that he had gotten rid of his sexual fantasies. However, I felt troubled. Something didn't seem quite right. I was not able to explain it back then, but now I understand the reason for my discomfort. For one thing, I have a strong suspicion that Daryl's sexual fantasies returned within a month, and his shattered expectation left him less able to cope with them than before. However, there's an even more basic reason why I am troubled by Elder Blank's solution to Daryl's problem.

We live in a quick-fix society. Is something wrong with your appendix? Take the problem to the doctor. Two weeks later, he'll have you back home as good as new. You'll never have to worry about your appendix again.

Something wrong with your car? Take it to the mechanic. Two days later, he'll return it to you as good as new. You won't have to worry about that problem for fifty-thousand miles.

Something wrong with the toaster? Throw it away. Go to the store. Two hours later, you'll be back home with a brand-new one that you won't have to worry about for at least two years.

Our quick-fix society wants snap solutions to all our problems. We think there's something wrong if we can't fix it, fix it, and go on. This attitude leads us to expect quick fixes for our character defects as well. We think something's wrong when we keep falling into sin. Besides, struggling against sin is painful, and who wants to endure pain when there's a quick fix for everything?

Daryl wanted a quick fix for his sexual problem. I must tell you, though, that in most cases God does not provide quick fixes for our character defects. The reason is not an unwillingness on His part to see us perfect, nor is He reluctant to deliver us from pain. The problem is that struggling against temptation is one of the best ways that we humans have for developing character. Anytime God removes a character defect instantly, we forfeit the opportunity of using that defect to develop character by struggling against it.

In chapter 22 I told you that surrender is the link between getting a change in our sinful desires and getting a change in our sinful behavior. We surrender our evil desires when we ask God to remove them at the very moment when we can't wait to enjoy them. And we surrender our evil behavior when we ask God to give us the power not to do it at the very moment when we want nothing more than to do it. I would like to share with you a prayer of surrender:

- Lord, this desire belongs to You now.
- It's Yours to remove when You want it to go away.
- It's not mine to remove when I want it to go away.
- I will wait patiently without acting on it until You remove it.

That is a powerful prayer. Write it down. Use it on the cherished sin that you are struggling against right now. It works.

Below is a diagram that you've seen before in this book, but with the addition of surrender:

Prayer for God to remove the desire		**The desire finally fades away**
	SURRENDER	
Clench the fists Grit the teeth		**Peace**

Abstinence—clenching the fists and gritting the teeth to keep from "doing it" while God is removing the desire—is a powerful act of surrender. Sin can only be overcome through bitter conflict, through wrestling with the sin and enduring the pain. Surrender means to:

- **Accept the pain.**
- **Let the pain happen without acting on the temptation.**
- **While God does His work in us in His time, not ours.**

Surrender—turning over to Jesus your strongest evil desire and your most cherished sinful behaviors regardless of how painful it may seem to do so—is one of your most important keys to conquering the dragon within. Without it, there is no victory. With it, there is the promise ahead of complete victory over every single temptation that you and I face.

DEVOTIONAL EXERCISES

Biblical reflection on chapter 28

1. Read Galatians 5:13-15. What does it mean to be "biting and devouring" each other? Have you ever seen this happen in a church you attended? Have you ever been a part of the biting and devouring? What feelings or desires will you have to surrender to overcome this problem? Ask God to give you insight and to help you to be honest in answering that last question.

2. Read Galatians 5:16, 17. Have you ever felt the conflict in yourself that Paul spoke about in these verses? What sinful feelings created the church conflict Paul referred to in verse 15? What feelings inspired by the Spirit were at war with the sinful feelings? (See verses 19-23.)

3. Read Galatians 5:24-26. In the context of the present chapter, what does it mean to "crucify" the feelings of the sinful nature that create church conflicts? What does it mean to "keep in step with the Spirit" in this context? Write a paragraph in which you honestly apply these principles to the church conflicts you have been a part of.

4. If you are part of a church conflict right now, ask someone on the other side to study this problem with you from Galatians 5:13-25. Talk to each other frankly, and try to listen honestly.

Devotional study of 1 Samuel 28:3-25

1. What emotion that Saul had experienced all his life possessed him on this occasion? How was this related to God's refusal to answer when Saul asked for His guidance? Write a paragraph or two reflecting on the relationship of this emotion to sin.

2. Why did Saul consult a witch, when all his life he had been very active in destroying witchcraft throughout the kingdom?

What kind of reasoning drove him to this? Was it purely a rational decision, or were his feelings involved?

3. Think of a time when fear of the future drove you to make an unwise decision. Write a paragraph about how to deal appropriately with fear of the future.

SECTION II
Part 4
Some Final Thoughts

Station Break 4

We are almost through with our discussion of how to conquer the dragon within. However, I do want to share with you a few thoughts that don't seem to fit in with the discussion of God's part and our part in getting a change in our sinful understanding, our sinful desires, and our sinful behavior.

Specifically, I want to share with you what I have learned about two things: How attitudes change and how we develop moderation. I will conclude the book with a final chapter about how to deal with failure.

Here is where we are right now:

Section II: How Jesus Helps Sinners Gain the Victory
  Part 1: Changing Our Sinful Understanding
  Part 2: Changing Our Sinful Desires
  Part 3: Changing Our Sinful Behavior
  Part 4: Some Final Thoughts

Chapter
Twenty-nine

CHANGING OUR ATTITUDES

I used to run around depressed most of the time. My first recollection of significant depression goes back to the 1959 to 1960 school year that I spent as a ministerial student at Potomac University—the name of the Seventh-day Adventist Theological Seminary when it was located in Washington, D.C. I would wake up in the morning, look in the mirror, and know that I didn't feel good about myself. The circumstances in my life weren't all that troubling or difficult. There was no logical reason why I should feel depressed. I just did.

During the second semester, I took a class in pastoral psychology from Dr. John Cannon. About two months before the school year ended, Dr. Cannon spent a class period or two explaining the symptoms of the major mental and emotional disorders. One of them in particular caught my attention. I don't remember the name he gave it—probably just plain old depression, but I can still remember him saying, "One of the characteristics of this disorder is a bad feeling that has no logical explanation in real life. The individual may wake up in the morning and look in the mirror and know that he doesn't feel good about himself. He can't give an objective reason why he feels miserable. He just knows that he does."

A light went on in my head. I made an appointment to talk to Dr. Cannon.

I can still remember the reason I gave for coming to see him. "In class yesterday," I said, "when you outlined the symptoms of the various emotional disorders, one of them was me."

I did not leave Dr. Cannon's office that day cured of my depression, but we did visit about once a week for the rest of the school year. By this time I had an invitation to work as a ministerial intern in the Southern California Conference, and Dr. Cannon advised me to seek professional help at the earliest opportunity.

The conference assigned me to the church in Pomona, about halfway between Los Angeles and San Bernardino. I was single at the time. The first order of business was to locate an apartment, which didn't take too long in those days. A week or two later, I asked a medical professional in the church with whom I had become acquainted for a referral to someone I could counsel with about my depression. He told me of a Seventh-day Adventist psychiatrist, Dr. Vernon Miller, whose office turned out to be just two blocks from the apartment I had rented.

I visited with Dr. Miller almost every week for about a year. He proved to be as much a friend and father figure as he did a counselor or psychiatrist. I will always remember him with very warm feelings. He did a lot of listening, and he helped me to sort through some of the confusing relationships in my life, including my relationship with my parents.

During the time I lived in Pomona, I also did a lot of journaling. Mostly, I did it on four-by-six cards. Often, I'd spend an hour or two putting my thoughts and feelings down on these cards. I think this is probably where I learned how to write—though I was not aware of it for another ten to fifteen years.

I wish I could tell you that I was over my depression when I terminated my visits with Dr. Miller. I wanted to believe that I was, but I wasn't. I continued living with these confusing emotions for many more years. I still get them once in a while.

I do remember the place and the exact moment when I believe my real healing began, though. I had returned to the seminary (this time at Andrews University in Michigan) to complete my Master of Divinity degree, still feeling very depressed much of the time. One day—I think it was the spring of 1969—I was walking across the campus between the James White Library and the university bookstore, when I noticed that my depression had lifted and I felt *really good*. I said to myself, "That's the way I'd like to feel all the time."

I had had these fleeting moments of peace in the past, but this time it dawned on me that this pleasant attitude was the healthy alternative to my usual depression. For the first time in my life,

I realized that this fleeting positive attitude was the way "normal" people felt all the time. In the past, whenever I had experienced this normal feeling, I simply enjoyed it while it lasted. It had never occurred to me until this day that I might actually be able to *live* this way all the time. On an impulse, I decided that instead of just enjoying the pleasure until it went away, I would see how long I could hang on to it.

It stayed around for a while, and then it left. However, because it had always returned before, I felt certain that in due time I would get it back. So I said a short prayer: "Lord, when it comes back, help me to hold on to it longer than in the past."

Sure enough, a few days later it came back, and this time I said, "Thank You, Lord, for bringing this healthy attitude back. Help me to hold on to it longer than last time."

I can't tell you whether there was any significant difference in the duration of this more healthy attitude on that occasion, but I do know that I kept saying that prayer; and each time the healthy attitude returned, I made a conscious effort to hold it in my mind as long as possible. For a number of years, whenever I was feeling depressed, I would look for a quiet place where I could be alone to pray. Often my retreat was a tiny, one-fixture restroom at the place where I worked. I would lock the door, kneel down, and say, "Lord, please bring back the normal attitude that I want to stay with me all the time, and when it returns, help me to hang on to it a little longer than before."

I rarely prayed more than a minute, and then I'd go back to work, still feeling very depressed but confident that the normal attitude would return. Sure enough, an hour or a day later, it would come back. I would thank the Lord for it and ask Him again to help me hang on to it longer than before.

Recovery was slow, but it was quite steady. As time went by, the up times increased, and the down times decreased. In less than ten years, I could honestly say that I felt normal most of the time. Today, I rarely feel depressed, but when I do, I know what to do about it. Mostly, I just say to myself, "This, too, shall pass," and wait for it to go away. It always does.

My depression was—and still is when it returns—a diseased way of thinking and feeling about life. It is an unhealthy *attitude*. Attitude is the spontaneous way we think and feel about ourselves, other people, and the events that happen to us from day to day. The person with a healthy attitude feels good about himself and others and is able to handle the stresses of life with relative ease. The person with an unhealthy attitude does not feel good about himself and finds life's stresses difficult to cope with.

Depression as emotional pain

Depression is also emotional pain, and when you have it, it's as real as a sore finger and often a lot worse. The pain in a sore finger can have a variety of obvious causes, including a cut, a burn, a bang with a hammer, or a splinter in the flesh. A variety of things also cause painful emotions, but unlike the sore finger, the cause of emotional pain is seldom obvious. It's more like a pain in the abdomen. The cause might be appendicitis, cancer, ulcers, or a diseased pancreas, but you have to go to the doctor to find out which.

I believe that three basic emotions—fear, shame, and anger—cause most of the depression we humans experience. I have already pointed out in this book that God gave us these emotions for protection, and they are healthy when we use them appropriately. Pain happens when they overwhelm us. God's plan was that these emotions should inform us of danger so we could take appropriate steps to protect ourselves. His plan was that our minds should be in control. Pain happens when shame, fear, and anger overwhelm our minds and take charge of our lives.

But like the pain in the abdomen, we only know that we're hurting. We don't know why. We feel afraid, ashamed, and/or angry, but these emotions are buried so deep inside of us that we don't recognize them. So we cope by acting in ways that feel good at first but in the long run make the pain worse. Alcoholics drink at the end of the day "to unwind." Drug addicts feel *so good* when they are on a high. Ask any addict—food, sex, shopping, anger—who knows he is an addict, and he will tell you that his addiction feels *so good*. Doing it brings such relief! But when he is through acting out his addiction, he also feels an incredible amount of anxiety and shame—the very thing that's driving the addiction in the first place.

If we do nothing to stop these habits, they will destroy us. People who have never been profoundly addicted cannot understand the insane power of addiction. The addict feels absolutely worthless, abandoned by God, hopelessly lost. He'd love to experience victory, and sometimes he does when he grits his teeth hard enough and clenches his fists tight enough. But it never lasts. A day or a week or a month later, he's back at it again. And then the pain, the shame, and the fear get even worse, which only ensures that he'll do it again.

That's the addictive cycle.

Healing our diseased attitudes

For me, healing began when I grasped the truth that my depression was actually a diseased attitude, a sick way of thinking and feeling, for which there was a healthy alternative. Healing progressed as I went in search of that healthy alternative and took appropriate steps to make it my own. Healing on that point was largely complete when the healthy attitude stayed with me most of the time and I was able to deal with the unhealthy attitude with relative ease when it returned.

If you feel depressed much of the time, as I used to, and if this depression is driving you into habits that you wish desperately you could break but haven't discovered how, then more than anything else, you need to understand that *there is a way out.* When you have found that way out, you will have a new, much happier attitude toward life. Your search today is for this new attitude, this new way of thinking and, especially, of feeling. If you have never experienced this new attitude before, it will probably seem impossible that you could ever achieve it, but let me assure you, you can.

To a great extent, the Christian life is a search for insight into the healthy alternative to our diseased attitudes and learning to live in these healthy attitudes all the time. Remember that God is on your side. He's anxious to show you the healthiest attitudes, the happiest way to live.

Recovery *does* work. Let me give you an example.

For about two years, my wife and I have been sponsors to a young woman who has been to The Bridge. We'll call her Martha. Martha went to The Bridge because of her extreme depression and her addiction to TV and novels, which she used to relieve the depression. For the first three months after she returned home from The Bridge, Martha called us every two or three days, and when she was really hurting, she'd call every day and sometimes two and three times a day. As we listened to her pain, we sometimes wondered whether she would ever get well. But we kept encouraging her to "stick with the program." "Trust the program," we said. "It works if you work it."

After about three months, Martha's calls slacked off to once every week or two. A few days ago, she called us in the evening. We talked for a while, and then she said, "You know, something's happening inside me. I don't know what it is, but I'm beginning to feel really good about myself. I'm also getting interested in things other than novels and TV."

I said, "Remember that we told you the program would work if you work it? Well, it's working."

I explained to Martha that she had now gained a little glimpse into the healthy, happy way she would feel all the time when she was well. "This good feeling will probably go away," I said. "You will experience more pain, and you may watch TV and read novels inappropriately again. But keep working the program. As long as you do that, this healthy attitude will *always* come back, and each time it does, it will be stronger and stay longer. Eventually, you will live in that attitude all the time."

Martha is fortunate. She has broken through the pain of depression enough that she has experienced an emotional goal to work toward, an attitude that she *knows* is "out there" for her.

You don't have to be a psychological expert to succeed

You may be thinking that you are too inexperienced at recovery to ever make it work for you, and since you haven't the money to go to a treatment center, what hope is there for you?

Plenty. Trust me.

When I started my journey out of depression thirty years ago, nobody knew about recovery in the modern sense of the term. Even the Twelve-Step program was still thought to be for alcoholics only. Yet as I reflect on my life back then, I realize that God led me to some strategies that I've since learned were right on target. I also know of some things I did back then that weren't so healthy, but frankly, not a soul in the world knows everything there is to know about recovery. We are all still learners. God will always teach us, though, if we ask Him to and start searching.

In the remaining pages of this chapter, I would like to reflect on my recovery from depression, calling attention to four points. First, I would like to mention one thing God did for me without my even asking. Second, I will share some of the things I did years ago that I now realize were good strategies. Third, I will share with you one thing I didn't do, which, had I done it, would have made my recovery much more rapid. Finally, I will point out one thing I did that slowed my recovery significantly, even though I did not realize it at the time. I will use these four points to show you both how my stumbling efforts worked and how they could have worked much better had I been better informed.

What God did for me. People in emotional pain do not usually understand the real cause of their depression, and they have even less of an idea what to do about it. So where did that glimpse of the healthy alternative to my depression that I received at Andrews University come from? Was it a mere fortuitous coincidence? Not at all. I believe God put this fleeting healthy attitude in my mind, and He helped me to understand that living that way all the time was a reasonable goal to set for myself. This was a change in my sinful,[1] diseased understanding, and He gave it to me without my even asking Him to.

What I did without understanding it. In a primitive way, I put into practice the three strategies I suggested earlier in this book as "our part" for getting a change in our sinful desires. First, I asked God to bring back this healthy attitude that He had given me a glimpse of, and I asked Him to help me hold on to it as long as possible. This was a very simple way of asking Him to "change my desire."

Second, at different times I talked to professional counselors, and during the first year or two after I entered the ministry, I journaled quite a bit. All of this was a form of "talking about it," and I'm sure it helped.

Third, I surrendered my depression. That is, after praying about it, I accepted it for the moment and returned to my work, refusing to worry about when or whether it would go away. I turned it over to God and said, in essence, "I can't make this depression go away. It's Yours to remove when You want it to go away. I will wait patiently without getting desperate about it until You choose to remove it." And then I went about my business.

In one sense, we should never accept our character defects. We must always believe there is a healthier, happier way to live and keep searching till we find it. On the other hand, we must always accept our defects "for the moment," recognizing that change takes time.

This is why the whole concept of justification that I presented in the first section of this book is so important. We must understand that God accepts us during the change process. It's impossible to accept our sinful condition "for the moment" if every time we make a mistake we are afraid that God is displeased with us or that our sins have broken our relationship with Him.[2] We will never overcome our imperfection until we can relax and recognize that God loves us and accepts us where we are.

What I didn't do. One of the most wonderful things about life is that we continually grow in our understanding. Today, at fifty-seven, I understand my life much better than I did when I was twenty-seven. So what have I learned in recent years that I wish I could have applied twenty years ago?

The most important principle I have learned is talking. With the exception of a few professional counselors with whom I consulted, I did not do a great deal of talking about my depression during the ten or fifteen years that I was recovering from it. Because I was afraid to admit my dysfunction, I tried handling it all by myself. I now know that this effort at total self-healing without the help of others is part of the denial, part of the disease.

There are two ways in which I would talk if I had it to do over again. First, I would find a sponsor—a mature Christian in whom I could confide my confused feelings and with whom I could discuss the crises in my life. And second, I would join a Twelve-Step group.[3]

The mistake I made. About halfway through my recovery from depression, I discovered that I could stop the pain by plunging into my work. I even advised a few friends who were depressed to "go to work in spite of the depression, and it will go away."

This may sound a great deal like the strategy of praying and returning to work that I had used a few years earlier, but there is a world of difference. Back when I prayed and returned to work,

I did not try to make the depression go away. I accepted it and let God remove it in His own time and way. This is surrender.

Several years later, I was using work as a way to fight the pain, as a way to *make* it go away. I was medicating the pain rather than surrendering it, and that is a straight path to work addiction.

The strategies I used to recover from depression twenty or thirty years ago were not perfect, but they were the best I had, and I believe God gave them to me. The strategies I am using today are still not perfect. I have much more to learn, and I know that a year and five years from now God will have helped me to learn more, and my recovery will continue at a much more rapid pace.

We should never worry about whether our recovery is rapid enough or whether we are using the right strategies and tools. Rather, we should do the best we can with what we have, asking God to show us more. We must never give up our goal of a better, happier life tomorrow, nor must we give up the faith that God will lead us to that life if we ask Him to and keep searching for it.

I truly believe that if you follow the principles I have outlined in this book for changing your attitudes, you will experience significant healing. You don't have to stay stuck in unhappiness and emotional pain. Your attitudes *can change*. You *can* conquer the dragon within.

---

[1] It is important to understand that depression is not sinful in the same sense that adultery, lying, and stealing are sinful. Depressed people are not guilty of "committing depression." Depression is more a result of our broken, sinful condition. No one should ever feel guilty that they are depressed.

[2] I am well aware of Isaiah 59:2, where God says, "Your iniquities have separated you from your God." However, the context of Isaiah's prophecy makes it very clear that the Israelites to whom Isaiah wrote were in such rebellion (see Isaiah 1, for example) that eventually God allowed them to be taken captive to Babylon. God treats repentant people much differently.

[3] Back then, I would have had to attend Alcoholics Anonymous, since nothing else was available. Fortunately, in the last fifteen to twenty years, the Twelve-Step concept has expanded and is now used to treat a wide variety of addictions and dysfunctions.

DEVOTIONAL EXERCISES

Biblical reflection on chapter 29

1. Read 1 Kings 19:1-18. Identify the attitude or emotion that caused Elijah to flee. Was this attitude and Elijah's response to it understandable? Was fleeing the appropriate response? What do you think would have happened had Elijah maintained the courage he had on Mount Carmel and stood up to Jezebel?

2. What attitude do you think Elijah was experiencing in verse 10? Was this attitude based on reliable information, or was it based on how he felt about the circumstances (see verse 18)?

3. Write a paragraph evaluating whether Elijah sinned by yielding to his fear and depression (see Matthew 25:24-30). Then write another paragraph evaluating God's response to Elijah in light of what you have learned in this book about how God treats Christians who make mistakes.

Devotional study of 1 Samuel 29 and 27

1. Review your reply to the questions about 1 Samuel 27. Did you conclude that it was appropriate for David to flee from the Philistines?

2. Was it appropriate for him to deceive Achish, the king of Gath? Write a paragraph explaining what you think David should have told the king and what might have been the result.

3. What does the Bible say about the moral implications of David's deception? What does it say about God's response to his deception? Write a paragraph evaluating God's relationship to David throughout the time he was deceiving Achish. Write another paragraph about whether God approved of David's deception. How do you relate these two ideas?

Additional Note to Chapter 29

There are two kinds of depression. One is the result of unresolved conflict in a person's life. That is the kind I experienced. The other is caused by a chemical deficiency in the brain and is best treated with medication. If you are severely depressed, you should not try to cope by yourself. Seek the help of a professional counselor or a psychiatrist. If you cannot afford the cost of treatment, call your county public health department and ask for a referral to a mental health clinic that charges according to the patient's ability to pay.

Chapter

Thirty

ACHIEVING MODERATION

St. Augustine was against sex.

Well, mostly.

He recognized, wisely, that the human race would soon die out if people didn't engage in sexual activity. He also knew that God commanded Adam and Eve to "be fruitful and increase in number; fill the earth" (Genesis 1:28), and he was smart enough to figure out that sexual activity was the only way they could possibly fulfill this command. Thus sex couldn't be all bad. The difference between right and wrong in sex, Augustine proposed, was in the motive. And procreation was the only right motive. He grudgingly conceded that it was all right for a married couple to engage in sexual activity if their purpose was to have children, but even then, they should try not to enjoy it!

You and I smile. Yet it's amazing how many of us agree emotionally with Augustine. We think that if it feels good, it must be bad. The solution to this problem lies, I believe, in learning to appreciate the gifts God has given us and in discovering the balance between addiction on the one hand and abstinence on the other—in other words, moderation. Ellen White once wrote that "it is carrying that which is lawful to excess that makes it a grievous sin" (TSB, 115).

Victory over some sins and addictions requires total abstinence. This is especially true of those that are foreign to our human nature such as alcohol, tobacco, and narcotics (including caffeine). I fully support the Seventh-day Adventist recommendation of total abstinence from the use of these substances.

On the other hand, food, sex, and buying and selling, along with a host of other common activities, are essential to our survival. They are not wrong in themselves. To the contrary, God gave them to us, and in most cases, we need to engage in them at least occasionally and sometimes frequently. But we must recognize that in a broken, sinful world it is possible to abuse them. Thus it is important that we learn how to use them in moderation.

Unfortunately, this is easier said than done. There are two extremes. One is total abstinence. The other is unrestricted license—"If it feels good, do it." Somewhere between addiction and abstinence lies the true path of moderation.

Our objective as Christians is to find that middle ground. But the addict can't just start living moderately. He has so lost control of his desires that when the desire to which he is addicted surfaces in his feelings, he can only say Yes. He cannot say No. He has no idea what moderation is like. He has no idea what it's like to say No appropriately, because he has never experienced it.

In order to overcome his addiction, the person who is addicted to that which is good in moderation needs three things. He needs to learn the truth about right and wrong in his area of addiction, he needs to understand the true nature of his addiction, and he needs to practice moderation till he has learned it. The rest of this chapter is a discussion of these three issues.

Learning the truth

Several years ago, I was discussing anger with a particular individual, and in the course of the conversation, I told him that I thought anger had an appropriate place in the life of Christians. My friend became visibly agitated. He insisted that "anger is always wrong!"

As you know from reading this book, I believe that God placed the capacity to experience anger within human beings when He created us. Anger protects us from being abused, and it helps us to protect others from being abused. Anger is wrong only when we use it to abuse others or when we internalize it as resentment.

Yet it's amazing how many Christians believe that all anger is wrong. When a child throws a temper tantrum, more often than not, his parents will tell him that he shouldn't get angry. Thus the child grows up thinking that it's wrong to feel angry, and every time he feels angry, he also feels guilty. The idea that anger is wrong is a part of our Christian culture. We probably get it from the fact that anger is a powerful emotion, and the Bible condemns "sinful passions" (Romans 7:5). It also condemns "works of the flesh," one of which is wrath (Galatians 5:19, KJV). Thus we conclude that any emotion as powerful and as potentially harmful as anger must surely be wrong in and of itself.

The first strategy for victory over sin that I shared with you in Section II of this book was called "Changing Our Sinful Understanding." Sometimes we need our sinful understanding changed in the sense of discovering the wrong attitudes and practices in our lives that we are unaware of and need to give up. However, it's equally important to understand the truth about the things we think are wrong that are not. I'd like to state a principle here:

The addict who thinks the object of his addiction is wrong when in itself it is not will never overcome his addiction until he learns the truth.

In chapter 19 I recommended that you ask God to remove your sinful desires. I will now qualify that recommendation. God will not remove any desire that is right in itself, for the simple reason that you and I don't need the victory over a desire that isn't wrong. We need victory only over its abuse. But we cannot gain the victory over the abuse of an otherwise right desire so long as we are deceived by the notion that the desire itself is wrong.

Let me illustrate. If you're struggling with anger, don't plead with God to remove the anger. What you need most at the moment is to understand the difference between the inappropriate use of anger that you've lived with all these years and the healthy experience of anger that He intended you to have. So pray that He will give you this insight and bring this healthy attitude into your mind, even if it's just for a moment, so that you can have a goal to work toward. When He does, you will have taken a major step toward getting a change in both your sinful understanding and your sinful desires.

One of the most common problems Christians face is the tendency to feel shame over something that is not shameful at all. Paul had to deal with this problem in the Corinthian church. In

1 Corinthians 8 he spoke about Christians with a "weak conscience" (verse 12), and his remarks are along the same lines that we have been discussing—people who think something is wrong when it really isn't, who feel guilty over something God gave them to enjoy. True Christian perfection requires that we understand clearly both what is wrong and what isn't, and that we rid our minds of false shame. The adage "Let your conscience be your guide" is actually dangerous, if by conscience we mean our feelings of shame and guilt. These emotions can lead us in the wrong direction. The only safe guide is the Bible. Unfortunately, we often study the Bible with our preconceived opinions and impose our shame values onto its words. It is in this context that I find Ellen White's advice so refreshing:

> Real experience is a variety of careful experiments made with the mind freed from prejudice and uncontrolled by previously established opinions and habits (3T, 69).

Sometimes the freedom that we need from prejudice and previously established opinions is freedom from traditional moral values that are not God's moral values. The New Testament provides an excellent example of this. The Jews of Christ's time were utterly bound up with picky rules and regulations that they had invented and to which they attached eternal moral consequences. They could not free their minds of these prejudices and previously established opinions long enough to hear what Jesus was saying.

A genuine Christian experience depends in part on our ability to evaluate our moral presuppositions apart from previously established opinions, which can easily get in the way of our learning the truth. Adventists need to learn this lesson as much as anyone. We have piled up our own share of cultural norms to which we attach moral consequences not found in the Bible.

At the risk of alienating some of my readers, I will suggest that our obsession with jewelry is a case in point. The Bible does not condemn jewelry in the harsh terms we have. This does not mean that our stand on jewelry all these years has been wrong. Abstinence from jewelry is a perfectly appropriate way for Christians to demonstrate their commitment to the principles of simplicity and stewardship. It's also all right for a group of Christians (a church) to decide that they will collectively demonstrate stewardship and the simplicity of the gospel through the nonuse of jewelry and to ask new members of the group (church) to do the same. But this does not make the moderate use of jewelry a sin. If the use of jewelry in itself is sinful, then a lot of Adventists who think it is all right to pin jewelry on their clothes need to rethink their position.

Once a group attaches moral significance to its cultural norms, its members pass these moral presuppositions on to their children and grandchildren. By the time the prohibition reaches the fourth and fifth generation, though, the original principle behind it, which was quite appropriate, has been totally lost sight of in most cases. All the great-grandchildren and great-great-grandchildren know is that their consciences feel shame over something that a careful study of the Bible tells them is not wrong at all.

This problem is not so serious with respect to the outward adornment of the body. But when we give our young people the idea that all anger is wrong or that all sexual desire is wrong, we set them up for terrible internal conflict that can break out in depression and addictions.

Why have I gone to the trouble to explain this matter in such detail? Because you cannot develop as rapidly in Christian perfection when you have confused ideas about God's requirements that are causing you emotional pain, depression, and guilt. Whatever area your addiction is in, you need to ask God to change your sinful understanding. Ask Him to give you insight into what's really right and what's really wrong with respect to that activity. Ask Him to help you understand the meaning of true moderation. It's essential, of course, that your new understanding arise out of Scripture. So as you read your Bible, ask God to help you put aside your shame and guilt long enough to understand what it really says.

Once you have begun to develop some new ideas about what's right and wrong, you must then experiment with them. A young man came up to me one evening after I had concluded a weekend seminar at a camp meeting in the Midwest. "Pastor Moore," he said, "is it all right for me to experiment with something that I used to think was wrong but now I'm thinking may not be wrong?" I said, "Yes, absolutely."

If that thought shocks you, read the rest of Ellen White's statement that I quoted above. I will begin with the part I quoted earlier:

> Real experience is a variety of careful experiments made with the mind freed from prejudice and uncontrolled by previously established opinions and habits. The results are marked with a careful solicitude and an anxious desire to learn, to improve, and to reform on every habit that is not in harmony with physical and moral laws. . . . There are more errors received and firmly retained from false ideas of experience than from any other cause, for the reason that what is generally termed experience is not experience at all; because *there has never been a fair trial by actual experiment* and thorough investigation of the principle involved in the action (3T, 69, emphasis added).

Please notice, though, the qualifiers that Ellen White placed around her advice about experimental religion. There must be "a careful solicitude and an anxious desire to learn, to improve, and to reform on every habit that is not in harmony with physical and moral laws"; and there must be a "thorough investigation of the principle involved in the action." Ellen White advocated carefully controlled religious experimentation, not reckless abandon.

What is likely to happen to those who do not engage in proper experimental religion? Notice what Ellen White said: "There are more errors received and firmly retained from false ideas of experience than from any other cause"! We tend to think of religious and spiritual error as false doctrine. But I suggest that some of the most destructive errors are lifestyle issues we humans have wrongly loaded down with shame and guilt. That was precisely the problem of the Pharisees. And one of the best ways to escape from this problem, Ellen White said, was experimental religion.

In a previous chapter, I said that you should ask God to change your evil desires. That is a good prayer, provided you understand what constitutes evil desire. Anger is not wrong. The desire for good food is not wrong. The desire to look attractive is not wrong. Sexual desire is not wrong.

Let's focus on sexual desire a bit more as an example of the point I am trying to make. Whether you are male or female, sexual desire is built into your nervous system. It's as much a part of you as your stomach, and it's as normal for you to feel the desire for sex as it is for you to feel the desire for food. If you have a sudden sexual impulse, you needn't feel shame over it, and you shouldn't ask God to remove it, because to do so, He would have to remove that which makes you male or female. Rather, thank God for the sexual impulse, and ask Him to help you enjoy it in an appropriate way. If you see an attractive person of the opposite sex, thank Him for the privilege of seeing that beautiful part of His creation, and ask Him to help you keep your thoughts toward that person within proper scriptural bounds. In this way, you will begin to learn the right attitude toward your sexual impulses.

My first experience many years ago with the healthy alternative to my depression was just a fleeting glimpse. That may be all you will get at first as an insight into the healthy alternative to whatever is troubling you. Thank God for it, ask Him to help you to hang on to it as long as possible, and when it goes away, ask Him to bring it back. Then believe that He will, go on with life, and don't worry that for now you are not able to experience this new attitude all the time. In this way, you will eventually break out of addiction and settle into moderation.

Understanding the true nature of addiction

Earlier I said the addict needs to learn three things. He needs to learn the truth about what's right and wrong in the area of his addiction, he needs to understand the true nature of his addiction, and he needs to practice moderation till he has learned it. We have completed our discussion of the first item—learning the truth about right and wrong. It's now time to discuss the second—discovering the true nature of our addiction.

If your anger is out of control, the problem is not anger. If your eating is out of control, the problem is not food. If your sexuality is out of control, the problem is not sex. *The basic problem is emotional pain that is caused by shame, fear, and anger.* This pain leads to excessive behavior in these other areas to anesthetize the pain.

Therefore, in addition to asking God to show you the healthy way to experience that to which you are addicted, you should also ask Him to show you the fear, shame, and/or anger that may be keeping you from this more clear understanding. As you begin gaining this insight, then in addition to asking Him to help you hang on to the healthier attitude toward that desire, ask Him to remove the shame, fear, and/or anger that your mind has been associating with it all these years.

It is imperative that you also apply to this problem the other principles for getting a change in your sinful desires that I discussed earlier in this book. Talk to other people, both one on one and in groups where you can be assured of confidentiality. And don't worry when the shame, fear, and anger keep recurring in your mind. Just trust that if you continue asking God to remove them, and if you keep talking to people in recovery, in due time, He will.

I know several people who embarked on a recovery program such as I have described in this book who struggled for several months with intense fear, shame, and anger. At first, they despaired of ever breaking free of these emotions. But those who trusted the program and practiced it consistently eventually broke free. As they say in Twelve-Step groups, It works, if you work it.

You may find it difficult at first to distinguish between shame, fear, and anger. Like the pain in the abdomen that we discussed in the previous chapter, all you know is that you're hurting. You have no idea why. I want to assure you, though, that it *is* possible to distinguish between them, especially if you will read widely in the area of addiction and codependence, talk with people who are in recovery (both one on one and in groups), and keep asking God to help you understand. I also want to assure you that the more specific you can be in asking God to help you with particular emotions, the more quickly and easily He can remove them.

I want to emphasize again that addiction is more than a particular wrong behavior such as food or sex. Addiction is more than the *desire* for these things. You need to ask God to remove the desire for the addiction, but it's also imperative that you and God deal as specifically as possible with the shame, fear, and anger that lie beneath the addiction and that drive the addiction.

I've seen people who felt absolutely certain in the emotional part of their nature that the Holy Spirit was trying to convict them of a "wrong" that their minds told them was not wrong at all. I have experienced this myself in several areas, one or two of them profound. When this happens, if you know that your mental understanding is based on a reasonable interpretation of Scripture, you must—*you absolutely must*—accept the fact that it is your shame talking to you, not God. And you must ask God to remove this false guilt and help you resist it till it goes away. Do not allow yourself to believe the Holy Spirit is talking to you when Scripture approves of what you feel so guilty about. You cannot recover from either your emotional pain or your addictions until you do this.

You may have to wrestle with these emotions and with God the way Jacob wrestled with the angel. You may have to say, "God, I refuse to believe that this shame I'm feeling is from You. I surrender it to You. Please remove it, because I can't." Do not be afraid to say to God, "I will not let You go until You bless me with freedom from this false guilt!"

When you have finished your prayer, don't worry if the false guilt stays around a while. Just go about your daily affairs, trusting that in His own time and way, God will remove it.

I can assure you that you will be surprised at how much more rapidly you gain the victory over your addiction when you do this.

Abstinence and moderation

The third thing you and I need to learn is the meaning of moderation, and to do that we must practice abstinence.

Abstinence means "doing without." With respect to alcohol, tobacco, and narcotics, Adventists recommend total abstinence. However, we humans often become addicted to practices that are appropriate in moderation. Almost no one recommends total abstinence from these practices, since to do so would in some cases, as with food, be a death sentence. But abstinence is still a vital part of overcoming our addictive-compulsive behavior in these areas.

The addict is so consumed with desire for his particular practice that death almost seems preferable to denial. He or she has a profound fear of losing it. Yet this fear is part of what is standing in the way of victory. God alone can remove the fear, but the addict must also do something about it, and abstinence is what you can "do." This abstinence should not be total, however. If the activity to which you are addicted is good in moderation, then moderation is what you need to learn, and total abstinence will not teach you that.

Let's use food addiction as an example. Suppose for a moment that you could abstain from food for a full year and survive. What would you have learned? You would have learned how to get along without food for a year. You would not have learned moderation. Moderation requires that you have the ability to say both Yes and No to food and to say it comfortably. Addiction, with which you are familiar, has taught you only how to say Yes. Total abstinence would teach you only how to say No. You will not learn moderation from total abstinence any more than you will learn it from addiction.

People who have fasted for several weeks at a time report that the overwhelming desire for food lasts only a few days. After that, they feel quite comfortable going without food. The same is true of total sexual abstinence. After a short time of saying No, the mind and body adjust to the new situation, and saying No is not hard at all. But that's not moderation. Moderation is not a continual No, No, No, No. Moderation means saying Yes, No, Yes, No, Yes, No.

The Yes part is no problem for the addict, but saying No fills her with terror. Breaking out of the addiction requires that she clench her fists, grit her teeth, and say No anyway, till saying No begins to feel comfortable. Then, if she is to learn moderation, she must say Yes and reenter the experience that has been addictive for so long, after which she will say No again for a time. Saying No still fills her with terror, though, so practicing moderation may require her to go through the pain of learning to say No over and over again.

It is essential that the addict practice abstinence long enough to discover that it won't kill him, then say Yes long enough to enjoy the activity for a while, and then say No again long enough to learn that the abstinence won't kill him. By doing this over and over, he will gradually learn to overcome his fear of saying

No. He will also begin to enjoy moderation, and eventually he will prefer it.

I need to warn you, though, that saying Yes after a period of abstinence often presents a curious problem of its own that you must learn to deal with. It's called *shame*. For years you have felt shame every time you said Yes to this particular activity, to the point that saying Yes and feeling shame are all bound up together in your head. You have programmed your mind to feel shame every time you say Yes.

Especially if you have thought that the area of your addiction was always wrong in and of itself (as some people do about anger and sex, for instance), you will not break this "shame program" in your mind just by coming to the rational conclusion that "it's OK after all." When you practice this round of Yes, No, Yes, No, you may discover yourself feeling profound shame each time you say Yes. Right here, it is crucial to understand that since the activity itself is appropriate in moderation, this feeling of shame over saying Yes is a major cause of your addiction, and *you must overcome it*.

I cannot emphasize this enough. I know of situations in which people have felt profound guilt in saying Yes to something that was perfectly appropriate for humans to do. The feeling of God's condemnation was so strong that they almost wanted to stay in the abstinence mode rather than experience the condemnation from saying Yes. It's so easy to think that if we *feel* guilty, the Holy Spirit must surely be trying to tell us that we *are* guilty. But we cannot, we dare not, go on feelings alone. Our consciences must be educated from the Bible, and if the Bible allows it and perhaps even commands it (as in the case of food and sex), then doing it and enjoying it are perfectly all right as long as we are within the Bible's guidelines.

Remember that your primary goal as a Christian is not relief from fear and guilt. Your primary goal is maturity in your Christian experience, because this and this alone will lead to genuine happiness. Now, it happens that you cannot experience Christian maturity so long as fear and false guilt control your mind. Therefore, you must get rid of these damaging emotions, not by shrinking into a hole so they can't bite you but by boldly confronting them and with God's help bringing them under the control of your mind and a properly educated conscience.

I promise you that you will not overcome your addiction as long as you allow this false guilt to control your mind. Therefore, it is just as important that you learn to say No as it is that you learn to say Yes, and it is just as important that you learn to say Yes as it is that you learn to say No. We can learn to say both appropriately through short periods of abstinence followed by short periods of practice.

The dragon wants nothing more than to confuse your mind over the good things that God has in this life for you. He doesn't really care whether you believe that something is right when God says it is wrong or whether you believe that something is wrong when God says it is perfectly all right, because either way he has you in bondage. With the exception of alcohol, tobacco, and narcotics, just about everything we humans become addicted to is perfectly all right in moderation.[1] Therefore, conquering the dragon means not just learning to say No but also learning to say Yes to the privileges God has given us and enjoying them to the fullest in moderation without shame or fear.

---

[1] Pornography is also wrong under all circumstances, and total abstinence from pornography is essential for recovery from sexual addiction.

DEVOTIONAL EXERCISES

Biblical reflection on chapter 30

1. Write a paragraph explaining the meaning of *temperance* the way you have always understood it. Then look up the words *temperance* and *temperate* in the King James Version of the Bible, using a KJV concordance (Cruden's, Strong's, and Young's are best). Does the Bible use these words in the way you defined them?

2. Look up these same verses in one or more modern speech translations of the Bible. Does this give you any new insight into the meaning of *temperance*?

3. Can you identify an area of your life over which you feel shame and guilt that your mind says is not wrong? Write a page or two stating the biblical principles involved in this problem and its solution (be sure to use actual verses,

stories, etc., from the Bible). Also, reflect on your feelings in light of these principles.

Devotional study of 1 Samuel 30

1. Imagine for a moment that a child of yours was abducted from your home. Write a paragraph explaining how you would feel. Write another paragraph describing the feelings of David and his men in verses 4 to 6.

2. What emotion(s) lay behind the talk by David's men of stoning him? How do you think David went about finding strength in God?

3. Have you ever had a trial in your life in which all you could rely on was God? Write a paragraph describing your feelings and what you did to strengthen your trust in God. Would you do differently today?

4. Describe the feelings of the men who did not want to share the loot with the soldiers who stayed behind. Was their perception of justice skewed (verses 21-25)? Why? Why was David able to have such a different attitude?

Chapter
Thirty-one

SUCCESSFUL FAILURE

Perhaps you've heard the story of the young banker who was named by the board of directors to replace the seasoned president, who was retiring. On the old president's last day at work, the young man came into his office, sat down, and said, "Sir, what's the secret of your success? What can you tell me that will help me to succeed?"

The veteran banker said, "Decisions."

"I understand, sir, that correct decisions are essential," the young man replied. "But how do I make right decisions?"

"Judgment."

"I understand that too," the young man said. "But I don't have your many years of experience. How do I get good judgment?"

The old bank president leaned back in his chair, drew a deep breath, and said, "Mistakes."

So far as I know, nobody has ever improved on mistakes as a way to learn. That's how children learn to walk. That's how Thomas Edison invented the light bulb. And that's how you will learn not to sin. *We overcome sin by learning from the times when we do sin.* This is what I call "successful failure."

I'm not excusing sin. I'm not saying you shouldn't feel guilty when you sin. Those who don't feel guilty are the ones who won't learn, because they won't see their mistakes as mistakes. They'll just think they had a good time and go do it over again. *Only those who understand that sin really is sin are in a position to learn from their sin.* Of course we should feel guilty for our sins, but we must never allow them to devastate us. We must recognize that we will make mistakes in the moral areas of our lives just as we make mistakes in every other area, and we must apply the treatment God has provided for correcting our moral mistakes.

My wife Lois spoke to a group of Adventist young people in church one Sabbath. Later, she told me that several of them felt perplexed about their Christian experience. "Why is it," they said, "that we keep making the same mistakes day after day? Why can't we really *live* the Christian life?"

This is another way of phrasing the question that we started out with in this book: "Just what *is* the solution when one has asked for forgiveness . . . and consecrated himself to God only to find himself falling right back into sin?"

Each of us who asks this question tends to look at the lives of other Christians and think, *Wouldn't it be wonderful to have* his or her *Christian experience! Mine seems so imperfect in comparison.* The flaw in this reasoning is that we can see only the externals of other people's lives—the front they put on in church. If we could read their minds, we would discover that in a great many cases, they are thinking the same thing about us!

The very worst thing you can do is to put this book down and expect total victory from this moment on. I can guarantee that you will *not* walk a perfect path from this day forward. You will *not* always gain the victory. You *will* fail some of the time. It will be two steps forward, one step back, two steps forward, one step back. The good news is that two steps forward, one step back is progress! Please review with me some wise comments by people who've been there:

- Wrong habits are not overcome by a single effort (4T, 612).
- We shall often fail in our efforts to copy the divine pattern (SM, 1:337).
- My children, I write this to you so that you will not sin. But if anybody does sin, we have one who speaks to the Father in our defense—Jesus Christ, the Righteous One (1 John 2:1).
- It is foolish not to anticipate relapses (*The Twelve Steps: A Spiritual Journey*, 26).

Some people feel very threatened by this. They think I'm compromising with sin. They think I'm denying the power of the gospel. They think I'm denying that complete victory over all sin is possible.

That is not true!

Now that you've nearly finished reading this book, I hope you understand that I have no intention of compromising with sin. I fully affirm the power of the gospel to give every Christian the victory over every single sin. But I happen to know that victory does not happen overnight. It hasn't happened that way in my own life, and it hasn't happened that way in the life of any Christian I've ever known.

If victory over sin is supposed to be instantaneous, then the gospel has failed in the lives of 99.99 percent of the lives of Christians down through the ages. At that rate, you wonder where God is going to find the 144,000! On the other hand, if victory over sin is a growth process, a learning curve, then there are millions of genuine Christians all over the world right now.

God does not expect our victory over sin to be instantaneous. He does not excuse sin, but He does forgive it. He doesn't tell us to slip and fall, but He doesn't abandon us when we do. He says to us what He said to the woman caught in adultery: "Neither do I condemn thee: go, and sin no more" (John 8:11, KJV).

So what should you do when you sin after you've started working on the plan that I've shared with you in this book?

Four things.

One: Ask God to forgive you

The Bible says that "if we confess our sins, he is faithful and just to forgive us our sins, and to cleanse us from all unrighteousness" (1 John 1:9, KJV). Two things happen when we confess our sins: God no longer holds us accountable for them, and the victory process goes on.

In some cases, our confession can be immediate. We can make things right as soon as we are aware that we did something wrong. However, often some time will elapse before we are able to make a confession. In some cases, circumstances may prevent us from confessing immediately. We may not be able to locate the individual we wronged, or we may need to wait until the situation we are dealing with works out more completely. In other cases, it will take a while for us to even realize that we did wrong, and when we do understand our mistake, it may take a while to get up the courage to make things right. We may have to wrestle with God for a few days or even a few weeks—maybe a few months!

As long as we are honest with God and committed to obeying His will, He is perfectly willing to work along with our human frailty. He does not demand that we be perfect. He only asks that we be honest.

Two: Give yourself time

You must give yourself time to gain the victory. This is a crucial point. Some Christians become very discouraged when they make the same mistakes day after day. They fail to understand that making mistakes day after day is part of being human—part of a normal Christian life. If victory is a process, then we must learn to let it be that way and not allow ourselves to be overwhelmed with guilt every time we make a mistake.

The issue is not whether we make mistakes day after day. The issue is whether we are seeking victory. The issue is not whether we've *achieved* victory but whether we are *progressing* toward it. The issue is whether victory is still our goal and whether we are actively pursuing it. So give yourself a break. Cut yourself some slack. God does not demand instant victory of you. Why should you demand it of yourself?

I believe that learning to accept our humanness and our imperfections and to be at peace with ourselves and with God is one of the greatest challenges of being human. It is one of the greatest lessons a Christian can learn. There is no peace without it.

Three: Ask God to show you what went wrong

Anytime we sin, something went wrong. The question is, What? Getting the correct answer is crucial to any Christian who is serious about victory. And I can tell you who knows the answer: God.

I wish I could assure you that you can get God's answer by praying, opening the Bible, and pointing to a text. I wish I could tell you that God will give you a vision or that you will hear voices in the night. However, God does not work in any of these ways to give us the answers to questions about our spiritual life. He is much more indirect, and since He is God, we can assume that

His way of giving us the answers is best even if it seems more frustrating to us.

So how can we find God's answer to our question about what went wrong?

By asking.

Let's review the three basic parts of Section II of this book:

Changing Our Sinful Understanding
Changing Our Sinful Desires
Changing Our Sinful Behavior

You know by now that the way you use your will to get a change in your sinful desires is different from the way you use your will to get a change in your sinful behavior. Suppose you've been experimenting with these two, but you've failed in spite of your most sincere desire to win. We can diagram it like this:

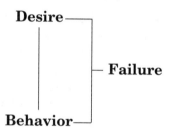

Notice that "understanding" is missing in this diagram. In order to understand your failure, you need to go back to the first part of the diagram and ask God to show you what went wrong. Then go back down to desire and behavior, and use what He showed you on your next temptation. Here's how we can diagram that:

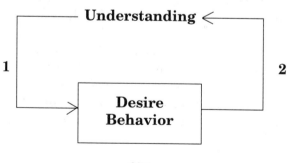

I want to assure you that God will respond to your request for greater understanding. However, as I pointed out earlier, you need not expect visions in the sky or voices in the night. God's answers are much more indirect. Let me illustrate with the analogy of the maze that I mentioned in an earlier chapter.

You're stuck in this giant maze with a bandanna tied around your head, covering your eyes. You're trying to escape by patting the walls on either side, and in due time, you come to a door, which you walk through. You then pat the walls on each side of that corridor till you come to another door, and you go through that one. Eventually, by trial and error, you emerge to the outside, where you are allowed to remove the blindfold.

Fortunately, you have the advantage of Someone who is eager to help you find the right doors to the outside. However, you need to understand that while He *could* take you by the hand and guide you straight to the outside (the "quick fix"), He has chosen *not* to do so. He helps by giving you strategies for discovering the outside more efficiently, but He lets you discover the outside for yourself through trial and error.

In this book I have shared with you many of the strategies for victory over temptation that have worked for me over the years. I can assure you that I did not come up with these strategies neatly worked out the way I have presented them to you in this book. I stumbled upon them one at a time, bit by bit, piece by piece, by trial and error. *These answers did not come easily, and they did not come fast!* But they did come.

And God is just as willing to show you the way out of your maze of temptations as He has been to show me the way out of mine.

Once you've asked God what went wrong, then you must go in search of the answer. Begin with your Bible. Pray as you read, asking Him to show you new ways to vary the experiment. The variation He shows you may be a new attitude, or it may be a new way to pray. Whatever it is, try it and keep coming back for more.

Get tough with yourself. Seek out a sponsor. Join a Twelve-Step group. Go to a bookstore, and look for books that deal with your particular temptation. Read everything you can about addiction and codependence. If you have to, go to The Bridge or a similar treatment center for recovering addicts and codependents. Remember God's promise:

> If you call out for insight
>> and cry aloud for understanding,
> and if you look for it as for silver
>> and search for it as for hidden treasure,
> then you will understand the fear of the Lord
>> and find the knowledge of God (Proverbs 2:3-5).

I would like to share an important promise with you:

VICTORY IS POSSIBLE
FOR YOU.

You must believe that! You must never give up believing it. Never allow yesterday's failures to blind you to the possibility of tomorrow's successes. Victory comes to believers, not doubters.

Neither must you give up trying. Victory will not come by wishing for it. You will not get it by sitting in church. It will not come to you by wringing your hands and wallowing in guilt. Victory comes to those who work for it, fight for it, and struggle for it.

Remember that the path to success is named Failure. Good people are good because they've come to goodness through failure. The term *experimental religion* means exactly what it says. When you fail, go back to the beginning and ask God how to vary the experiment, and then try again. If that fails, ask God to show you another way to vary the experiment, and try again. You may not conquer at every try, but *you will make progress.*

Four: Remember that Jesus still accepts you

In a faraway country is a railroad bridge over a deep chasm. The chasm is one thousand feet deep, and the bridge is a half mile long. One day a traveler wants to cross the bridge on foot, but the way is long, the chasm is deep, and he does not know when a train might come by. By good fortune, he finds a citizen of that country who knows the train schedule and who has crossed the bridge many times. This man offers to guide our traveler across the bridge. He shows him how to step carefully from tie to tie.

Then, holding the traveler's hand tightly in his own, he begins guiding him across. Suddenly, halfway across the bridge, the traveler's foot slips between two of the ties, and he starts to go down.

Tell me, what do you think the guide will do? Will he let go of the traveler's hand, or will he grip his hand tighter?

You know the answer, don't you?

But it's amazing how many people believe that anytime they stumble along life's journey to victory, Jesus lets go of their hand. There are those who will say, "Jesus hasn't let go of your hand, you've let go of His." I'll grant you that it's possible for you and me to let go of Jesus' hand. But we don't do that by sinning. We do it by refusing to repent of our sins. We do it by refusing to even try to overcome. We do it by becoming discouraged and deciding that we *can't* overcome. The name for that is unbelief, and God said that the Israelites failed to enter the Promised Land because of *unbelief* (see Hebrews 3:19).

We have now come full circle in this book. We started out with justification, and now we are back to justification. Justification is a secure platform on which we can makes mistakes while learning not to make mistakes. Does that idea make more sense to you now? Maybe you felt threatened by it when you read it in the first part of this book, fearful that I was lowering the standard, compromising with sin, excusing evil. I hope you realize, after reading Section II, that I do *not* excuse sin. I do not treat it lightly. Sin is extremely serious, and God expects us to do everything we possibly can to overcome it. But He understands the reality of *how* we overcome. He knows that victory over sin comes through character development, which takes time. And He gives us the time. He does not demand instant victory over sin. He only asks that we pursue the victory process seriously.

Please read again the two promises from Ellen White's writings that I shared with you in Section I:

> When it is in the heart to obey God, when efforts are put forth to this end, Jesus accepts this disposition and effort as the best service that man has to offer, and He makes up for the deficiency with His own divine merit (SM, 1:382).

To go forward without stumbling we must have the assurance that a hand all-powerful will hold us up, and an infinite pity be exercised toward us if we fall. God alone can at all times hear our cry for help (SD, 154).

With promises like that, and with all the help that God has provided, you and I cannot help but conquer the dragon within. And the more we learn to conquer the dragon within, the better qualified we will be to conquer the dragon without.

DEVOTIONAL EXERCISES

Biblical reflection on chapter 31

1. Name three Bible promises that can help you cope in a time of moral failure. Write a sentence or two explaining the practical application of each one.
2. Make a list of all the biblical principles for victory over temptation that you can think of. Use this list to prepare a strategy of three or four points that you will follow next time your besetting sin tempts you.

Devotional study of 1 Samuel 31

1. Write a page in which you reflect on Saul's life and the feelings that prompted his behavior. Conclude with your comment on the manner of Saul's death in light of the life that he lived.
2. Write a paragraph or two in which you apply what you learned about Saul's way of dealing with his feelings to your own way of dealing with feelings in the past. What have you learned that can help you to deal more successfully with your feelings in the future?
3. Why do you think it was the men of Jabesh Gilead who recovered the bodies of Saul and his sons from the Philistines and not the citizens of some other city? (See chapter 11.) In view of Saul's life and especially of his final days (see chapter 28), was their act appropriate? Explain your answer.

EPILOGUE

Imagine with me for a moment that you are sitting in your living room one afternoon several years from the time you are reading this book, watching the evening news. Events in the world suggest quite clearly to you that probation has probably closed, and this evening's news report is particularly convincing in this regard. Suddenly, the doorbell rings, and when you answer it, you find a close friend from the church standing on your front porch. You welcome him in and invite him to be seated. After you've chatted for a few minutes, your friend turns to you and says, "Does it seen to you that probation has closed?"

"Interesting that you should ask," you say. "I was just watching the evening news and wondering the same thing myself. I believe the answer to your question is probably Yes."

Your friend pauses. Then he turns to you with a concerned look on his face, and he says, "Do you feel good enough for the close of probation?"

That question seems almost unreal today, doesn't it? I can assure you, though, that if our Adventist understanding of the end time is in any way realistic, you and I will all be pondering it with great interest one of these days!

As you reflect on that question today, what answer do you think you would give to your friend? Would you say, "Why, of course I'm ready! I'm feeling really *perfect* these days."

I hope you would not say that today, because I can assure you that you *won't* be able to say it then. The only answer I can give to the question of how perfect you and I must be after the close of probation is this: Our characters must be as perfect as Jesus can make them as we struggle with Him to modify them now.

I want to assure you that if you are faithfully doing your part to develop a character like Christ's before the close of probation, He guarantees to do His part and get you ready in time. You won't know when you are ready, but He will, and that's all that matters. Trust that He isn't going to close probation till you are ready, because *He won't!*

This brings up one final issue that we need to deal with in this book—the idea of "absolute perfection."

Every now and then, someone says to me, "Pastor Moore, those who live after the close of probation without a Mediator must be absolutely perfect!" Some people call this "final generation theology." Maybe you've heard about it too.

I've found the perfect answer for those who challenge me with this teaching. I say to them, "You may be right. I really don't know, because I can't define perfection, and therefore I'll never know when I'm good enough." I go on to point out that if we are faithful in doing our part, God guarantees to do His part and get us ready on time.

If God can see that absolute perfection is what you and I must have in order to live without a Mediator after the close of probation, then He's going to get us "that good." If He can see that something short of absolute perfection is adequate to live without a Mediator, He'll get us "that good." Since I won't know when I'm perfect enough, I must simply trust that if I do my part, God will do His part and get me as ready as I need to be, and He'll do it on time.

To put it another way, Seventh-day Adventists and all other Christians need to spend a great deal of time getting honest with God and each other about their lives and doing their best to overcome their sins and character defects. But I do not hesitate to say that *we have no business spending one minute worrying about how perfect we are or how perfect we must become.* This is not to deny the reality or the importance of perfection. It is only to state the logical conclusion that if we cannot define perfection, and if we will never know when we are perfect enough to live without a Mediator, then there is nothing to worry about.

And in any case, character perfection alone will never be enough to carry you and me through the close of probation and the seven last plagues. During those final days of earth's history, we will need the justifying robe of Christ's righteousness just as much as we do now, and probably more.

In conclusion I would like to share with you the best definition of perfection I have ever seen. I found it in *Christ's Object Lessons,* page 384:

> The completeness of Christian character is attained when the impulse to help and bless others springs constantly from within.

Please notice the last word of that statement, and then compare it with the last word in the title of this book. Perfection happens *within.* You and I need most of all to conquer the dragon *within.* Jesus especially wants to change your impulses and mine *within.* We will not be ready for the close of probation and living without a Mediator until we are ready *within.* I hope above all else that what you have learned from this book will help you every day to grow more and more like Jesus *within.*

Appendix A

PRAYERS AND CARDINAL PRINCIPLES

Section II of this book gives prayers for help in changing sinful attitudes, sinful desires, and sinful behaviors. There is also a prayer of surrender. For your convenience, these prayers are given below, exactly as they appear in the main text of the book.

Also, four cardinal principles appear in Section II, and these are also listed below.

PRAYERS FOR VICTORY

Prayers for a change in our sinful understanding
- Lord, please show me the flaws in my character that I'm not aware of.
- Lord, please help me understand why I yield to (name the temptation).
- Lord, help me understand the defects that keep me from being like Jesus.
- **And especially help me to understand my wrong motives.**

- Lord, please show me what I can start doing right now that will help me to conquer (name the temptation).
- Lord, please help me to understand anything I'm doing that's hindering my efforts to overcome.
- Lord, help me to understand the principles that lead to victory.
- **And especially help me to understand the motives that are interfering with my efforts to overcome.**

- Lord, show me the things I need to know in order to be ready for the close of probation.
- Lord, show me what I need to know in order to be among the 144,000.
- Lord, show me the things I need to know in order to reflect the image of Jesus.
- **And especially help me to understand my wrong motives.**

A prayer for a change in our sinful desires

Lord, please remove my desire for this sin, and replace it with a desire for what is right.

A prayer for a change in our sinful behavior

Lord, please remove the desire for this sin, and please give me the power not to do it right now.

A prayer of surrender

- Lord, this desire belongs to You now.
- It's Yours to remove when You want it to go away.
- It's not mine to remove when I want it to go away.
- I will wait patiently without acting on it until You remove it.

CARDINAL PRINCIPLES

Cardinal Principle 1

Victory is possible for those who believe that it is.

Cardinal Principle 2

To gain the victory, you must get honest with yourself and with God.

Cardinal Principle 3

Ask God to remove the desire for sin when you want nothing more than to enjoy it and act on it.

Cardinal Principle 4

Practice abstinence—clench your fists and grit your teeth—when you want nothing more than to yield.

Appendix B

THE TWELVE STEPS OF ALCOHOLICS ANONYMOUS

1. We admitted we were powerless over alcohol—that our lives had become unmanageable.
2. Came to believe that a power greater than ourselves could restore us to sanity.
3. Made a decision to turn our will and our lives over to the care of God *as we understood Him*.
4. Made a searching and fearless moral inventory of ourselves.
5. Admitted to God, to ourselves, and to another human being the exact nature of our wrongs.
6. Were entirely ready to have God remove all these defects of character.
7. Humbly asked Him to remove our shortcomings.
8. Made a list of all persons we had harmed, and became willing to make amends to them all.
9. Made direct amends to such people wherever possible, except when to do so would injure them or others.
10. Continued to take personal inventory and when we were wrong promptly admitted it.
11. Sought through prayer and meditation to improve our conscious contact with God *as we understood Him*, praying only for knowledge of His will for us and the power to carry that out.
12. Having had a spiritual awakening as the result of these steps, we tried to carry this message to alcoholics, and to practice these principles in all our affairs.

Several objections have been raised to the Twelve Steps by some Christians, including Seventh-day Adventist Christians. Following is a brief response to some of the most common objections.

Christians should not confess to each other

Two objections have been raised to the fifth step by some Seventh-day Adventists. The first is that the fifth step is the same as the Catholic confessional. The second is that Ellen White says we should confess our sins only to God. I have responded to these objections in chapter 16.

There is only one God

Some Christians object to the steps 3 and 11, which speak of "God as we understood Him." They claim that this step leads to a multiplicity of gods, whereas the Bible speaks of only one God. I will respond to this objection in two ways.

First, while for Christians the statement that the only true God is the God of the Bible is correct, there are many perceptions of the biblical God in the minds of Christians. The Twelve Steps do not say there are many gods. They ask the addicts to pray to God as they understand Him.

Second, the Twelve Steps were not written for Christians per se. They were designed to help people of all religious faiths and even those of no faith. Buddhists, Muslims, and Hindus have found recovery from alcoholism through the Twelve Steps. The Twelve Steps deal with spiritual rather than religious principles, on the assumption that spiritual principles cross denominational and religious boundaries. Christians who wish to use the Twelve Steps from a strictly Christian point of view need to start a Christian Twelve-Step group, and advertise it as such.

The originator of the Twelve-Step program was a spiritualist

Alcoholics Anonymous was founded in the late 1930s by Bill Wilson of New York City and Dr. Robert Smith of Akron, Ohio. Initially, there were only six steps, but in 1938 Bill Wilson expanded them to the present twelve. Over the next few years, slight modifications were made, primarily to avoid offending people of certain religious groups. Thus today's Twelve Steps can be said to have originated in 1938 with Bill Wilson.[1]

There is some evidence that Wilson dabbled in spiritualism

during the early 1940s. However, it is quite certain that he was not doing so in 1938 when he wrote the Twelve Steps.

And in any case, the Twelve Steps must be judged for what they say, not for other beliefs that their originator may have held. If the Twelve Steps do not mention spiritualistic principles—and they do not—then they are not based on spiritualism.

The Twelve Steps and justification by faith

Some people have objected to the Twelve Steps on the grounds that they are contrary to the biblical principle of justification (or righteousness) by faith. The response to this objection is simple. Salvation, as Protestant Christians (including Seventh-day Adventists) understand it, is based on justification by faith, not by works of the law. Alcoholics Anonymous makes no claim that the Twelve Steps will provide eternal life. They are a pathway for sobriety in this life and nothing more. However, many Christians, including many Seventh-day Adventist Christians, have found that the Twelve Steps provide an excellent way to overcome besetting and cherished sins. I have pointed out repeatedly that victory over sin is not the basis of our salvation. Thus there is no contradiction between the Twelve Steps and justification by faith.

I have also pointed out in this book that there is a great similarity between the Twelve Steps and the biblical principles for victory over sin. I have found no contradiction between these two.

In view of the fact that character development is the work of a lifetime, I used to wonder how God was going to develop necessary character strengths in those who accept the truths we proclaim during the loud cry and the final warning. Now I know. I believe God is using the Twelve Steps to accomplish that purpose right now in the lives of millions of honest-hearted people, both Christian and non-Christian. At the last minute, they will add the finishing touch of doctrine that they need to pass through earth's final crisis, and they will be as ready for the close of probation and the second coming of Jesus as those of us who have walked in the more complete light of truth for many years.

---

[1] For a more complete account of the origin of Alcoholics Anonymous and the Twelve Steps, see chapter 24 of Carol Cannon's book, *Never Good Enough*.

Appendix C

HOW TO FIND A TWELVE-STEP GROUP

Since about 1970, a number of organizations have been established that apply the recovery concepts of Alcoholics Anonymous, including the Twelve Steps, to other addictive behaviors. I have verified the names, addresses, and telephone numbers of the organizations in the list below. They are accurate as of September 1994. All of these organizations publish literature on their particular addiction. They also maintain a list of Twelve-Step meetings around the United States and Canada. If you call them, they will give you the address and time of the meeting closest to you and the name and telephone number of a contact person in your area. They can provide information on starting a group in your area, and they will send you a price list of the books, pamphlets, and video and audiotapes they produce. In some cases, you may be able to order with a major credit card over the telephone.

Alcoholics Anonymous (AA)
P.O. Box 459
Grand Central Station
New York, NY 10163
(212) 870-3400
AA has both open and closed groups. Anyone is welcome to attend an open group. Only persons who are addicted to alcohol are allowed to attend closed groups. AA groups are everywhere in the United States and Canada and in many other parts of the world.

While AA is especially for alcoholics, if you are struggling with another addiction for which no Twelve-Step group is available in your area, you can almost certainly find an AA open group where you will be welcome to discuss your issues. Look in the white pages of your telephone book under Alcoholics Anonymous, or call the AA number in New York City for information and referral to a group in your area.

Alanon/Alateen Family Group
P.O. Box 182
Madison Square Station
New York, NY 10159
(800) 356-9996

The purpose of this Twelve-Step group is to provide support for friends and relatives of alcoholics. It helps these people relate to the alcoholic in such a way that they do not enable the disease, but rather help the victim to face his or her problem and seek help.

Codependents Anonymous (CODA)
P.O. Box 33577
Phoenix, AZ 85067-3577
(602) 277-7991

CODA differs from most other recovery organizations in this list in that it does not deal with addiction to a specific substance or behavior. It focuses more specifically on codependence and recovery from codependence than does EA. It is a good general group to attend if you cannot identify a specific issue you are struggling with.

Emotions Anonymous (EA)
P.O. Box 4245
St. Paul, MN 55104
(612) 647-9712

Like Codependents Anonymous, EA differs from most other recovery organizations in this list in that it does not deal with addiction to a specific substance or behavior. EA groups provide support for people who are experiencing depression, anxiety, fear, shame, etc. It is a good general group to attend if you cannot identify a specific issue you are struggling with.

Gamblers Anonymous (GA)
P.O. Box 17173
Los Angeles, CA 90017

(213) 386-8789

The name describes the issue that the organization deals with. They provide information and literature and can refer you to groups and persons in your area.

Narcotics Anonymous (NA)
P.O. Box 9999
Van Nuys, CA 91409
(818) 780-3951

Like AA, NA has both open and closed meetings. Look in the business white pages of your telephone book under Narcotics Anonymous, or call the NA number above for information and referral to a group in your area.

Overeaters Anonymous (OA)
P.O. Box 44020
Rio Rancho, NM 87174-4020
(505) 891-2664

OA is for people who are struggling with food issues, especially overeating. Bulimics and anorexics will find support in OA but may need professional treatment as well, with attendance at OA as part of a recovery program.

Sexaholics Anonymous (SA)
P.O. Box 300
Simi Valley, CA 93062
(805) 581-3343

SA support groups are available in all major cities in North America and many smaller communities as well. SA defines sobriety as no fantasy or sex with self or another person except a marriage partner. In addition to books, pamphlets, and tapes, they publish a newsletter.

Sex Addicts Anonymous (SAA)
P.O. Box 70949
Houston, TX 77270
(713) 869-4902

Like Sexaholics Anonymous, Sex Addicts Anonymous provides support for sex addicts trying to break free of their addiction. The major difference between the two groups is in their definition of sobriety. Where SA defines sobriety for the addict (see above), SAA encourages the addict to define sobriety for himself and to continue modifying that definition as he progresses in recovery.

Sex and Love Addicts Anonymous (SLA)

P.O. Box 119, New Town Branch

Boston, MA 02258

(617) 332-1845

Sex and Love Addicts Anonymous is the group for relationship addicts. If you are in an abusive relationship, or if your worth as a person is tied to a relationship with another individual, SLA can help you. Call them for a referral to a person and group near you and for literature.

Workaholics Anonymous (WA)

P.O. Box 289, Station A

Menlo Park, CA 94026-0289

(510) 273-9253

As its name implies, Workaholics Anonymous exists to help people who work compulsively, whether on the job or at home. An answering machine will respond to your telephone call at the number listed above, and you will be asked to leave your telephone number and authorization to receive a collect call if you live outside that telephone number's calling area. Be sure to state your need—whether a literature list, a referral to a group nearest you, or information on starting a WA group.

The Bridge

1745 Logsdon Road

Bowling Green, KY 42101

(502) 777-1094

The Bridge is a treatment center for healing from emotional and spiritual disease. Their approach is group instruction and group therapy based on the concepts of recovery from codependence and addition. I have been through their two-week codepency treatment program, and I highly recommend both it and their three-month program for recovery from chemical addition.

Appendix D

HOW TO START A TWELVE-STEP STUDY GROUP

If you would like to attend a Twelve-Step group but none that deals with your issues exists close enough to where you live, you may want to consider starting one. I recommend that before you start a group, you attend Twelve-Step meetings at least once a week for six months to a year. This will give you the "feel" for what a Twelve-Step group is like. It would be best that you attend a variety of groups.

The following suggestions for starting your own group arise out of the experience that my wife and I had starting a Twelve-Step Christian group in our home church of Caldwell, Idaho, in February 1993. The group is still going strong in September 1994.

Getting Started

What kind of group do you want to start?
The first thing you need to decide is the kind of Twelve-Step group you will start. If you have a particular addiction, such as food, anger, or sex, you may want to start a group for that issue. However, often it is easier to find people with a variety of addictions who are willing to start a general Twelve-Step group. Most readers of this book will probably want to start a Christian Twelve-Step group.

Alcoholics Anonymous sponsors three types of groups: (1) lecture groups, in which one individual talks to the entire group for about an hour; (2) discussion groups, in which the group members choose a topic and discuss it for an hour or more; and (3) study groups, in which the members agree on a book they will study. Most study groups also do a lot of discussing. I recommend that you start a study group.

If you decide to start a study group and have decided whether it will be specific or general, you need to select a book for study. Appendix E lists several possibilities, among which are the following:

The Twelve Steps: A Spiritual Journey (Christian)
The Twelve Steps: A Gentle Path (spiritual but not Christian)
Codependents' Guide to the Twelve Steps (spiritual but not Christian
Facing Codependence (spiritual but not Christian)
Any of the books under specific categories in Appendix E

Who will attend?

Once you have determined the book that will be the basis for discussion in your group, you need to find several people who want to meet together for recovery. If you and several others (at least three and preferably six to twelve) have already decided to start a group, then all you need to do is agree on a time and place. If only one or two people want to start a group, you will need to advertise for more members. In order to announce a specific time and place, you will have to begin by finding a suitable location to meet. Most churches are willing to provide a room, perhaps for a small monthly fee that can be covered by taking up an offering at the meeting. Be sure to arrange for the hour to meet at the same time you arrange for the location.

Your advertising should state the specific purpose of the group—whether it is a general Twelve-Step group or specific for alcoholics, workaholics, sexaholics, etc. If you are starting a Christian Twelve-Step group, you should also state that. Following are good places to advertise:

Radio and TV announcements
Church bulletins of various denominations
Christian bookstores
Grocery-store bulletin boards
Newspapers (many newspapers run a weekly announcement
    of Twelve-Step groups in their area)
Hospital addiction-recovery centers

A comfortable group size is eight to twelve people, but don't worry if more people attend the first night. You will almost certainly lose at least half of them within the first month.

How to Conduct a Meeting

The opening night

Some, and perhaps most, of those who attend on the opening night will very likely never have attended a Twelve-Step meeting before, so after welcoming everyone, you should spend a bit of time explaining how a Twelve-Step group operates. Walk them through the introductory exercises that any Twelve-Step group always follows. These are listed below.

You must—you absolutely must—emphasize that all Twelve-Step groups are anonymous. That is, anything that is said in the group is held in strictest confidence. Group members should also agree never to mention outside the group the name of anyone in the group. Within the group, members should use first names only.

One person should lead out in each meeting. If one or two of you started the group, you will naturally be the leaders, at least to begin with. If possible, two or more people should take turns leading from one meeting to the next. That way, the group will always have a leader when one of the leaders has to be away for an evening.

The meeting format

Meetings should last for one to one-and-a-half hours. Unless someone is deep into the discussion of a personal issue, the group leader should plan to bring the meeting to a close at the agreed-upon time. Following is a format for a Twelve-Step study group, followed by an explanation of each one:

1. A moment of silence followed by the serenity prayer
2. Introductions
3. Reading of the Twelve Steps (and in a Christian group, of the Bible texts associated with the Twelve Steps)
4. Reading of the group's ground rules or traditions
5. Reading of the promises

6. Discussion of "burning issues" (individual problems)
7. Reading of the study book
8. Offering
9. Close with the Lord's Prayer

In order to get on with reading and discussing, your group may be tempted to skip items 1 to 5 in the list above. *Do not succumb to this temptation.* These items are extremely important and should be a part of every meeting. You do not have a Twelve-Step meeting if you do not do this.

A moment of silence and the serenity prayer
The group leader should call the meeting to order and say, "Let's begin with a moment of silence followed by the serenity prayer." After half a minute to a minute of silence, the leader should say, "God," and pause. Then he or she and the group as a whole will say the serenity prayer:

God, grant me the serenity to accept the things I cannot change,
The courage to change the things I can,
And the wisdom to know the difference.

Introductions
Introductions should always be by first names only. The group leader should ask one person to begin the introductions, and each person should introduce himself or herself in order clockwise around the group. Some groups encourage members to mention their addiction or addictions after they say their name. Introductions often go something like this:

"Hi, my name is John, and I'm a perfectionist and a workaholic."
"Hi, my name is Cindy, and I'm a love and relationship addict and a people pleaser."
"Hi, my name is Ernestine, and I'm an overeater and a religion addict."
"Hi, my name is Sam, and I'm a drug addict."

Reading the Twelve Steps and Bible texts
After introductions, the first activity in all Twelve-Step groups

is to read the Twelve Steps. The Twelve Steps of Alcoholics Anonymous are listed in Appendix B. The first step says, "We admitted we were powerless over alcohol—that our lives had become unmanageable." Groups other than Alcoholics Anonymous usually substitute the name of their addiction in place of the word *alcohol* in this step. General groups such as Emotions Anonymous, Codependents Anonymous, and Christian Twelve-Step groups insert something like "We admitted we were powerless over our emotions," "We admitted we were powerless over our relationships with others," or "We admitted we were powerless over our separation from God."

Christian Twelve-Step groups usually alternate the reading of each step with an appropriate Bible verse. One person reads the first step, and another person reads the appropriate Bible verse. The first person then reads the second step, and the other person reads the second Bible verse, etc. Following are Bible verses that can be used after each step:

Step 1: Romans 7:18
Step 2: Philippians 2:13
Step 3: Romans 12:1
Step 4: Lamentations 3:40
Step 5: James 5:16a
Step 6: Romans 7:22-24
Step 7: James 4:10
Step 8: 1 John 1:9
Step 9: Matthew 5:23, 24
Step 10: 1 Corinthians 10:12
Step 11: Colossians 3:16a
Step 12: Galatians 6:1

Reading the group's ground rules or traditions

After the reading of the Twelve Steps should come the reading of the group's ground rules or traditions. Following are some sample ground rules:

1. The only requirement for membership in our group is a desire for recovery from addiction and codependence.
2. We agree to maintain absolute confidentiality. What we see,

hear, and say here stays here.

3. We do not give advice or try to "fix" the problems of others.
4. Our purpose is to share our experience, strength, and hope. We are here to search for answers, not to complain.
5. We use first names only.
6. Every group ought to be fully self-supporting, declining outside contributions.
7. Our common welfare should come first. Personal recovery depends on unity.
8. For our group purpose, there is but one ultimate authority— a loving God as He may express Himself in our group conscience.
9. The only requirement for membership is a desire for recovery from addiction and codependence.
10. Our public-relations policy is based on attraction rather than promotion.

A word of explanation is in order about ground rules 3 and 4. The "advice giving" and "fixing" mentioned in number 3 happen when one person says to another, "I think this is what you ought to do." If you believe you have an insight that might help the other person, share it in terms of your own experience. Instead of saying, "This is what I suggest you do," say, "Here's how I handled a similar situation," or "Here's what I do when that happens to me."

One of the major problems you want to watch for in a group is the tendency for members, in sharing their burning issues, to complain. Complaining happens when all we do is feel sorry for ourselves over our miserable circumstances or the way others are treating us with no effort to search for solutions. The group should agree that if a member starts complaining, they will encourage him or her to search for solutions.

Reading of the promises

Various promises have been used by Twelve-Step groups. The "Big Book" of Alcoholics Anonymous has many good ones, among which are the following:

If we are painstaking about this phase of our development,

we will be amazed before we are halfway through. We are going to know a new freedom and a new happiness. We will not regret the past nor wish to shut the door on it. We will comprehend the word serenity and we will know peace. No matter how far down the scale we have gone, we will see how our experience can benefit others. That feeling of uselessness and self-pity will disappear. We will lose interest in selfish things and gain interest in our fellows. Self-seeking will slip away. Our whole attitude and outlook upon life will change. Fear of people and of economic insecurity will leave us. We will intuitively know how to handle situations which used to baffle us. We will suddenly realize that God is doing for us what we could not do for ourselves.

Are these extravagant promises? We think not. They are being fulfilled among us—sometimes quickly, sometimes slowly. They will always materialize if we work for them (*Alcoholics Anonymous*, 83, 84).

Henry Ford once made a wise remark to the effect that experience is the thing of supreme value in life. That is true only if one is willing to turn the past to good account. We grow by our willingness to face and rectify errors and convert them into assets. The . . . past thus becomes the principle asset of the family and frequently it is the only one!

This painful past may be of infinite value to other families still struggling with their problems. . . . Showing others who suffer how we were given help is the very thing which makes life seem so worthwhile to us now. Cling to the thought that, in God's hands, the dark past is the greatest possession you have—the key to life and happiness for others. With it you can avert death and misery for them (*Alcoholics Anonymous*, 124).

Discussion of "burning issues"

A "burning issue" is anything that a member of the group wants to discuss. It may be a victory experienced during the past week, or it may be a painful experience the member needs to share. Sometimes one person's burning issue will take up half or even all of the group's time that day. Other times two or three people may have burning issues to share. These issues are the most important reason for the group's existence and should be given priority.

This last statement needs a word of qualification, though. Until a group has learned the basic principles of addiction and codependence, reading may need to take precedence over the sharing of burning issues. This may not be quite so important when one or two people are well enough acquainted with these principles that they can comment appropriately when an issue arises that illustrates the principles of addiction, codependence, and recovery. However, they need to be sure always to make their comments in harmony with ground rule number 3.

Reading of the study book

Group members should read their book through from beginning to end. Starting with chapter 1, paragraph 1, they should take turns reading a paragraph at a time until everyone has had a chance to read one paragraph. Then they should stop and discuss what they have read. Group members should be encouraged to share any thoughts from the reading that were especially meaningful to them. When discussion lags, the group leader should start another round of reading. Some groups take turns reading a page at a time rather than a paragraph at a time, in which case they should pause for discussion after the reading of each page.

The group should read and discuss until closing time. Every effort should be made to close on time.

Offering

Shortly before the conclusion of each meeting, the group leader should pass a basket, envelope, or other receptacle for receiving donations. Usually members will drop in a dollar, though some will not put in anything, and that is all right too. Giving must never be a requirement for membership in the group.

Donations can be used to pay rent on the meeting room and to purchase refreshments and literature for the group. Groups that are part of a larger organization such as Alcoholics Anonymous, Overeaters Anonymous, etc., may have an arrangement with their parent group for passing on a part of their weekly receipts to the parent organization.

The Lord's Prayer

When closing time has come, the group leader should inform the group that it is time to say the Lord's Prayer. In the groups I have attended, the members stand in a circle and hold hands. The group leader then says, "We hold hands to symbolize that we can do together what we cannot do alone." Or he or she may say to one of the group members, "Why do we hold hands?" and the group member says, "To show that we can do together what we cannot do alone."

With everyone's head bowed, the leader then says, "Whose Father?" The group replies, "Our Father, . . ." and continues with the Lord's Prayer. After the prayer, many groups like to shake their hands up and down (as they hold hands) as they say, "Keep coming back. It works if you work it!"

The meeting is now over.

Appendix E

HELPFUL BOOKS TO READ

Understanding an addiction is one of the first steps toward overcoming it. The following books will give you insight into various types of addictions and emotional problems. Any of them that are out of print can be obtained from your local library. If your library does not have it, they can obtain it through interlibrary loan.

Where a book is written from a Christian perspective, I have said so. I have also identified books that are written from a spiritual but not necessarily Christian perspective. All others are from a secular perspective.

ADDICTION IN GENERAL

Transferring Obsessions
Judi Hollis, Ph.D.
Hazeldon, 1986
The author explains how addicts substitute one addiction for another instead of overcoming the problem that is driving the addiction in the first place. People switch from the addiction they grew up with to sex, food, caffeine, work, shopping, etc.

Never Good Enough: Growing Up Imperfect in a "Perfect" Family
Carol Cannon
Pacific Press, 1993
Cannon is a therapist who works with addicts at The Bridge in Bowling Green, Kentucky. She explains the foundation of addiction and codependence and examines the various addictions in detail. This book is written from a Christian perspective.

When Too Much Is Never Enough
Gaylen Larsen with Marita Littauer
Pacific Press, 1992
Larsen is a professional therapist who has worked with many addicts. He explains that people can become addicted to more than substances such as alcohol and drugs. He examines in detail the various nonsubstance habits that people can become addicted to and offers suggestions for overcoming them. This book is written from a Christian perspective.

The Twelve Steps: A Spiritual Journey
Written by a group of addicts in recovery
Recovery Publications, 1988
This is a workbook. Each chapter is based on one of the Twelve Steps. Chapters consist of Bible texts followed by two to four questions, below which is space for writing answers. An appendix tells how to start a Twelve-Step study group. This book is written from a Christian perspective.

ALCOHOL ADDICTION
Alcoholics Anonymous (The Big Book)
Alcoholics Anonymous World Services, Inc., 1939, 1986
This book was written by the people who first learned to break out of alcohol addiction in the mid-1930s. It is *the* classic in the field of addiction recovery. It is must reading for anyone who has an alcoholic addiction, and it is useful for those in other addictions as well. It is available through any AA center. This book is written from a spiritual perspective.

The Twelve-Steps and the Twelve Traditions
Alcoholics Anonymous World Services, Inc., 1953
"The Twelve and Twelve," as it is called by those in recovery from addiction, is a guided tour through the Twelve Steps and the principles that underlie them. This is an excellent primer for understanding addiction. It is available through any AA center. This book is written from a spiritual perspective.

ANGER AND ANGER ADDICTION
The Dance of Anger
Harriet Goldhor Lerner, Ph.D.
Harper & Row, 1985
Anger issues involve both anger that is out of control (anger addiction) and anger that is stuffed and never expressed. The author explains why anger is a healthy emotion when it is experienced appropriately and shows how to break out of the dysfunctional expression of anger. While the book is written for women, it is valuable reading for both men and women.

The Angry Book
Theodore Isaac Rubin, M.D.
Collier Macmillan Publishers, 1970
This is one of the early books in the recovery movement (outside of Alcoholics Anonymous). The author explains how anger arises out of our past experience as children, the dysfunctional expression of anger in the present, and how to change.

CODEPENDENCE
Codependents' Guide to the Twelve Steps
Melody Beattie
Simon and Schuster, 1990
The author reflects on the Twelve Steps a chapter at a time with practical suggestions for implementing them. This is a book about how to live humbly, honestly, and at peace with yourself. This book is written from a spiritual perspective.

Facing Codependence
Pia Melody
Harper & Row, 1989
Melody is a therapist at The Meadows, an addiction treatment center in Arizona. She explains codependence, its effects, and how to recover. The book is a comprehensive overview of codependence in nontechnical language. This book is written from a spiritual perspective.

FOOD ADDICTION
Overeaters Anonymous
Overeaters Anonymous World Service Office
This is the "Big Book" of overeaters anonymous. It should form the foundation of any effort to use the Twelve Steps to bring obsessive eating habits under control. It is also a good book to use for an Overeaters Anonymous study group.

Feeding the Empty Heart
Barbara McFarland and Tyeis Baker-Baumann
Hazeldon, 1988
This book explains the dynamics of eating disorders. It shows the relationship between these disorders and childhood family dysfunction and offers help for recovery.

Fat Is a Family Affair
Judi Hollis
Harper/Hazeldon
The author describes eating disorders and addictions and explains why overeaters eat too much and undereaters eat too little. It confronts addicts with their dysfunctional behavior and attitudes and offers specific help for recovery.

RELATIONSHIP ADDICTION
Men Who Hate Women and the Women Who Love Them
Dr. Susan Forward and Joan Torres
Bantam Books, 1987
This book describes men who hate women and helps women to recognize when they are being controlled. It also suggests ways that women can break out of such relationships and how they can heal from the codependence that got them into such relationships in the first place.

Women Who Love Too Much
Robin Norwood
Pocket Books, 1986
This book explains the dynamics of abusive relationships and helps women who are in a destructive relationship with a man to understand why. It shows how women get themselves into such

relationships as adults because of the abuse they experienced in childhood and provides tools for changing their lives.

Sex and Love Addicts Anonymous
Sex and Love Addicts Anonymous, Inc.
This is the "Big Book" of Sex and Love Addicts Anonymous. It is available through their organization. Their address is listed in Appendix C.

RELIGIOUS ADDICTION
Healing Spiritual Abuse
Kenneth Blue
InterVarsity Press, 1993
While this book is as much for the victims of religious abuse as it is for religion addicts, religion addicts can gain a great deal of insight into religious abuse by reading it. Also, many people who are abused religiously become religious addicts.

The Gospel Versus Legalism
Marvin Moore
Review and Herald, 1994
This book is primarily a study of Paul's letter to the Galatians. However, the primary problem in Galatia was legalism, and the author draws many lessons for legalistic Christians today. In the last five chapters, the author examines modern legalistic attitudes, which are a form of religious addiction, and provides suggestions for overcoming this problem. This book is written from a Christian perspective.

SEXUAL ADDICTION
Sexaholics Anonymous
SA Literature, 1989
This is the "Big Book" of Sexaholics Anonymous. It is published by the Sexaholics Anonymous organization. The book is profoundly spiritual. While it is written especially for sex addicts, it is outstanding reading for anyone who is struggling to break free of any addiction. It will be mailed in a plain envelope. It is available through the SA office in California. The address is given in Appendix C.

Out of the Shadows: Understanding Addiction
Patrick Carnes, Ph.D.

CompCare Publishers, 1985

The author is a professional counselor and therapist for sexual addicts. He explains the anatomy of sexual addiction and how to break free. He writes with empathy for the sexual addict's emotional needs.

SHAME AND FALSE GUILT

Facing Shame: Families in Recovery
Merle A. Fossum and Marilyn J. Mason

Norton, 1986

The authors are family therapists who provide insight into where shame comes from and how it creates dysfunction in families. They describe the anatomy of shame, how to recognize shame-based attitudes and relationships, and how to break free.

Understanding Shame
Eunice Cavanaugh, M.Ed., M.S.W.

Johnson Institute, 1989

This book explains healthy and unhealthy shame and how unhealthy shame and false guilt control our lives. The author shows how to recognize and overcome unhealthy shame and how to allow healthy shame to shape our lives positively.

WORK ADDICTION

Working Ourselves to Death and the Rewards of Recovery
Diane Fassel, Ph.D.

Harper Paperbacks, 1990

Because work addiction is so widely approved and rewarded in our culture, it is one of the more difficult addictions to recognize and deal with. The author describes the characteristics of work addiction in detail and provides suggestions for recovery.

Meditations for Women Who Do Too Much
Anne Wilson Schaffe

HarperCollins, New York, 1990

Schaffe's book is written for women but is just as useful for men who are addicted to work and a "keep busy" attitude. The book is less of an effort to analyze work addiction and more a resource of spiritual help for coping with the stresses that create the addiction in the first place.

Appendix F

ADDICTION, CODEPENDENCE, AND CHRISTIANITY

Beginning in the 1930s and increasingly on into the present, Alcoholics Anonymous has brought the world's attention to addiction. Since about the mid-1980s, codependence theory has flourished alongside addiction as an explanation of human problems. Some Christians criticize both addiction and codependence theory on the grounds that they compromise the Christian view of humanity, God, and sin. As you know, in this book I talk a great deal about addiction and codependence. I have found a great deal of help in these theories. To respond to the concerns of the critics of addiction and codependence in the main body of this book would have gotten us off the track of the book's main purpose. However, these concerns do need to be addressed, and I have chosen to do so in this appendix.

I will begin by stating that in some ways, the concerns of those who criticize addiction and codependence theory are legitimate. Christians need to be careful how they relate to ideas about the human mind and emotions that originate outside the Bible. Unfortunately, some Christians carry this idea to such an extreme that they insist on all truth originating in the Bible. If the Bible didn't say it first, they refuse to consider it. They are so afraid of pollution by the world that they avoid the world altogether.

My approach is to look at what the world says with a mind that has been informed by the Bible and let this biblical understanding help me to pick and choose, accepting some ideas and rejecting others.

It would take a book the size of this one to address all the objections that have ever been raised against addiction and codependence theory. In this short appendix, I will address two issues and ask you, the reader, to use my method of evaluating these criticisms as a model for your own assessment of whatever criticism comes your way. Remember that some criticisms of addiction and codependence theory will be valid and others will not. You must decide, based on your biblically informed reason.

Addiction as disease

Some Christians attack addiction theory on the grounds that it reduces sin to a mere disease. As one critic put it:

> Codependence theory, like the theory behind Alcoholics Anonymous and other "recovery" groups, depends on the concept of disease. Disease is a neat, if unpleasant concept, suggesting the rational processes of diagnosis, treatment, and recovery. Codependence gurus say that whatever is wrong with you or society is simply a symptom of a sickness. The human condition thus requires only the right therapy. This is a devastating thing to suggest to non-Christians, since Scripture teaches that the human condition is death, not sickness, requiring regeneration, not healing (Kenneth A. Myers, *SPC Journal*, 18:3).

This author confuses the issue by making the disease concept of sin the whole piece of cloth. If we think of sin as disease and nothing else, then his statement is true. However, if we think of disease as one way of looking at sin among others, and if we take from the disease concept what is useful and refuse to carry the concept to its extreme, then it can be very helpful.

The truth is that the Bible itself defines sin as disease. "Your whole head is injured, your whole heart afflicted," wrote Isaiah in describing the sinful condition of the Jewish people at his time. "From the sole of your foot to the top of your head there is no soundness—only wounds and welts and open sores, not cleansed or bandaged or soothed with oil" (Isaiah 1:5, 6).

In the New Testament, the word for salvation and the word for healing from disease are the same. The New Testament compares sin to leprosy, and modern Christians often compare sin to cancer.

When we say that sin is a disease, we are simply using a metaphor, an illustration, to help us understand the fallen, broken human condition. Many metaphors could be used to define sin. We could use computer language and call sin a "bug" or a "virus" in the system. As long as we don't press the analogy to all of its logical ramifications, as long as we restrict it to one or two simple concepts, such a comparison can be helpful. No one analogy of sin can encompass all that sin is. We are best served by using a variety of analogies, taking from each one what is helpful and refusing to press any of them to their logical extreme.

Even our most biblical definitions can be carried to an unhealthy extreme. Adventists typically define sin as the transgression of the law (see 1 John 3:4). That is a good definition of sin, but it does not encompass all that sin is, and we get into trouble when we try to make it so. The Pharisees were experts at defining sin in terms of law, but in the Sermon on the Mount, Jesus explained that sin is much more than a written code. He expanded the definition of sin to include the condition of the mind and heart.

The disease concept of sin can be helpful to those who are suffering from unhealthy shame and false guilt. Some addicts report that thinking of their addiction as a disease relieves them of the moral implications of their problem enough that they can overcome it. What they mean is that they felt such intense and unhealthy shame over their condition that the shame kept them locked in it. Looking at their problem as a disease relieved them of the shame enough that they could break out of both the unhealthy shame and the addiction itself.

However, it would be a serious mistake to press this idea to say that addiction has no moral implications whatsoever or that addicts should never feel the slightest bit guilty over their addictions. To claim this would be an example of incorrectly carrying an analogy to its logical extreme.

Codependence and the New Age

A common objection to codependence theory is that it is New Age philosophy. There is an element of truth to this, just as there is an element of truth to the statement that God, prayer, and meditation are a part of New Age philosophy. You will find a number of books on codependence that are written from a New Age perspective. (I tried to avoid listing any such books in Appendix

E.) This does not make codependence itself New Age any more than the fact that New Agers write on meditation and prayer makes these devotional activities "New Age."

The point at which Christians must be on their guard is not whether both Christian and New Age authors write on meditation and prayer or codependence. The point to watch for is what each is saying about these ideas. A Christian book or magazine article on meditation and prayer will express ideas that are radically different from New Age books and articles on the same subject. The same is true of Christian and New Age books on codependence.

I have tried, in this book, to give you Christian, biblically based insights into codependence. Or, to put it another way, I have tried to draw biblically sound ideas from addiction and codependence theory that can help Christians understand their human condition a little better. As long as we keep close to the Bible, I believe it is perfectly appropriate for Christians to search for ideas "out there" in the world.

Let me give you an example of what I mean. One of the common ideas propounded by New Age thinkers is that the self is god. Everything depends on self-understanding, they say. All knowledge is within you. The solution to the problem of evil is for human beings to develop the goodness that is already inherent within them.

Christians also think of the self, but in a radically different way. We begin by saying that the self is corrupted by a sinful nature. However, we do not therefore say that the self has no value or that a Christian should not take care of his or her "self." It was Jesus Himself who said, "Love your neighbor as your*self*" (Matthew 22:39). Many Christian writers have pointed out that we cannot love our neighbors if we do not also love ourselves. We must not love ourselves more than our neighbors, but neither must we love our neighbors more than ourselves. The spiritually and emotionally healthy Christian is the one who knows how to take care of both himself *and* his neighbor.

Some people criticize codependence theory because of its view that healthy self-care must come first and care of others second. For example, Carol Cannon at The Bridge emphasizes that a parent's first obligation to a child is to take care of himself or herself. Carol is not telling parents to be selfish, much as it may sound that way. She is merely stating the obvious truth that an emotionally diseased parent cannot give adequate care to a child. If an emotionally unhealthy parent could read all the books in the world about the techniques of child care, he or she would still be an inadequate parent. Parents *must* resolve their own emotional issues first. Then they can help their children to develop in emotionally healthy ways.

This points up the fact that it is very easy to misread an author. Just because a statement sounds unchristian doesn't mean that it is. I will illustrate the point by showing you two statements that I read recently in a magazine article that was critical of codependence theory. In each case, the statement I quote was not original with the author of the magazine article. He was quoting two writers on codependence to prove his point that codependence theory is bad. In my opinion, one of the quotations he used is indeed a valid criticism of codependence theory as it is understood by some people, and the other one is not. See if you can identify which statement I agree is a valid criticism of codependence theory and which is not. (The statements appear in an article by Edward T. Welch, "Early Roots of the Codependence Movement," *SCP Journal*, 18:3, 25.) Here are the two statements:

> To honor the self is to be in love with our own life, in love with our possibilities for growth and for the experiencing joy (sic.), in love with the process of discovery and exploring our distinctively human potentialities.
>
> Thus we can begin to see that to honor the self is to practice selfishness in the highest, noblest, and least understood sense of that word. And this, I shall argue, requires enormous independence, courage, and integrity (Nathaniel Branden, *Honoring the Self* [Boston: Houghton Mifflin, 1983], 4).

> *My* individuality is found in Soul. Soul is the sense that *I* am and *I'm* pretty terrific and *I* want to feel like this all the time. . . . *My* holy sacred self is in place and *I* want to see that self here and now (Lynne Bundesen, *God Dependency* [New York: Crossroad, 1989], 106).

Which statement do you think is appropriate, and which is objectionable from a Christian point of view? My choice is the first as the appropriate statement and the second as the objectionable one.

Why?

The first author is encouraging us to honor our love of life and the infinite possibilities that lie within us for growth and for experiencing joy. He advises us to be "in love with the process of discovery and exploring our distinctively human potentialities." This is the same lesson that Jesus taught in the parable of the talents. Which man was condemned in the parable—the man who loved life and all the God-given possibilities within himself for growth or the one who, out of fear, rejected his potential?

I would feel uncomfortable with this author's second paragraph without the qualifications of the first. But if we limit his use of the terms *self-care* and *selfishness* to the definition he gave us in the first paragraph, then I can even agree with his statement that "thus we can begin to see that to honor the self is to practice selfishness in the highest, noblest, and least understood sense of that word. And this, I shall argue, requires enormous independence, courage, and integrity."

The second author, on the other hand, sounds very New Age to me. He begins by saying that "*my* individuality is found in Soul," and right there I get nervous. Is my nervousness a gut-level reaction to the word *soul* that arises out of my Adventist conditioning? Absolutely—just as in the previous statement my initial reaction to the author's use of the word *selfishness* arose out of my Adventist roots. *We need this "gut-level" response to the things we read.* That's the value of having a solid grounding in the Christian faith. It makes the flags go up instantly to warn us of moral danger. But the wise Christian will read carefully to be sure that his gut-level reaction is valid. If it is, he will reject what he reads. But if a careful examination of the author's words shows that the author's ideas are valid from a Christian point of view, as in the case of the first statement above, then the wise Christian will accept what the author says as valid.

As I read the second author's full quote, I find that he is glorifying self and the feelings of his "self." He is calling his self "holy" and "sacred." His constant emphasis on "I" and "me" reminds me of Satan's claim in Isaiah 14:13, 14 that "*I* will ascend to heaven; *I* will raise my throne above the stars of God; *I* will sit enthroned on the mount of the assembly." All of this is New Age philosophy that I reject absolutely.

One of the most interesting things about the two statements I quoted above is that the first one appears in a book by a secular publisher while the second one appears in a book by a Christian publisher!

We must be very careful what we read!

In conclusion, I would offer the following guidelines for reading books, both secular and Christian, on addiction and codependence.

1. Know your Bible. Ground yourself in Christian doctrine. If you are a new Christian, or if as a long-time Christian you have neglected to ground yourself thoroughly in the Christian faith, then check out the ideas you read with more mature Christians. I suggest that you ask the advice of more mature Christians about what to read.

2. Pray that God will help the warning flags to go up in your mind. Don't assume that if the author and publisher are Christian, it must be all right. Be cautious, but not paranoid, about reading books both by Christians who are not of your denomination and by authors who are not Christians.

3. Be as cautious about paranoid Christians as you are about secular authors. By this I mean, watch out for the Christian whose criticism is extreme, who labels everything as total black or white, whose language suggests that he or she has a bias or an agenda to promote. Watch out for the Christian who uses emotional language. For example, one of the authors I mentioned above who is critical of codependence theory referred to "codependency gurus." *Guru* is an emotionally laden word that tells me I need to question this author's objectivity, especially in view of the fact that his entire article has this tone.

4. Pray that God will give you insight into yourself, first from the Bible, and then from other sources. Ask Him to help you recognize genuine truth wherever you find it, regardless of

who said it or who wrote it.

5. You should definitely avoid reading entire books or even magazine articles when you know that the author is a New Age adherent. However, I also suggest that you avoid rejecting an entire book because of one statement or even an entire chapter that you may not agree with, when the rest of what the author says is sound from a Christian point of view.

An Eleventh-Hour Wake-Up Call to God's Sleeping Army

A storm is coming. But despite the sound of distant thunder, most don't know what's ahead.

In *The Crisis of the End Time*, Marvin Moore suggests that history's climax is about to break upon us with startling speed and ferocity. He also shows how we can keep our relationship with Jesus during earth's darkest hour.

The Crisis is a forceful yet easy-to-understand explanation of the vital issues facing our church and our world on the eve of Christ's return.

US$10.95

THE Crisis OF THE End Time

Marvin Moore

To order, call TOLL FREE **1-800-765-6955**, or visit your local ABC.

Prices subject to change without notice.

A revival is coming. Will you be a part of it?

What would happen in our homes, churches, and communities if we followed God's counsel in 2 Chronicles 7:14, humbled ourselves, and prayed? That question is explored and answered in Randy Maxwell's *If My People Pray*, a book infused with a passion for prayer as God's chosen method for establishing His kingdom through us and supplying our greatest needs.

If you've had it with status quo Christianity and thirst for a genuine prayer experience that results in revival, get this book and begin praying today. Paper, 192 pages. US$10.95/Cdn$15.90.

Available at your local Adventist Book Center, or call toll free 1-800-765-6955.

© 1994 Pacific Press Publishing Association 799/9834

IF MY PEOPLE PRAY

An Eleventh-Hour Call to Prayer and Revival

If My People Who are called by My Name will humble themselves and pray and seek my face, and turn from their wicked ways, THEN I will hear from heaven, and will forgive their sin and heal their land.

Randy Maxwell

A CURE FOR BLINDNESS!

Laodicea
by Jack Sequeira

Poor, miserable, blind, and naked! A pathetic condition for anyone—but for a church? Could Christ truly be speaking about your church and mine? About you and me?

Laodicea looks closely at Christ's urgent counsel to lukewarm Christians in the last days and upholds the sure and only cure for Laodicea's blindness— righteousness by faith alone. A powerful call for Adventists to open their hearts, ears, and eyes to the healing only Christ can give.
US$10.95/Cdn$15.90.
Paper.

Available at your local ABC, or call toll free 1-800-765-6955.

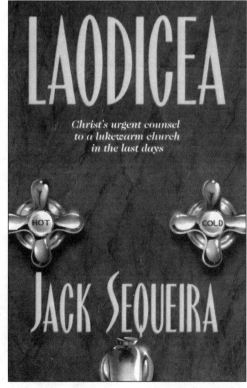